Translation and Cultural Change

Benjamins Translation Library

The Benjamins Translation Library aims to stimulate research and training in translation and interpreting studies. The Library provides a forum for a variety of approaches (which may sometimes be conflicting) in a socio-cultural, historical, theoretical, applied and pedagogical context. The Library includes scholarly works, reference works, post-graduate text books and readers in the English language.

EST Subseries

The European Society for Translation Studies (EST) Subseries is a publication channel within the Library to optimize EST's function as a forum for the translation and interpreting research community. It promotes new trends in research, gives more visibility to young scholars' work, publicizes new research methods, makes available documents from EST, and reissues classical works in translation studies which do not exist in English or which are now out of print.

Volume 61

Translation and Cultural Change:
Studies in history, norms and image-projection
Edited by Eva Hung

Translation and Cultural Change

Studies in history, norms and image-projection

Edited by

Eva Hung

The Chinese University of Hong Kong

John Benjamins Publishing Company

Amsterdam/Philadelphia

The paper used in this publication meets the minimum requirements of American National Standard for Information Sciences – Permanence of Paper for Printed Library Materials, ANSI Z39.48-1984.

Library of Congress Cataloging-in-Publication Data

Translation and Cultural Change : Studies in history, norms and
      image-projection / edited by Eva Hung.
            p.   cm. (Benjamins Translation Library, ISSN 0929–7316 ; v. 61)
      Includes bibliographical references and index.
            1. Translating and interpreting. 2. Language and culture. 3. Social
      change.

      P306.2.T7359 2005
418'.02--dc22   2004062772
ISBN 90 272 1667 3 (Eur.) / 1 58811 627 1 (US) (Hb; alk. paper)

John Benjamins Publishing Co. · P.O. Box 36224 · 1020 ME Amsterdam · The Netherlands
John Benjamins North America · P.O. Box 27519 · Philadelphia PA 19118-0519 · USA

Contents

Editor's preface   vii

Notes on contributors   xiii

Translation as an agent for change

Enhancing cultural changes by means of fictitious translations   3
  Gideon Toury

Translation and cultural transformation: The case of the
Afrikaans bible translations   19
  Jacobus A. Naudé

Cultural borderlands in China's translation history   43
  Eva Hung

Cultural perception and translation

Translating China to the American South: Baptist missionaries and
Imperial China, 1845–1911   65
  Ray Granade and Tom Greer

Translating the concept of "identity"   91
  Eva Richter and Bailin Song

Translation and national cultures: A case study in theatrical translation   111
  Alain Piette

The Japanese experience

The reconceptionization of translation from Chinese
in 18th-century Japan   119
  Judy Wakabayashi

Translationese in Japan   147
  Yuri Furuno

The selection of texts for translation in postwar Japan:
An examination of one aspect of polysystem theory   161
  Noriko Matsunaga-Watson

Case studies from China

Translation in transition: Variables and invariables   175
  Lin Wusun

On annotation in translation   183
  Han Jiaming

Index   191

Editor's preface

Translation and interpreting as human activities may be as old as human civilization, but these activities did not come under the purvey of intellectual investigation or systematic research until the second half of the 20th century. Granted, translation has always had an academic role in the teaching of languages: from the old Latin classes in European schools to the learning of English in present-day China. But this role only served to create the impression of translation as a rudimentary tool for the unpolished learner. It concentrated attention on fragments of texts as linear sequences of units which can be switched into another language without reference to contexts and purpose. At the other end of the scale, we have religious translation work which penetrated the lives of ordinary people and should have aroused more awareness of inter-lingual activities. But the nature of religious translation itself called for the downplaying or obliteration of the translators' existence to facilitate the illusion that the Almighty and the prophets speak directly to the faithful. Thus, despite the frequent contact people had with translation work through religion, they were not always aware it.

Given this background, it was only natural that translation was thought of, if at all, as a secondary and rather lowly pursuit. Nor does it surprise us that in the early days when translation aroused certain intellectual interest it was subsumed under applied linguistics, and that until the 1970s the theoretical explorations were all along the lines of linguistic theories. One of the main concerns was to establish the exact mechanism of linguistic transcoding/transference so that the task of translating could be both understood and carried out smoothly and flawlessly. The belief that understanding the process of translation would lead to the unveiling of the secrets of 'the translator's black box' (i.e. her mind) is still with us as part of the process-oriented approach in translation and interpreting research. This belief assumes that if the precise process and procedures can be mapped, analyzed and replicated, then trainees need only be taught how to replicate this *process* for them to become fully competent translators and interpreters. Even more importantly, perhaps, precisely replicable processes will facilitate the development of programmes for computer translation which will produce texts that are qualitatively comparable to those done by the best human translators, but at much quicker speed and less cost.

The research orientations described above are grounded in the practical needs of translation and interpreting as a job to be done, and the focus, perhaps naturally, is on how the job should be accomplished. But history tells us that translation played a part in the development of all cultures. In the cases where translated works had an impact on their host cultures, that impact was not dependent so much on how the work was *done* as on how they were *conceived* prior to the translation act and how they were *received* after it. Moreover, historical cases also show us repeatedly that the idealized concept of a 'good translation' (one that conveys the contents of the original without omission, addition, or deviation, and in a style which a bilingual person would find appropriately reminiscent of the original's) bears no direct relationship to the impact a translation has on its host culture. After all, translations which had such cultural impact were used by people who were not bilingual, and who were much more interested in how the work fit into their own agenda than how it functioned in its original culture. The awareness of such phenomena aroused our intellectual curiosity to explore and explain them, and in that lay the seed of the discipline now called Translation Studies.

In terms of the development of translation as an intellectual discipline, a demarcation line was drawn by James Holmes in 1972 with his mapping of the discipline and his proposal of its name.[1] This led to a rapid expansion of our lines of enquiry from the text-oriented (often source-text oriented) to a multitude of foci, and to the development of new theories based on socio-cultural, rather than linguistic, considerations. In the last quarter century, *skopos* theory, polysystems, and the descriptive investigation of translation norms have become standard points of reference for the translation researcher in many parts of the world. The new thinking drew inspiration from such disciplines as communication theory, comparative literature and literary theories, anthropology, history and, most recently, gender studies and cultural studies. The new emphasis is on context rather than text.

However, one context which rarely comes under investigation is how the academic enquiries now called Translation Studies are themselves subject to the cultural environment and social structures that govern them in different countries and regions of the world. For example, a country with a strong tradition of written literature would be naturally predisposed to place literary translation in a central position, this despite the fact the most influential contemporary translation activities in that country may not fall under the category of literature at all. Similarly, a country where history is written according to rules stipulated by a dominant ideology would not see much new thinking coming out of translation historiography. The differences that exist between countries and regions suggest that such trends in "pure translation studies" as "descriptive study" and "the cultural turn" may not be feasible in some countries, or may only be adapted in a form that is acceptable to the dominant ideology of these countries. Like a translator faced with culturally sensitive material, the majority of academics who are used to a highly regulated education system may choose to stay on the safe path when faced with ideologically sensitive approaches of enquiry. For the great majority, that path is "applied translation studies" — particularly the training and assessment of students who will become professional translators or language workers. Hence, a study of the national discourse among translation studies circles tells us more than the discipline's state of development; it also reveals cultural and ideological preferences and taboos.

For this reason, though most of the chapters in this volume fall under the category of "pure translation studies", we have not entirely excluded case studies which seem to be pedagogical or prescriptive in approach. Instead we have selected a small number of papers to illustrate how the concerns of the field is communicated in one country at one specific period in time — China in the late 20th century. The People's Republic of China (PRC) is a country which emerged in the early 1980s from decades of isolation, with many of the characteristics and practices of an ideologically authoritarian government still intact. On the other hand, the state has put 'modernization' on the agenda and academics in many disciplines are dazzled by the brave new world of western theories. Translation as a tool that enables communication between cultures has gained endorsement from the state, but intellectual investigations which challenge the concept of translation as a neutral tool are not as welcome. These objective factors mean that Translation Studies in China is developing in a culture conspicuously different from those in many other parts of the world.

The first section of this book deals with translations as agents of change. Gideon Toury is a prominent figure in effecting the shift of focus from the translated text to the relationship between translations and the cultures that generate them. One of the ways he highlights translations as products of the host culture is through the study of psuedo-translations (or fictitious translations). More recently, he has also become interested in the role of translation in cultural planning. In showing how various fictitious translations were invented to serve new needs specific to their cultural and historical contexts, his chapter "Enhancing Cultural Changes by Means of Fictitious Translations" brings these cases into the province of cultural planning.

Drawing from the experience of another continent and other eras, Jacobus Naude's comprehensive study of different Afrikaans translations of the Bible gives us a clear picture of the interaction between the production of significant cultural texts and their immediate social and cultural environment. His detailed contrastive analysis of specific lines of the Bible in successive translations, in one case to justify apartheid and in another to enhance a new social consciousness of racial and gender equality, is one of the best illustrations of how translations and their cultural environment shape and are shaped by each other.

In "Cultural Borderlands and China's Translation History", Eva Hung attempts to define the various types of cultural borderlands which generated translation activities in historical China (2nd to 19th century), and to trace their relationship with the cultural centre. This chapter gives us a panoramic view of the translation movements that had the greatest impact on the development of Chinese culture over some 2,000 years, and also draws attention to the fact that much of the cultural translation work was initiated and done by non-Chinese translators.

The second section of this volume contains studies of how translations are done and perceived in specific cultural contexts. Ray Granade and Tom Greer, who have conducted in depth studies of Baptist missionaries in China, deal here with the issues of translation as representation. Nineteenth century missionaries had to tell their constituents in the U.S. about the China missions, not just for the sake of cross-cultural communication, but to justify the effectiveness of their work and seek funding for its continuation. Against this background, "Translating China to the American South" tells us what the missionaries concentrated on in their portrayal of China, and why.

The chapter by Eva Richter and Bailin Song has its roots in personal experience: the concepts of 'identity' and 'self' as culturally specific and therefore incomprehensible concepts to students in the PRC. Using representative texts in American culture, and with the help of bilingual Chinese people as well as translations, they explore the concept of identity and the obstacles anyone faces in trying to bring it into Chinese culture.

Alain Piette's chapter "Translation and National Cultures: the Case of Theatrical Translation" is another example of how concepts and styles are sometimes perceived as native to one culture and alien to another, thus affecting the translation selection process. Here the case is whether the farcical genius of the French playwright Crommelynck is indeed too foreign to be appreciated by an Anglo-American audience. The author's use of theatrical reviews and contextualization against theatrical traditions give the chapter an added edge.

The third section in this book is on the Japanese translation experience. Japan provides fertile ground for investigation in terms of translation studies if just for two reasons: (1) its long tradition of modelling itself culturally first on China and since the mid-19th century on the West means that it has always been culturally open to new and foreign ideas and had used translation work to facilitate its cultural development; (2) Japanese translation norms are very different from those current in the cultures after which it modelled itself, and has traditionally shown not just tolerance of but often actual preference for source-oriented translations.

Japan's early adoption of Chinese texts for the education of the elite produced a special way of marking Chinese texts in accordance with Japanese syntax so that Japanese people who did not know Chinese could nevertheless read such texts. Whether this method of notation and reading called *Kambun kundoku* can be classified as a form of translation is a subject still under debate. Whether it had an influence on Japanese translation norms is perhaps even more worthy of investigation. Judy Wakabayashi's chapter on "The Reconceptualization of Translation from Chinese in 18th Century Japan" explains in detail the method of *Kambun kundoku*, investigates its status and traces its conflict with the budding paradigmatic shift towards what we tend to think of as 'normal' translation. This is an extremely illuminating study that throws light on the factors which may influence translation norms.

Traditionally the issue of 'translationese' was not an important one in Japan, for it was the accepted norm that translations should read differently from works written originally in Japanese. This situation, however, has been changing, and a debate about the acceptability of translationese emerged in the last two decades of the 20th century. In "Translationese in Japan", Yuri Furuno traces the arguments pertaining to this debate. She then presents results from her own survey on this issue in order to identify the key elements which indicate to a reader whether a text is a translated one or an original.

Noriko Matsunaga-Watson's chapter "The Selection of Texts for Translation in Post-war Japan" is based on a survey of how translated titles perform in sales terms. While her analysis is grounded in the polysystem theory, through an examination of her data she also challenges some of the hypotheses of that theory. As the author points out, the literary polysystem is not isolated from other systems, and her survey results again illustrates that the factors — cultural,

economic and political — which influence the selection and reception of translations vary from country to country and from period to period.

The last section of this volume presents two case studies which illustrate the
primary concerns of translation academics in China at the end of the 20th century. Their desire to keep up with the theoretical discourse in the Western world
is shown in the many brief introductions and critical introductions to Western
translation theories that make up a substantial part of the translation studies
discourse in the PRC. However, while text-linguistics and semiotics have made
considerable headway in Chinese translation research, the historical-descrip-
tive approach still faces a considerable number of obstacles, one of which is the
ideological taboos that govern humanities research in China even now. Since
translation is still regarded as a tool for modernization, both practitioners and
teachers are under tremendous pressure to establish modes of operation conducive to enhancing the quantitative and qualitative performance of actual translation work. The two case studies below illustrate such mainstream concerns in
the PRC.

Lin Wusun's position in his chapter "Translation in Transition: Variables and
Invariables" represents that of the experienced practitioner knowledgeable
about the role translation is expected to play. Lin's own background as a veteran
translator and translation administrator at the national level means that his
concerns — like the government's — is primarily in meeting quantitative and
qualitative challenges. Given the fact that the PRC changed in twenty years
from a completely closed society to one of the economic engines of Asia, such
challenges are indeed enormous. It is these challenges — rather than intellectual investigations which may unsettle the established perception of 'Chinese'
and "other" — which will generate possible financial and structural support for
translation as a field of study. Lin's analysis of the current trends in the translation and interpreting professions in China and the application of new translation aids and tools in terms for future training is aimed at this direction.

Han Jianming's approach to his chapter on annotation is influenced by the
problems he faces as a teacher of English language and literature for whom the
translation course is a small part of the curriculum. Its prescriptive orientation
is rooted in the basic needs of undergraduates who are trying to master translation as a skill. This situation is in fact very representative, and is one of the main
reasons why many conference papers presented in China show a similar orientation. Han draws on his experience as translator in different contexts to rein-
vestigate the use of annotation in various types of literary texts. The examples he
cites not only reveal scholarly and readership considerations, but also how con-

tractual and legal obligations now play a role in translation work. The latter is a relatively new element that Chinese translation scholars have yet to investigate.

Eva Hung

Acknowledgements

The papers collected in this volume represent a very small percentage of those presented at the International Conference on Culture and Translation which took place in Beijing in 1999. The conference was jointly organized by the English Department, Peking University and the Research Centre for Translation, The Chinese University of Hong Kong. I would like to express my gratitude to my co-organizers Professors Gu Zhenqun, Han Jiaming, Shen Dan, and particularly Professor Liu Shuseng, for the amount of work they put in to make the conference a success. In preparing this volume for publication, I am also indebted to my secretary Alena Chow for her help in word-processing and scanning, and to my research assistants Audrey Heijns and Florence Li, whose help in proofreading and indexing proved invaluable.

Note

1. "The Name and Nature of Translation Studies", *Translated! Papers on Literary Translation and Translation Studies*, Amsterdam: Rodopi, 1988, pp.66–80.

Notes on Contributors

Yuri FURUNO received her Ph.D. degree from Queensland University with a thesis on "Changes in Translational Norms in Postwar Japan". She received her M.A. in Japanese Interpreting and Translation from Queensland University and her Bachelor of Laws from Keio University, and is an accredited NAATI English–Japanese translator. Her publications include "G. Toury's Translation Theory and English–Japanese Translation" (in Japanese) *Tsuuyaku Riron Kenkyu* (Interpreting Research) 14, Vol. 7 No. 2 (1998).

S. Ray GRANADE is Director of Library Services and Professor of History at Ouachita Baptist University in Arkansas, USA. His research publications focus on American social and intellectual history. He has considered the uses of force ("Violence: An Instrument of Policy in Reconstruction Alabama", "Slave Unrest in Florida", and "The Shoemaker Flogging Case: Tampa, 1936"), education ("Higher Education in Antebellum Alabama" and "Forty Years of Frustration: Higher Education in Antebellum Florida"), and religion ("A System & Plan: The Arkansas Baptist State Convention, 1848–1998", "An Enlarged Tent: Arkadelphia First Baptist Church, 1851–2001", "The 'Cross Case': Church Discipline, the Law, and Arkadelphia's Second Baptist Church", and "Among the Last: An Arkansas Missionary Confronts a Changing China").

Tom GREER is Chair of the Humanities Division, Ouachita Baptist University. He and Ray Granade are compiling a directory of 650 Baptist missionaries from the American South active in China from 1846 to 1950. He is also engaged in the research of American utopian societies, with special focus on 'New Harmony' in Indiana and 'Germantown' in Louisiana. He is the co-author of the school textbook *Arkansas: The World Around Us*, New York: Macmillan/McGraw-Hill, 1991.

HAN Jiaming teaches English at Peking University. A graduate of Jilin University, he received his Ph.D. from Cornell University. He is the author of *Henry Fielding: Form, History, Ideology* (Peking University Press, 1997) and a co-translator of *The Short Oxford History of English Literature* (People's Literature Press, 2000). He has published articles on English literature, comparative literature, and translation studies.

Eva HUNG received her B.A. and M.Phil. from the University of Hong Kong and her Ph.D. from London University. She has been the Director of the Research Centre for Translation, Chinese University of Hong Kong and Editor of *Renditions* for some nineteen years. Her research interests are translation history, literary translation, and early Chinese Republican women. Her works in translation studies include *Translation • Literature • Culture* (Peking University Press, 1999) and (ed.) *Teaching Translation and Interpreting 4* (John Benjamins, 2002). Her latest research project is the rewriting of Chinese translation history.

LIN Wusun was a long-serving Vice-President of the Chinese Translators Association and a veteran translator and translation administrator. He retired in 2001.

Noriko MATSUNGA-WATSON is a Ph.D. candidate working on her dissertation in the area of Cultural Studies at the Department of English Media Studies and Art History, University of Queensland.

Jacobus A. NAUDÉ obtained his D.Litt. in Near Eastern Studies as well as an M.A. in Linguistics and an M.Th. in Old Testament Exegesis and Theology. He is a professor in the Department of Near Eastern Studies, University of the Free State, Bloemfontein, South Africa, where he teaches Translation Studies, Linguistics (Syntax), Dead Sea Scroll Studies, Hebrew and Aramaic Grammar. He is co-editor of *Contemporary Translation Studies and Bible Translation. A South African Perspective* (Bloemfontein, 2002), co-author of *A Biblical Hebrew Reference Grammar* (Sheffield, 1999) His research interests include the translation of religious literature into the eleven official languages of South Africa, and the application of modern linguistic theory (minimalist programme) on the description and explanation of syntactic structures in non-living languages.

Alain PIETTE is Professor of English and Director of the American Studies Center at the State University of Mons, Belgium. He is the author of numerous essays on drama, cinema, translation, and education published in the United States, Canada, Asia, and Europe in such journals as *Modern Drama, Literature/Film Quarterly, BELL, Theatre Journal, Studies in the Humanities,* and *Le Soir.* His book-length works include *The Crommelynck Mystery – The Life and Work of a Belgian Playwright* as well as the translation *The Theater of Fernand Crommelynck: Eight Plays,* both published by Susquehanna University Press.

Eva RICHTER is retired from the City University of New York, where she taught English for more than thirty years. She was on the editorial board of *Studies in Medievalism* and has published articles on medievalism and on education. She translated *Die Ritter der Tafelrunde*, a play by the German writer Christoph Hein, which received its American premiere at the University of Delaware in 1994. Professor Richter taught English at Hebei Teacher's University in China from 1986–1987 and is currently working for a non-government organization at the United Nations.

Bailin SONG is an Associate Professor of English at Kingsborough Community College of the City University of New York. Her research interest is mainly in English as a Second Language reading and writing instruction and assessment. She has published articles in *College ESL*, *Journal of College Reading*, *Journal of Second Language Writing*, and *Writing Center Journal*.

Gideon TOURY is M. Bernstein Chair of Translation Theory at the Tel Aviv University where he fist began his academic studies in 1966. He is best known as a major proponent of the descriptive approach in Translation Studies. His works include *Translational Norms and Literary Translation into Hebrew*, 1930–1945 (Tel Aviv 1977), *In Search of a Theory of Translation* (Tel Aviv 1980), and *Descriptive Translation Studies and Beyond* (Amsterdam 1988). He is also a prolific literary translator who has made available in Hebrew the works of F. Scott Fitzgerald, Gunter Grass, Hemingway, Steinbeck, J.D. Salnger, Thomas Mann, and C.S. Lewis.

Judy WAKABAYASHI is currently an associate professor of Japanese translation at Kent State University in Ohio, after teaching Japanese–English translation at the University of Queensland in Australia for fifteen years. Her research interests focus on Japanese–English translation, the history of translation in Japan, translation theory and translation pedagogy, and she has published various articles in these fields.

Translation as an agent for change

Enhancing cultural changes by means of fictitious translations

Gideon Toury
Tel Aviv University

I

At this point in the evolution of culture theory, very few would contest the claim that **change is a built-in feature of culture**. Implied is not only that cultures are changeable in principle, so to speak, but also that, given the time, every single cultural system would indeed undergo some change. In fact, a culture which would have failed to show change over a considerable period of time is bound to get marginalized and become obsolete, if not stop functioning as a living culture altogether. At the same time, cultural systems are also prone to manifest **a certain resistance to changes**, especially if they are deemed too drastic. When renewal seems to involve such changes, they may well be rejected in an attempt to maintain what has already been achieved; in other words, retain whatever equilibrium the culture has reached. Innovation and conservation thus appear as two major contending forces in cultural dynamics.

One 'big' hypothesis which has been put forward in an attempt to reconcile these two extremes claims that new models do manage to make their way into an extant cultural repertoire in spite of the system's inherent resistance to changes if and when those novelties are **introduced under disguise**; that is, as if they still represented an established option within the culture in question. Inasmuch as the cover is effective, it is only when penetration of products and production processes pertaining to the new model has been completed that the receiving culture would appear to have undergone change, often bringing it to the verge of a new (and different) state of equilibrium. Needless to say, the process as such may take a while. Also, it tends to involve a series of smaller, more intricate changes, which may not be recognized as changes as they are occurring. Even something which appears to represent a cultural "revolution" would thus normally be found to have followed an *evolutionary* process (Shavit 1989: 593–600).

A lot of this tends to go unnoticed by the average person-in-the-culture, precisely because many of the potentially new products s/he may encounter in daily life have been disguised as standing for something else, much more established, much less alien, and hence much less of a threat to the culture's stability. By contrast, those who act in accordance with the new model, and produce the behaviour which will be paving the way for its ultimate reception, often do realize its explosive potentials. It is precisely out of such a realization that they may decide to conceal the true nature of their behaviour, namely, in an attempt to introduce whatever innovations they may entail in a controlled way, and in smaller doses, so that they may go unnoticed by the masses, or those who dominate the culture while all this is happening, until the innovations have been [partly] incorporated into the culture and are no longer felt as a potential threat.

My intention in this paper is far from claiming that this is the only way a new model may make its way into a cultural repertoire (because I don't believe it is). On the other hand, I have no wish to devote too many efforts to modifying — and necessarily complexifying — the 'disguise' hypothesis either (for instance, by specifying the conditions under which it is more or less likely to gain [or lose] validity). What I'll be doing instead would amount to adding some weight to the very feasibility of such a 'big', overarching hypothesis as a possible explanation of cultural dynamics; and I will do so on the basis of one kind of evidence: **the creation and utilization of fictitious translations** (also known as pseudo-translations); a recurring type of cultural behaviour which I have been preoccupied with for almost twenty years, and from changing points of view.[1]

II

As has been demonstrated so many times, translations which deviate from sanctioned patterns — which many of them certainly do — are often tolerated by a culture to a much higher extent than equally deviant original compositions. Given this fact, the possibility is always there to try and put the cultural gatekeepers to sleep by **presenting a text as if it were translated,** thus lowering the threshold of resistance to the novelties it may hold in store and enhancing their acceptability, along with that of the text incorporating them as a whole. In its extreme forms, pseudo-translating amounts to no less than **an act of culture planning** — a notion which, as I have been claiming lately, deserves to be given much higher prominence in Translation Studies than has normally been the case; at least while trying to account for translation behaviour under specific circumstances, that is, as a descriptive-explanatory tool. (See Toury 1998, forthcoming.)

Be that as it may, it is clear that recourse to fictitious translations entails **a disguise mechanism** whereby advantage is taken of a culture-internal conception of translation: not an essentialistic 'definition' (that is, a list of [more or less] fixed features, allegedly specifying what translation inherently 'is'), but a functional conception thereof which takes heed of the immanent *variability* of the notion of translation: difference across cultures, variation within a culture and changes over time.

The underlying assumption here is that a text's systemic position (and ensuing function), including the position and function which go with a text's being regarded as a translation, are determined first and foremost by considerations originating in the culture which actually hosts it. Thus, when a text is offered as a translation, it is quite readily accepted *bona fide* as one, no further questions asked. By contrast, when a text is presented as having been originally composed in a language, reasons will often manifest themselves — for example, certain features of textual make-up and verbal formulation, which persons-in-the-culture have come to associate with translations and translating — to at least suspect, correctly or not, that the text has in fact been translated into that language.

Within such a so-called 'target culture', any text which is regarded as a translation, on no matter what grounds, can be accounted for as a cluster of (at least three) interconnected postulates:

(1) The Source-Text Postulate;
(2) The Transfer Postulate;
(3) The Relationship Postulate.[2]

Regarded as postulates, all three are *posited* rather than factual; at least not of necessity. It is precisely this nature of theirs which makes it so possible for producers of texts, or various agents of cultural dissemination, to offer original compositions as if they were translations: neither the source text nor the transfer operations (and the features that the assumed 'target' and 'source' texts are regarded as sharing, by virtue of that transfer), nor any translational relationships (where the transferred — and shared — features are taken as an invariant core), have to be exposed and made available to the consumers; not even in the case of genuine translations. Very often it is really the other way around: a 'positive' reason has to be supplied if a text assumed to be a translation is to be deprived of its culture-internal identity as one.

Thus, it is only when a text presented (or regarded) as a translation has been shown to have *never* had a corresponding source text in any other language, hence no text-induced 'transfer operations', shared (transferred) features and accountable relationships, that it is found to be 'what it really is': an original composition disguised as a translation. To be sure, this is a far cry from saying that a translation proved to be fictitious has 'no basis' in any other culture, which is not necessarily true either: like genuine translations, fictitious ones may also serve as a vehicle of imported novelties. However, to the extent that such a basis can be pointed to, it would normally amount to a whole *group* of foreign texts, even the [abstractable] *model* underlying that group, rather than any individual text.[3]

From the point of view of any retrospective attempt to study pseudo-translating and its implications, a significant paradox is precisely that a text can only be identified as a fictitious translation after the veil has been lifted, i.e., when the function it was intended to have, and initially had in the culture into which it was introduced, has already changed; whether the fact that it used to function as a translation still has some reality left or whether it has been completely erased from the culture's 'collective memory'. Only then can questions be asked as to why a disguised mode of presentation was selected in the first place, and why it was this particular language, or cultural tradition, that was picked as a 'source', as well as what it was that made the public fall for it for a longer or a shorter period of time. At the same time, if any historically valid accounts are to be attempted, the text will have to be properly contextualized. In other words, it will have to be reinstated in the position it had occupied *before* it was found out to be fictitious. (Of course, there may exist myriad fictitious translations, with respect to which the mystification has not been dispelled, and maybe never will be. These texts can only be tackled as translations whose sources have remained unknown; but then, so many *genuine* translations are in that same position, especially if one goes back in time. Moreover, there is no real way of distinguishing between the two, which — in terms of their cultural position (that is, from the internal point of view of the culture which hosts them) — tend to be the same anyway.)

By contrast, the lifting of the veil itself, and the circumstances under which it occurred, form an integral part of the story we are after. Thus, when an undercover mission has been accomplished, there is little need for that cover any more. On the contrary, sometimes a wish may arise precisely to *publicize* the way by which the new dominating group (or individual) have managed to 'outsmart the establishment' and smuggle in its own goods. All this does not rule out the possibility that the veil could also be lifted prior to a successful fulfilment of the task: This may certainly happen. After all, a strategy's success is never guaranteed. In

cases like this, fulfillment may well be stopped, or even reverted, which constitutes another important aspect of any attempt to study cultural dynamics.

III

To be sure, a fictitious translation is not necessarily just *presented* to the public as
if it were a genuine one (which — based as it is on make-believe alone — would
still represent a disguise, but a rather superficial one indeed). In many cases, the
text is *produced* 'as a translation' right from the start. Entailing as it does the possibility of putting the claim that the text 'is' indeed a translation to some kind of
test, this would certainly count as a far more elaborate form of disguise.

Thus, features are often embedded in a fictitious translation which have come
to be habitually associated with genuine translations in the culture which would
host it, and which the pseudo-translator is part of, on occasion so much as a
privileged part; whether the association is with translations into the hosting
culture in general, or translations into it of texts of a particular type, or, more
often, translations from a particular source language/culture. By enhancing
their resemblance to genuine translations, pseudo-translators simply make it
easier for their textual creations to pass as translations without arousing too
much suspicion.

Interestingly enough, due to the practice of embedding features in fictitious
translations which have come to be associated with genuine translations, it is
sometimes possible to 'reconstruct' from a fictitious translation bits and pieces
of a text in another language as a kind of an 'possible source text' — one that
never enjoyed any textual reality, to be sure — as is the case with so many genuine translations whose sources have not (or not yet) been identified. In fact, as is
the case with parodies (which are akin to them in more than one respect), fictitious translations often represent their fictitious sources in a rather exaggerated
manner, which may render the said reconstruction quite easy as well as highly
univocal. It is simply that the possibility, if not the need, to actually activate an
'original' in the background of a text is often an integral part of its proper realization as an 'intended translation', and hence of the very disguise involved in
pseudo-translating.

No wonder, then, that fictitious translations are often in a position to give a
fairly good idea as to the notions shared by the members of a community, not
only concerning the *position* of translated texts in the culture they entertain, but
concerning the most conspicuous *characteristics* of such texts as well; in terms of

both textual-linguistic traits as well as putative target-source relationships. "The point is that it is only when humans recognize the existence of an entity and become aware of its characteristics that they can begin to imitate it" (James 1989: 35), and overdoing-in-imitation is a clear, if extreme, sign of such a recognition.

One final remark of a general nature: there is no doubt that putting forward, even producing a text as if it were a translation always involves an *individual* decision. However, such a decision will inevitably have been made within a particular cultural setup which is either conducive to pseudo-translating or else may hinder recourse to it. No wonder, then, that there seem to be circumstances which give rise to a *multitude* of fictitious translations, often from the same 'source' tradition, and/or executed in a similar way, thus introducing into the culture in question a true model whose cultural significance is of course much greater than that of the sum-total of its individual (i.e., textual) realizations. Such a proliferation always attests to the internal organization of the culture involved and very little else. In particular, it bears out the position and role of [genuine] translations, or of a certain sub-group thereof, within that culture, which the pseudo-translators seem to be putting to use, trying to deliberately capitalize on it.

For instance, Russian literature of the beginning of the 19th century was crying out for what became known as "Gothic novels". In order not to be rejected, however, the texts put forward as novels of this type had to draw their authority from an external tradition, and a very particular one at that: the English Gothic novel. As Iurij Masanov has shown, in response to this requirement — a reflection of the internal interests of Russian literature itself which had very little to do with the concerns of the English culture — a great number of books were indeed produced in Russia itself — and in the Russian language — which were presented, and accepted, as translations from the English. Many of those were of "novels by Ann Radcliffe", who was at that time regarded in Russia as the epitome of the genre (Masanov 1963: 99–106).[4]

In a similar vein, a former Tel Aviv student, Shelly Yahalom, has argued convincingly that one of the most effective means of bringing about changes in French writing of almost the same period was to lean heavily on translations from English, genuine and fictitious alike, with no real systemic difference between the two (Yahalom 1978: 42–52, 74–75). As a third example of an overriding tendency towards pseudo-translating I would cite the work of another former student at Tel Aviv University, Rachel Weissbrod, who demonstrated the decisive role fictitious translations, mainly "from the English" again, have played in establishing particular sectors of non-canonized Hebrew literature of the 1960s, most notably westerns, novels of espionage, romances and porno-graphic novels, where — as previous attempts had shown — *un*disguised texts of domestic origin would almost certainly have been considered inappropriate and relegated to the culture's extreme periphery, if not totally ejected from it (Weissbrod 1989: 94–99, 354–356).

IV

If by 'culture planning' we understand any attempt made by an individual, or a small group, to incur changes in the cultural repertoire, and the ensuing behav-iour, of a much larger group,[5] pseudo-translating would surely count as a case of cultural planning, especially in its most radical forms. Let me conclude by outlining three instances of pseudo-translating exhibiting growing extents of planning along various dimensions.

(a) *Papa Hamlet*

In January 1889, a small book was published in the German town of Leipzig, whose title-page read:

Bjarne P. Holmsen

PAPA HAMLET

Uebersetzt

und mit einer Einleitung versehen

von

Dr. Bruno Franzius

The book opened with the translator's preface — the *Einleitung* announced on the cover — a rather common habit at that time, especially in translations which made a claim of importance. The preface itself was typical too. In the main, it consisted of an extensive biography of the author, Bjarne Peter Holm-sen, claimed to be a young Norwegian, but one of the central passages of the preface discussed the difficulties encountered by the translator while dealing with the original text and the translational strategies he chose to adopt. It even expressed some (implicit) concern that a number of deviant forms may have crept into the German text in spite of the translator's prudence, forms which would easily be traceable to Norwegian formulations.

During the first few months after its publication, *Papa Hamlet* enjoyed relatively wide journalistic coverage. It was reviewed in many German newspapers and periodicals, where it was invariably treated as a translation. The claim was thus taken at face value, precisely as could have been expected. At the same time, none of the reviewers, mostly typical representatives of the German cultural milieu of the turn of the 20th century, had any idea about Bjarne Peter Holmsen and his literary (or any other) career. In fact, all of the information they supplied — which current norms of reviewing encouraged them to do — was drawn directly from the preface supplied by the translator, whose doctoral degree must have enhanced the trust they placed in it, as did the fact that the author's biography seemed to correspond so very closely to what would have been expected from a contemporary Scandinavian writer. Comical as it may sound, at least one reviewer went so far as to draw conclusions from the author's portrait, which appeared on the book's jacket. Quite a number of reviewers also referred to the translation work and its quality, in spite of the fact that none of them detected — or, for that matter, made any serious attempt to detect — a copy of the original; all on the clear assumption that a book presented as a translation actually is one. Unless, of course, there is strong evidence to the contrary.

And, indeed, a few months later, counter-evidence began to pile up, until it became known that *Papa Hamlet* was not a translation at all. Rather, the three stories comprising the small book were original German texts, the first results of the joint literary efforts of Arno Holz (1863–1929) and Johannes Schlaf (1862–1941). (The portrait on the jacket — a visual aspect of the overall disguise — belonged to a cousin of Holz's, one Gustav Uhse.)

Thus, towards the end of 1889 it was the *uncovered* disguise which became a literary fact (in the sense assigned to this notion by the Russian Formalist Jurij Tynjanov [1967]) for the German culture. However, an essential factor for any *historically* valid account of the case is that, for several months, *Papa Hamlet* did serve as a translation. Although factually wrong, this identity had been functionally effective; among other things, in enhancing the acceptance of what the two authors wished to achieve, and for whose achievement they decided to pseudo-translate in the first place.

Thus, Holz's and Schlaf's main objective was to experiment in freeing themselves — as German authors — from what they regarded as the narrow confines of French naturalism and getting away with this breach of sanctioned conventions. And they chose to do so by adopting a series of models of contemporary Scandinavian literature as guidelines for their writing, which were considered "naturalistic" too, only in a different way.

At that time, Scandinavian literature was indeed rapidly gaining in popularity and esteem in Germany. As such, it was in a good position to contribute novelties to German literature, and ultimately even reshape its very centre. However, when Holz and Schlaf were writing *Papa Hamlet*, German original writing was still firmly hooked to the French-like models. This made it highly resistant to the new trends, so that Scandinavian-like models were still acceptable only inasmuch as they were tied up with actual texts of Scandinavian origin; in other words, translations.

Disguising a German literary work which took after Scandinavian models as a translation was thus a most convenient way out of a genuine dilemma, where both horns — giving up the very wish to innovate as well as presenting the unconventional text as a German original — were sure to yield very little. Nor was this the only case of fictitious translation in modernizing German literature at the end of the 19th century, notably in the circles where Holz and Schlaf then moved, which may well have reinforced their decision to pseudo-translate.

The two authors were quite successful in attaining their goal too: *Papa Hamlet* indeed introduced "Scandinavian-like" novelties into German literature, many of them disguised — at least by implication — as instances of interference of the Norwegian original. A non-existent original, to be sure. In fact, the book came to be regarded as one of the most important forerunners of so-called *konsequenter Naturalismus*, a German brand of naturalism which owes quite a bit to Scandinavian prototypes. A successful instance of transplantation by any standard, due to an ingenious act of planning!

(b) *Book of Mormon*

A more extreme case of planning is represented by the *Book of Mormon* (1830): here, the innovations which were introduced by means of a text presented (and composed) as a translation gave birth to an altogether new Church, which brought in its wake a redeployment of much more than just the religious sector of American culture. One cannot but wonder what history would have looked like, had Joseph Smith Jr. claimed he had been given golden plates originally written in English, or had everybody taken the claim he did make as a mere hoax! (According to one Mormon tradition, the golden plates looked very much like a piece of 19th century office equipment, a kind of a ring binder.)

To be sure, it is only those who bought the claim that the *Book of Mormon* was a genuine translation from an old, obsolete (or, better still, obscure) language nicknamed 'reformed Egyptian' — in spite of the enormous difficulties in accepting such a claim[6] — who were also willing to accept its contents as well as the sacredness associated with it. As a result, it was not the entire American culture which absorbed the innovation. Rather, a relatively small group partly detached itself from mainstream culture and formed what became known as "the Church of Jesus Christ of Latter-day Saints". Moreover, the new Church developed not only due to a marked refusal to lift the veil connected with the *Book of Mormon*, but actually due to an ongoing struggle to *improve* the disguise and fortify it; in other words, to make the *Book* look more and more like a genuine religious book, which — according to previous traditions in the Anglo-American cultural space — had to be a translation.

Another aspect of the novelty of the *Book of Mormon* could well be literary. Thus, it has been claimed that

> the book is one of the earliest examples of frontier fiction, the first long Yankee narrative that owes nothing to English literary fashions . . . its sources are absolutely American.   (Brodie 1963: 67)

In fact, in the 19th century there have been persistent allegations that use had been made of a lost manuscript of a novel by one Solomon Spaulding, which was supposed to have been stolen and passed on to Joseph Smith (Brodie 1963: 419–433).

The possible literary intentions notwithstanding, it is clear that the producers of the *Book of Mormon*, struggling to establish a third *Testament*, took advantage first and foremost of large portions of the tradition of Bible translation into English. Regard the way the *Book* as a whole was divided into lower-level 'Books', and especially the names that were given to the latter; for instance,

first (and Second) Book of Nephi
Book of Jacob
Book of Mosiah.

Obviously, there is nothing 'natural' about that division or the book names, nor can there be a doubt that both conventions were taken over from the *biblical* tradition.

As to the subdivision of each individual 'Book' to 'Chapters' and 'Verses', it too was modelled on the Bible (more correctly, on its English translations, because Smith didn't even claim to know either Hebrew or Greek). However, this subdivision didn't even exist when the *Book of Mormon* first came into being. Rather, it was imposed on the English text some fifty years later, not even by the original pseudo-translator himself. There can be little doubt that this was done in a (rather successful) attempt to further reduce the difference between the *Book of Mormon* and the other two Testaments, thus enhancing its "authenticity" and adding to its religious authority — within the group which had already formed around the *Book*, that is. Can there be any doubt that what we are facing here is a whole series of gradual planning moves connected with a particular conception of translation?

To be sure, it is not all that clear what Smith had in mind when the Church was not yet in existence; not even whether he initially planned a religious work with a historical narrative at its base or just a historically-oriented narrative with some religious overtones. Moreover, in spite of the detailed story about how he received the golden plates and translated them, on the title-page of the first edition of the *Book of Mormon* he chose to refer to himself as "author and proprietor". Only in later editions was the reference changed to "translator". By contrast, it is very clear what happened to the *Book* in future times; namely, in a secondary, much more focussed act of planning. In the same vein, references were later added to "prophecies" mentioned in the *Book*, which "had come true", as so many missionary groups have been doing in their versions of the New Testament (and "the Church of Jesus Christ of Latter-day Saints" has indeed adopted a strong missionary orientation).

The names used in the *Book* constitute another feature which reveals a biblical model:

> Of the 350 names in the book he [Smith] took more than a hundred directly from the Bible. Over a hundred others were biblical names with slight changes in spelling or additions of syllables. But since in the Old Testament no names began with the letters F, Q, V, W, X, or Y, he was careful not to include any in his manuscript. (Brodie 1963: 73)

To which one could add those names (such as *Mosiah*) that end with the syllable *ah*, imitating a common ending in Hebrew whose retention has become part of standard transliteration of truly biblical names even in cases where the Hebrew closing *h* is silent, and hence phonetically superfluous.

Finally, in terms of its linguistic formulation, the *Book of Mormon* is an extreme case of what I have called "overdoing it *vis-à-vis* the source it is modelled on", which is so typical of fictitious translations. Take, for example, the way quotations from the Bible were used in the *Book*. As is well known, occasional quotation from the Old Testament has already been one of the literary devices of the New Testament, but it was used quite sparsely. By contrast, about 25,000 words of the *Book of Mormon* consist of passages from the Old Testament, and about 2,000 more words were taken from the New Testament. As Fawn Brodie,

Smith's biographer, put it, it is almost as if, whenever "his literary reservoir . . . ran dry . . . he simply arranged for his Nephite prophets to quote from the Bible" (1963: 58). To be sure, Smith often "made minor changes in these Biblical extracts, for it seems to have occurred to him that readers would wonder how an ancient American prophet could use the exact text of the King James Bible". However, "he was careful to modify chiefly the italicized interpolations inserted for euphony and clarity by the scholars of King James; the unitalicized holy text he usually left intact". In the same vein, the phrase "and it came to pass" [= it so happened], which is typical to the book's style, appears at least 2,000 times (1963: 63), which is really a lot!

(c) The "Kazakh Poet" Dzhambul Dzhabayev

In the most extreme of cases, planning may be so much as imposed on a society from above, by agents endowed with the power to do so; most notably political institutions in a totalitarian society. This is precisely the way pseudo-translating was used, misused and abused in Stalin's Soviet Union, a famous case in point being the patriotic poetry of Dzhambul Dzhabayev.

During the first decades after the Soviet Revolution, an old Kazakh folk singer named Dzhambul Dzhabayev (1846–1945) became famous throughout the Empire. Yet, nobody has ever encountered that man's poems in praise of the regime in anything but Russian, a language he himself didn't speak. Several of those poems were translated into other languages too, most notably in East Germany, always from the Russian version.

Now, at least since the memoirs of the composer Dmitri Shostakovitch "as related to and edited by Solomon Volkov" (Shostakovitch 1979: 161ff.) it has become common knowledge that the Russian 'translations' of Dzhambul's poems were in fact written "by an entire brigade of Russian poetasters" (derogatory noun — Shostakovitch's), who, in turn, didn't know any Kazakh. Some of the real authors were actually rather well-known figures in Soviet letters, which is why they were assigned the job in the first place: they knew only too well what the authorities expected of them and of their poems. The team "wrote fast and prolifically", Shostakovitch goes on, "and when one of the 'translators' dried up, he was replaced by a new, fresh one". "The factory was closed down only on Dzhambul's death", which was made known throughout the world; that is, when he could no longer be taken advantage of in person. Luckily enough (for the planners), he lived to be ninety-nine.

Evidently, the Soviet authorities resorted to this practice in a highly calculated attempt to meet two needs at once, each drawing on a different source: the poems had to praise 'the great leader' and his deeds in a way deemed appropriate. People of the Russian *intelligentsia* were in the best position to do that. On the other hand, the new norms which were then being adopted in the Soviet Union demanded that "the new slaves . . . demonstrate their cultural accomplishments to the residents of the capital", in Shostakovitch's harsh formulation (1979: 164). Consequently, an author for the concoction had to be found in the *national republics* such as Kazakhstan, and not in the Russian centre; and in case a suitable one couldn't be found, one had to be invented.

In this case, as in many others, the invention was not *biographical*: a forgery of such magnitude — the invention of a person that has had no form of existence whatsoever — would have been too easy to detect, with all the ensuing detrimental consequences. However, it most certainly was a *functional* kind of invention: the required figure was thus not made up as a person, but rather as a persona; namely, the 'author' in the Kazakh language of a growing corpus of poems which, in point of fact, came into being in Russian. The invented persona was superimposed on an existing person, among other things, in order that someone could be present in the flesh on selected occasions, thus enhancing the 'authenticity' of the poems as well as that of their [fictitious] author.

Significantly, comparable methods were used in music, [folk] dance, and several other arts too, which renders the use of fictitious translations in Stalin's Soviet Union part of a major culture-planning operation, and a very successful one, at that (from the point of view of those who thought it out): mere disguise systematically turned into flat forgery.

Notes

1. E.g. Toury (1982, 1984, 1995a: Excursus A). Others have also tackled this phenomenon although from slightly different angles; most notably Santoyo (1984) and Sohár (1998).

2. For more details see Toury (1995a: 31–35; 1995b: 135–147).

3. Thus, one possible way of settling the long dispute over the authenticity of Macpherson's Ossianic poetry — one of the most influential cases of pseudo-translating in the history of European Literature — is precisely to maintain that it is various elements of a whole *tradition* of Gaelic oral poetry which underlies it rather than a finite number of instances of performance, let alone one particular (source) text in the Gaelic language for each and every English (target) text. See Stafford and Gaskill (1998).

4. By an interesting coincidence, a few decades earlier, the English Gothic novel itself had come into being at least in part under disguise, most notably another famous fictitious translation, Horace Walpole's *The Castle of Otranto* (1764). But this was truly a historical 'accident'.

5. See the sources mentioned in n. 2 as well as Itamar Even-Zohar, "Culture Planning and Cultural Resistance". URL: http://www.tau.ac.il/~itamarez/papers/plan_res.html.

6. To be sure, all this occurred a short while after the Egyptian part of the famous 'Rosetta Stone' had finally been deciphered. Even laymen heard about this achievement, mostly through the local press. Many developed 'romantic' ideas towards it, which may serve as a partial explanation for Smith's selection of his 'source language'; especially as a substantial part of the truly biblical stories took place in Egypt or in connection with it anyway. At the same time, even if they saw some blurred pictures of the Stone in a newspaper, the majority had very little idea as to what the deciphered languages were like, either in form or in usage. In fact, when Smith was later asked to present some of the 'Egyptian' characters he had seen on the original golden plated, he produced a piece of paper which resembled nothing; certainly no hieroglyphs. (The paper is reproduced e.g. in Brodie's biography of Smith [Brodie 1963: facing p. 51].)

Works cited

Brodie, Fawn M. 1963. *No Man Knows My History: The Life of Joseph Smith, the Mormon Prophet*. Eyre & Spottiswoode (Frontier Library), [1945].

Even-Zohar, Itamar. "Culture Planning and Cultural Resistance". URL: http://www.tau.ac.il/~itamarez/papers/plan_res.html

James, Carl. 1989. "Genre Analysis and the Translator". *Target* 1:1, 29–47.

Masanov, Ju. I. 1963. "Lozhnye perevody". In *V mire psevdonimov, anonimov i literaturnykh poddelock*. Moskva, 99–106

Santoyo, Julio César. 1980. "La Traducción Como Técnica Narrativa". In *Actas del IV Congreso de la Asociación Española de Estudios Anglo-Norteamericanos (Salamanca, del 18 al 21 de Diciembre de 1980)*. Salamanca: Ediciones Universidad.

Shavit, Zohar. 1989. "The Entrance of a New Model into the System: The Law of Transformation". In: Karl Eimermacher, Peter Crzybek and Georg Witte, eds. *Issues in Slavic Literary and Cultural Theory*. Bochum: Brockmeyer, 593–600.

Shostakovitch, Dmitri. 1979. *Testimony: The Memoirs of Dmitri Shostakovich, as Related to and Edited by Solomin Volkov*. Tr. Antonina W. Bouis. London: Hamish Hamilton.

Sohár, Anikó. 1998. "'Genuine' and 'Fictitious' Translations of Science Fiction and Fantasy in Hungary". In Lynne Bowker, Michael Cronin, Dorothy Kenny and Jennifer Pearson, eds. *Unity in Diversity?: Current Trends in Translation Studies*. Manchester: St. Jerome, 38-46.

Stafford, Fiona and Gaskill, Howard. eds. 1998. *From Gaelic to Romantic: Ossianic Translations*. Amsterdam/Atlanta: Rodopi.

Toury, Gideon. 1982. "Pseudotranslation as a Literary Fact: The Case of *Papa Hamlet*". *Hasifrut/Literature* 32 (1982), 63–68 [in Hebrew].

Toury, Gideon. 1984. "Translation, Literary Translation and Pseudotranslation". *Comparative Criticism* 6. Cambridge: Cambridge University Press, 73–85.

Toury, Gideon. 1995a. *Descriptive Translation Studies and Beyond*. Amsterdam and Philadelphia: John Benjamins.

Toury, Gideon. 1995b. "The Notion of 'Assumed Translation': An Invitation to a New Discussion". In Henri Bloemen, Erik Hertog and Winibert Segers, eds. *Letterlijkheid/Woordelijkheid: Literality/Verbality*. Antwerpen and Hermelen: Fantom, 135–147.

Toury, Gideon. 1998. "Culture Planning and Translation". Alberto Álvarez Lugrís and Anxo Fernández Ocampo eds. In *Anovar/Anosar: Estudios deTraducción e Interpretación*. Vigo: Servicio de Publicións da Universidade de Vigo, 13–25.

Toury, Gideon. 2002. "Translation as a Means of Planning and the Planning of Translation: A Theoretical Framework and an Exemplary Case. In Saliha Paker ed., *Translations: (Re)shaping of Literature and Culture*, İstanbul: Boğaziçi University Press, 148–165.

Tynjanov, Jurij. 1967. "Das literarische Faktum". In *Die literarischen Kunstmittel und die Evolution in der Literatur*. Tr. Alexander Kaempfe. Frankfurt am Main: Suhrkamp, 7–36 [Russian original: 1924].

Weissbrod, Rachel. 1989. *Trends in the Translation of Prose Fiction from English into Hebrew, 1958–1980*. Tel Aviv: Tel Aviv University [Ph.D. Dissertation; in Hebrew].

Yahalom, Shelly. 1978. *Relations entre les littératures française et anglaise au 18e Siècle*. Tel Aviv: Tel Aviv Universtiy [MA Thesis; in Hebrew].

Chapter 2

Translation and cultural transformation

The case of the Afrikaans bible translations

Jacobus A. Naudé

University of the Free State

Introduction

Historically speaking, translation activities played a crucial role in redefining and regenerating cultures worldwide (Delisle et al. 25–100). This paper is the forerunner of a much larger project dealing with the relationship between translation and culture as it arises from the influence of the Afrikaans Bible translations on the cultural-political transformation of the Afrikaner. The influence of Afrikaner nationalist ideology on these Afrikaans translations accomplished by male Afrikaner scholars, deriving from a neo-Calvinist middle-class background, formed the topic of at least one previous investigation (Payle 1988: 122–132). The process of translating the Bible into Afrikaans was not a politically, socially or theologically isolated event. Specifically, this paper seeks to investigate the translation strategies used to transfer aspects of culture that influenced the cultural transformation of the Afrikaner in South Africa at grass-roots level. A cultural model for translation criticism, used within the descriptive translation studies paradigm is adopted in order to conduct a comparative analysis of selected aspects. In a comparative analysis, the translation critic has to take into account a complex network of relations between, on the one hand, the source text and the political, social, cultural, literary and textual norms and conventions of the source system, and, on the other hand, the target texts and the political, social, cultural, literary and textual norms and conventions of the target system.

Historical context

South African history is capable of a structural division into four principal epochs namely Dutch (1652–1795), British (1795–1924/1948), Afrikaner (1924/1948–

1990) and Democratic (since 1994). These divisions coincide roughly with the structural periods in the vicissitudes of Western economy: a mercantilist world order where slavery was an accepted institution (1350–1770); a 19th century world order (1770–1914) bringing in its wake the philosophy of emancipation and revolution; a contemporary western order (1914–1990) with the preponderance of human rights as its hallmark and the new world order or global village era, where cultural and political borders diminished markedly (since 1990) (Adapted from Terreblanche 1980: 258–259).

The Dutch period

South Africa was inhabited by the San (Bushmen) and the Khoe-Khoe (Hottentots) at that point in history when the Dutch East India Company (VOC) selected Table Bay as its mainland base for merchant ships plying the trade routes between European ports and the Far East (Bredekamp 1986: 102–103). With this sole purpose of sustenance in mind the first community of Dutch settlers was established at the Cape in 1652, to be followed by the French Huguenots in 1688 and numerous German immigrants ever since 1691 (Boucher, 1986: 61–66). Gradually the European settlers ousted the indigenous peoples from their land and their water resources—possibly as the result of their unfamiliarity with Khoe-Khoe notions of ownership and utilisation of land (Bredekamp 1986: 104–106). The settlers employed the Khoe-Khoe as farm labourers and drafted them into the army. The VOC suffered such an acute shortage of labour that it found itself compelled to import slaves from the Malay archipelago and from regions situated in both West and East Africa (Angola, Guinea and Madagascar). The Cape rapidly developed into a society with distinct stratifications of legal and social status (servants and white landowners) (Boucher 1986: 67–71). The status of the white population continued unabated for almost three and a half centuries.

Driven by their desire to hunt, to settle or to escape from VOC supremacy, the Dutch settlers, or Boers as they are sometimes called, penetrated the frontier zone already frequented by San hunters and further inland to the north and to the south into regions occupied by Bantu-speaking pastoralists. In the year 1778, the Fish River (1,000 kilometers to the East of Cape Town) was fixed as the eastern boundary of the then Cape Colony (Boucher 1986: 67).

The British period

England seized the Cape in the course of the wars unleashed by the French

Revolution and accorded colonial status to this addition to its empire. White-hall continued to administer the Cape from 1795 onwards, except for a brief interval between 1803 and 1806 when it reverted back to Dutch rule (Le Cor-deur 1986: 75–93). In 1820, 5,000 immigrants, later known as the 1820 settlers, arrived at the Cape (Butler 1986: 100–101). Their presence as well as the rigid authoritarianism of British rule equal to that of the demised VOC was bitterly resented by the Boers.

During the period 1836 to 1838, tensions rose on the frontier and unmiti-gated British oppression led to a systematic emigration of the Boers (subse-quently known as the Afrikaners). Organized parties of Boers accompanied by their Khoe-Khoe retainers and servants travelled towards the north to estab-lish their own republics (the Republic of the Transvaal and the Republic of the Orange Free State) on what was believed to be vacant land (Heydenrych 1986: 143–160). This was the much-vaunted Great Trek and represents a way the Bo-ers adopted to vent their anger at the more general philanthropic aspects of British colonial policy. As the desire for access to Africa among the European powers increased, the determination to maintain British hegemony in the area grew apace, no doubt spurred on by the thought of the untold riches buried be-neath the crust of the earth in the diamond fields of Kimberley and the gold fields of the Witwatersrand. This led to the South African (Anglo-Boer) War (1899–1902) which engulfed the Republic of the Transvaal and the Orange Free State (Pakenham 1986: 200–219). The conflict involved the entire population of South Africa in one way or another. It was a savage cataclysmic strife where the entire population was drawn into the inferno. Boer women and children evicted from farms or villages which were pillaged and put to the torch were lodged in concentration camps where vast numbers succumbed to the scourge of disease and malnutrition. African farm labourers were likewise placed in camps, or drafted into labour gangs by the British Army.

The Afrikaner period

In 1910, the former Boer republics, now two British colonies, joined the Cape Colony and Natal in forming the Union of South Africa, a dominion of Great Britain (Spies 1986: 231–248). However, the wounds inflicted on the Afrikaner by the war still chafed. The agonised poetry of this era reflects a much more intense nationalism than the Afrikaner had ever felt before. Earlier efforts in the seventies and eighties of the previous century seeking to consolidate the Afrikaner behind cultural and political movements were resuscitated, and drew their renewed strength from a reaction against imperial rule. A new Afrikaner republicanism and a host of cultural and welfare societies sprang up. All of them had Afrikaner interests at heart and in particular those of the vast number of Afrikaners impoverished by the war (Murray 1986: 249–259).

The National Party, which was formed in 1914 to foster the political development of the Afrikaner until parity with the English-speaking part of the population was achieved, won the general election of 1948. Be that as it may, after 1948 the National Party committed itself to the apartheid ideology, which had been refined into a formula that would ensure the political future of the white minority well into the next millenium (Stadler 1986: 260–270). The basic underlying idea was to create a permanent white political majority by establishing homelands for Africans in which alternative political provision could be made for them eventually leading to self-government and a measure of independence. In 1961, the country became a republic and left the Commonwealth.

The democratic period

Black militancy waxed perceptibly during the 1980s and particularly 1985 and 1986. The tidal wave of African liberation finally reached South Africa's borders. The fervour of conflict in Africa dropped rapidly with the collapse of the Soviet Union, making the American policy of constructive engagement a realistic alternative all of a sudden. A new generation of the Afrikaner, tired of conflict and driven by a sense of social justice introduced a change in society. Between 1988 and 1989 white leaders across the spectrum decided to engage the ANC's exiled leaders in exploratory conversations. The break-through was brought about by a decision of the then State President F W de Klerk to release the incarcerated ANC leader, Nelson Mandela, unconditionally in February 1990, after the latter had served twenty-seven years in prison. This led to South Africa's first democratic election in April 1994 and to a Government of National Unity (Burger 1998: 28–31).

The emergence of Afrikaans

When the settlement at the Cape was founded, the first Dutch settlers spoke different dialects resulting from a lack of uniform written or spoken language as in the Netherlands. Dutch remained the dominant language, which was in due course adopted by all foreigners. The broken Dutch of the foreigners, who outnumbered the Dutch during most of the VOC's rule, also simplified the language spoken by the Dutch colonists. It is generally accepted that the presence of English cannot be held to account for the origin of Afrikaans, since the vernacular spoken at the Cape had obviously assumed its modified guise prior to the arrival of the British in 1795. By the end of the 18th century, it had probably attained most of the distinctive characteristics to identify it as a (separate) language distinct from Dutch to the extent that newcomers from the Netherlands were not conversant therewith (Van Rensburg 1994: 166–179). Thus, Afrikaans the youngest member of the Germanic family of languages, sprang from the Dutch dialects of the 17th century and developed into a separate language during the century and a half of the Dutch East India Company's sway at the Cape. Although Afrikaans was widely spoken, Dutch remained the written and cultural tongue of scholars and urban dwellers (the standard language) until the end of the 19th century. Afrikaans (non-standard Dutch) was the language of the lower classes of the society namely the Dutch settlers (or Boers) in the interior, the destitute, the slaves and the landless. For them standard Dutch amounted to nothing more than a closed book. Until the end of the 19th century Afrikaans enjoyed no language rights due to the fact that English became the language of the government and officialdom in 1822.

The use made of Afrikaans by a secessionist political movement in the Eastern Cape (Meurant) and as a medium for Islamic religious instruction (Abu Bakr) failed to strengthen the claims of Afrikaans as a written or spoken language (Davids 1994: 110–119). During the 1870s a movement with the main object and incentive to translate the Bible into Afrikaans was initiated. By then the Dutch Bible was well beyond the reach of the average speaker of Afrikaans. This went hand in hand with the establishment of an association known as the Afrikanerbond (Afrikaner Society) which used Afrikaans to promote the political ideals of the Afrikaner, and to campaign for official recognition of the language. The goals set for themselves by both movements came to naught. The Boer War gave a fresh impetus to the language movement to the extent that from 1905 onwards, literary works appeared in Afrikaans for the first time. In 1918 Afrikaans was accorded the status of an official language of the Union and in 1925 it replaced Dutch as one of the languages of Parliament. By 1919 Afrikaans had been fully recognised as the official language of the Church by all the Dutch Reformed Churches, to be followed in 1933 by the publication of a complete translation of the Bible in Afrikaans (Hofmeyer 1987: 95–123).

Three manifestations of Afrikaans are distinguishable: Southwestern or Cape Afrikaans, based on the non-standard Dutch of the slaves and the Khoe-Khoe; Northwestern (Namaqualand) Afrikaans or Orange River Afrikaans influenced to a considerable extent by the Khoe-Khoe in the Orange River basin; the Afrikaans of the rural non-standard speakers of Dutch in the Eastern Border of the Cape on which the northern vernaculars of Afrikaans (Transvaal and Free State) are based. The Afrikaans, accepted as standard language in 1925, is based on the northern variety of the last-mentioned and adapted to suit the model of standardised Dutch (Du Plessis 1994: 120–129). The standardisation process of Afrikaans started in 1914 and continued after 1925 to develop into the Afrikaans academic, technical and religious language.

The Afrikaans bible translations

Early endeavours

The Bible of the Afrikaans speaking community was the Dutch Authorised Version (State-Bybel), representing an overwhelming influence on the religious life of the Afrikaner. In 1872 concern was voiced over the fact that the meaning of the Dutch Bible was at that stage beyond the grasp of ordinary Afrikaners. The idea of translating the Bible into Afrikaans was the main object and incentive of the Society of True Afrikaners established with this purpose in mind. Their plea was flatly refused by both the British and Foreign Bible Society as well as the Dutch Reformed ministers. A few books of the Bible were nevertheless translated into Afrikaans, mainly by S. J. du Toit and his associates. His translations never became popular, because they reflect Cape Afrikaans, a variant not acceptable to the Afrikaans speakers in the interior. This period ended on the demise of S. J. du Toit in 1911 (Smit 1970: 225–229).

The first complete translation (1933) and its revision (1953)

Prof. B. B. Keet championed the cause of the Bible in Afrikaans in the course of a lecture delivered in 1914, which was followed up two years later by a resolution of the Free State Synod of the Dutch Reform Church to the effect that the Bible should be translated into Afrikaans. This resolution represents for all practical purposes the first positive decision emanating from the church authorities. A translation was made from the Dutch Authorised Version and checked against the Hebrew and Greek. This publication, in 1922, of the Four Gospels and the Psalms encountered fierce criticism (Smit 1970: 229–231).

Due to this criticism levelled at these efforts a return to the original texts

and a source text oriented translation from the Greek and the Hebrew was re-
solved upon. This resulted in the 1929 translation of the Four Gospels and the
Psalms in which various translators from the sorority of Afrikaans churches
participated. The translation was finally brought to completion in 1933. In that
very same year, the Bible was officially put into service by the three Afrikaans
Churches (Nienaber 1935: 108–182).

A decision to revise was taken as early as 1933. Originally expected to take
about three years to complete, a full twenty years elapsed before the revision
made its début in 1953. The differences between the revised version and the original 1933 translation manifest themselves mainly on a linguistic level and can
be divided into four categories namely punctuation, spelling, choice of words
and the construction of sentences. The demand for a more fundamental revision was heard shortly after this publication. However, the revision process
progressed at snail's pace and gradually the idea of a brand-new translation as-
serted itself (Smit 1970: 233–235).

However, the first translation and its revision had an impact on the development, enrichment and promotion of the Afrikaans language and its recognition
as a national language.

The new translation (1983)

The development of Afrikaans; the advances made in the field of biblical science
(archaeological discoveries casting light on the cultural and historical background of the Bible, the progress made in the field of textual research and the
development of textual criticism as a science); and the emergence of translation
science (under the influence of Eugene Nida) all contribute to the decision to
translate the Bible into contemporary Afrikaans.

The Bible Society of South Africa arranged a large translator's seminar during
July 1967. Eugene Nida, then secretary for translation of the American Bible Society, was one of those who conducted the seminar. When Nida suggested that
a new translation would be received with much more enthusiasm than a revision, this novel idea was born (Wegener 1985: 228–238). The decision in favour
of a new target text oriented translation was ratified by the Bible Society in 1968.
The synods of the sorority of Afrikaans churches followed suit. Advisors in the
field of philology and a final editorial committee consisting of philologists and
theologians were appointed.

The first three books from the Old Testament and three from the New Testament were finished during 1971 and published. *Die Blye Boodskap* consist-

ing of the Four Gospels, the Acts of the Apostles and the first fifty Psalms, was published in 1975. Steady progress was made and the final manuscript of the New Testament and the Psalms was handed over to the Bible Society of South Africa in 1979. Four years later (1983) the complete Bible in its most recent translation was completed. This Bible was released fifty years subsequent to the publication of the first Bible in Afrikaans (Wegener 1985: 231–238).

The publication of the two complete official Afrikaans Bible translations co-incided each with a transition stage in the history of the Republic of South Africa. The first translation (1933) and its revision (1953) saw the light of day simultaneously with nascent Afrikaner nationalism, while the second translation (1983) reached completion in an epoch best described as the twilight of Afrikaner nationalist supremacy and the advent of the first democratically elected government of the Republic of South Africa. In the next section the epistemological traditions within which the translations were done as well as the sanctioning and dismissal of apartheid are overviewed.

Epistemological traditions

Epistemological traditions and the Afrikaans translations

Two epistemological traditions in the Dutch Reformed Church can be identified since 1920: naïve and critical realism (Deist 1994: 63). Naïve realism or Calvinism as represented by the conservative stream in biblical science originated from the fundamentalist theology of Amsterdam and Princeton. They claim that the Biblical stories are historically reliable and infallible and may be seen as a vehicle to promote the intention of the Almighty (Bible = Word of God) (Deist 1994: 112–113). Critical realism is a much more sophisticated approach regarding theology as a science to be studied critically. The existence and revelation of God was regarded as axiomatic, but the unequivocal and facile acceptance of the Bible as the Word of God came under fire. Until 1935 (marking the completion of the first Afrikaans translation), an uneasy truce existed between the proponents of the two opposing traditions. The translators of the first complete Afrikaans translation were from both traditions. However, after 1935, the conservative group with their naïve-realistic theology gained the upper hand and the critical group departed from the scene in disarray. The epistemology of naïve realism contributed to the uncritical support provided by the Dutch Reformed Church for the apartheid policies of the Nationalist Government (Deist

1994: 155–260). The story of creation and the tower of Babel were seen as historical events and formed *inter alia* the argument for apartheid by Christian/Cal-
vinistic politics. Pivotal to the Afrikaner way of thinking was their conviction
of being God's chosen people and thereby merging their own national identity
with that of Old Testament Israel—a people separated from the rest of the nations (Du Toit 1983: 920–952). Beginning in the sixties critical realism made a
come back, experiencing a high tide—in the seventies so as to restore the equilibrium which existed between the two rival groups prior to 1935 (Deist 1994:
261–318). It goes *pari passu* with acquiescent social consciousness among the
Afrikaners. The new complete translation of the Afrikaans Bible was undertaken in these days by proponents from both groups.

The sanctioning of apartheid by the church

Until 1930 biblical justification for the differentiation among nations was found
nowhere. A moral basis for the idea of apartheid was taken over from Kuyper
and was introduced into South Africa via the Free University of Amsterdam.
According to Kuyper, God rules, manages and determines creation in its diversity of sovereign spheres of authority (for example state, society, church) by
means of creation ordinances (principle of diversity) which give to each different sphere a certain authority and character (Loubser 1987: 39–41). In the
1940s the popularity of Kuyper's theology was to reach its climax in South Africa. Each ethnic group was seen as an organism, which formed part of the body
of humanity. Each people were seen as a sovereign sphere, normative in itself
and directly responsible to God for its own household. Unity and diversity are
accommodated by holding on to the unity of creation in the mystical body of
Christ and also ascribing the diversity to the ordinance of God (Loff 1983: 10–
23). This duality of concepts, diversity and unity, was to form the future framework for the Dutch Reformed Church's vision of apartheid. As early as 1943 at
a meeting of the Council of Dutch Reformed Churches a decision was taken
whereby biblical proofs for apartheid were accepted. In 1962 a commission was
appointed to establish a scriptural justification of apartheid. Time and again
reports were turned down because of their controversial nature. The Landman
concept resulted in the historic document *Human Relations and the South African Scene in the Light of Scripture* (*Ras, Volk en Nasie*) accepted by the Church
in 1974. Quotes from this bear eloquent testimony that the nature of the first
translation encouraged this view.

The dismissal of apartheid and the emerging of social consciousness

At the seminal synod of the Dutch Reformed Church in South Africa (representing 38% of the White and 60% of the Afrikaner population) in October 1986, the biblical justification for apartheid, as upheld during the past forty-three years, was retracted as stated in a document *Church and Society* (Kerk *en Samelewing* (1986)). A revised edition was published in 1990.

The new translation (1983) introduces a new vocabulary of reconciliation, clearly apparent from the quotes contained in the document on church and society. This reconciliation vocabulary provided moral support for the Afrikaner to submit to a new dispensation.

Support for this view is that a small group of Afrikaners who inimical to the new dispensation either acknowledges only the first translation and its revision (the Afrikaner Protestant Church) or opts for a new source-oriented translation (some members of the Reformed Church).

In the next section, the comparison of proof texts will be presented, which will justify the above hypotheses concerning the influence of the Afrikaans Bible translations on culture. It will also be shown which translation strategies are followed by each translation.

Comparison of the proof texts

Theoretical assumptions

The realisation that translations are never produced in a vacuum, regardless of time and culture, and the desire to explain the time- and culture-bound criteria which are at play, resulted in a shift during the early eighties towards a descriptive approach to translation criticism (Hermans 1985). The descriptive translation theorist starts with a practical examination of a corpus of texts and then seeks to determine those norms and constraints operating on these texts in a specific culture and at a specific moment in history. In other words, the theorists attempt to account not only for textual strategies in the translated text, but also for the way in which the translation functions in the target cultural and literary system. The greatest advantage offered by this approach is that it enables us to bypass deep-rooted source-oriented and normative traditional ideas concerning fidelity and quality in translation. Stated otherwise, the researcher describes (i.e., explains) the specific characteristics of a translated text (or multiple translations of the same original) in terms of constraints or norms reigning in the target system at a particular time, which may have influenced the method of translating and the ensuing product. The quality of equivalence between translations and their originals may be described in terms of shifts or manipulations that have occurred.

The question is how does one set about comparing anything. The first step is to make sure that like is compared to like: this means that the two (or more) entities to be compared, while differing in some respect, must share certain attributes (James 1980: 169). This requirement is especially strong in the process of contrasting, i.e., looking for differences, since it is only against a background of similarity that differences are significant. This similarity is called the constant and the difference variables. The constant has traditionally been known as the tertium comparationis (TC). In the light of the above, a TC will therefore comprise an independent, constant (invariable) set of dimensions in terms of which segments of the target text (TT) and source text (ST) can be compared or mapped on to each other (adapted from Toury 1995: 80). In this paper the Afrikaans TTs are compared to the Biblical Hebrew (BH) or Greek New Testament (GNT) ST in terms of the cultural dimensions of words for division, justice, truth, etc. as functioning in the proof texts of the documents *Human Relations* and *Church and Society*.

In the next two sections proof texts for the justification of apartheid and of social consciousness are compared with the first (OAV) and the new Afrikaans versions (NAV). It will be shown that the first Afrikaans translation utilises the strategies of explication/intensification. The result is that apartheid vocabulary is highlighted. The new Afrikaans translation utilizes the strategy of substitution, paraphrase, generalization and deletion. The apartheid vocabulary is downplayed.

Proof texts for the justification of apartheid

Texts were used in an arbitrary and cavalier way to illustrate the theme of diversity. The weightiest item of proof was adduced from a passage in Genesis 11 relating the building of the Tower of Babel (Ras 1974: 14–18). It is the first verse *par excellence* which reveals the error made (Bax 1983: 112–143). The most important inference drawn was that differentiation is God's purpose for creation. From this finding, the principle of apartheid was derived.

(1)   Genesis 11:1

    (a) BH   וַיְהִי כָל־הָאָרֶץ שָׂפָה אֶחָת וּדְבָרִים אֲחָדִים

              The whole earth was one lip and one set of words.

    (b) OAV   En die hele aarde het dieselfde taal gehad en een en dieselfde woorde.

              And the whole world had the same language and one and the same words.

    (c) NAV   Die hele wêreld het net een taal gepraat.

              The whole world spoke only one language.

As a source text oriented translation, the OAV explicates the ST by replacing *one* with the *same* in the first part of the verse and adds *same* to the second part. However, NAV (as a target text oriented translation) transfers *one* of the ST into the TT and deletes the last part of the verse, which is a repetition of the first part (see Kerk 1986: 21).

Genesis 1:28 is seen as a command of God in order to justify a positive differentiation (Ras 1974: 14–15). A logical leap was made to quote the multiplication of mankind as substantiation of a cultural differentiation. OAV transfers *fill* of the ST. NAV substitutes it with a general term *inhabit* (see Kerk 1986: 31).

(2)   Genesis 1:28 (also Genesis 9:1, 7)

    (a) BH   פְּרוּ וּרְבוּ וּמִלְאוּ אֶת־הָאָרֶץ

              Be fruitful and multiply, and fill the earth.

    (b) OAV   Wees vrugbaar en vermeerder en vul die aarde.

              Be fruitful and increase and fill the earth.

    (c) NAV   Wees vrugbaar, word baie, bewoon die aarde...

              Be fruitful, become many, inhabit the earth...

In earlier documents the concept of diversity drew considerable support from the qualification of everything created *after its own kind* (Genesis 1:11, 21 (2×), 24, 25 (3×)) (Loubser 1987: 56–57). OAV explicates the ST item by replacing it with *sort*. NAV substitutes the ST item by a general term *nature*.

(3)   Genesis 1:11

    (a) BH   לְמִינוֹ

              after its own kind

    (b) OAV   volgens hulle soorte

              after their sorts/species

(c) NAV   elkeen NAV sy aard
          everyone after its nature

A similar conclusion is drawn from Genesis 10 containing the table of nations where mention of a spontaneous diversification of the human race into different generations is made (Genesis 10:5, 20 and 31) (Ras 1974: 12–14).

(4)   Genesis 10:5
      (a) BH   מֵאֵלֶּה נִפְרְדוּ אִיֵּי הַגּוֹיִם בְּאַרְצֹתָם
               From these the coastlands of the nations were branched off
               into their countries.
      (b) OAV uit hulle het verdeel geraak die kuslande van die nasies, in
               hulle lande...
               out of them the coastal regions of the nations became sep-
               arated, according to their countries...
      (c) NAV Uit hulle het die mense wat nou die kusstreke bewoon, daarna-
               toe versprei...
               Out of them humans now inhabiting the coastal regions,
               spread thereto...

The ST item *branch off* is explicated by the OAV item with *separated/divided*. NAV substitutes the ST item by *spread*. In addition, NAV substitutes the ST item *nations* by *humans* and deletes *to their countries* (see Kerk 1986: 21).

From Deuteronomy 32:8 and Acts 17:26 the conclusion is drawn that the history of the nations is not beyond the will or intervention of God. Occasionally He allotted each of them its own area of habitation. The view of the diversity of peoples flows directly from this tenet (Ras 1974: 20–24).

(5)   Deuteronomy 32:8
      (a) BH   בְּהַפְרִידוֹ בְּנֵי אָדָם יַצֵּב גְּבֻלֹת עַמִּים
               When He branching off the sons of man, He set the boundaries
               of the peoples...
      (b) OAV ...toe Hy die mensekinders van mekaar geskei het, het Hy die
               grense van die volke vasgestel...
               and when He separated the children of man from each other,
               He fixed the boundaries of the nations...
      (c) NAV ...toe Hy die mense in volke opgedeel het, het Hy vir hulle
               hulle grense bepaal...
               ...and branching off the people into nations, He fixed bounda-
               ries for them...

OAV explicates the ST item *branch off* with the TT item *separated/divided*. NAV transfers the ST item *branch off* (see Kerk 1986: 31).

(6)   Acts 17:26
    (a) GNT   ὁρίσας προστεταγμένους καιροὺς καὶ τὰς ὁροθεσίας τῆς
                      κατοικίας αὐτῶν
                      having determined their appointed times, and the boundaries
                      of their habitation...
    (b) OAV   ...terwyl Hy vooraf bepaalde tye en grense van hulle woon-
                      plek vasgestel het.
                      ...while he set fixed times and the boundaries of their habita-
                      tion.
    (c) NAV   Hy het bepaal hoe lank hulle sal bestaan en waar hulle sal woon.
                      He decided how long they would exist and where they would
                      live.

OAV transfers the ST items. NAV paraphrases the ST items with the result that *appointed times and boundaries of their habitation* of the ST merged into the rest of the passage (see Kerk 1986: 31).

The prohibition on Israel to mix with other peoples was adduced as proof of the maintenance of a diversity of cultures, peoples and races. This conclusion was drawn from *inter alia* the texts in (7)–(11) (Ras 1974: 95).

(7)   Deuteronomy 7:3 (also Joshua 23:12–13)
    (a) BH   וְלֹא תִתְחַתֵּן בָּם
                  You must not become a son-in-law with them.
    (b) OAV   ...Jy mag jou ook nie met hulle verswaer nie.
                      ...You must not become a son-in-law with them.
    (c) NAV   Jy mag nie met hulle ondertrou nie.
                      You shall not intermarry with them.

OAV transfers the ST item *you must not become a son-in-law with them*. NAV paraphrases the ST item.

(8)   Deuteronomy 23:2
    (a) BH   לֹא־יָבֹא מַמְזֵר בִּקְהַל יְהוָה
                  No child born out of wedlock shall enter the convocation of
                  the Lord.
    (b) OAV   Geen baster mag in die vergadering van die Here kom nie.
                      No bastard shall come into the convocation of the Lord.

(c) NAV   Niemand wat gebore is uit ontoelaatbare geslagsgemeenskap
mag lid van die gemeente word nie.
Nobody born from an inadmissible sexual union is allowed to
become a member of the congregation.

OAV explicates the ST item for *a child born out of wedlock* as *a bastard*, which
means in Afrikaans a child born from parents belonging to different racial
groups. This translation caused untold harm in South Africa. NAV substitutes
the ST item with the term *illegitimate birth* and adds a footnote referring to Le-
viticus 18: 6–20, which deals with illegitimate relationships. The ST item for *the
convocation* is explicated by the NAV by placing it within the religious sphere
(*member of the congregation*) (Kerk 1986: 35).

In (9)–(11) the intermarriage terminology of OAV which could be misunderstood as functioning within the political or judicial sphere is explicated by
NAV where it is placed in the religious sphere. Intermarriage is not forbidden
among nations but between believers and non-believers (Kerk 1986: 36).

(9)   Ezra 9:2
    (a) BH   וְהִתְעָרְבוּ זֶרַע הַקֹּדֶשׁ בְּעַמֵּי הָאֲרָצוֹת
... so that the holy race has become mixed with the nations of
the earth.
    (b) OAV   ... sodat die heilige geslag hom met die volke van die lande
vermeng het.
... in order that this holy generation does not intermingle with
the peoples of the countries.
    (c) NAV   Hulle het hierdie volk hom laat vermeng met heidene
They allowed this nation to intermingle with the heathen (=
non-believers).

(10)   Ezra 10:2
    (a) BH   וַנֹּשֶׁב נָשִׁים נָכְרִיּוֹת מֵעַמֵּי הָאָרֶץ
... that we made foreign women from the nations of the earth
residents.
    (b) OAV   ... dat ons vreemde vroue uit die volke van die land getrou het.
... that we married foreign women from the peoples of the
land.
    (c) NAV   ... ons het met vreemde vroue getrou, vroue uit die heidenna-
sies.
we married foreign women, women from the heathen nations.

(11)   Nehemiah 13:25
    (a) BH   אִם־תִּתְּנוּ בְנֹתֵיכֶם לִבְנֵיהֶם
             . . . you shall not give your daughter to their sons.
    (b) OAV   Julle mag julle dogters nie aan hulle seuns gee. . .
             You shall not give your daughters to their sons.
    (c) NAV   Julle sal julle dogters nie laat trou met die heidene se seuns
             nie. . .
             You shall not allow your daughters to marry the sons of the
             heathen. . .

Proof texts for social consciousness

NAV explicates social consciousness terminology (12)–(13).

(12)   Acts 10:34 (Kerk 1986: 26)
    (a) GNT Ἐπ᾽ ἀληθείας καταλαμβάνομαι ὅτι οὐκ ἔστιν προσωπολήμπτης
           ὁ θεός,ἀλλ᾽ ἐν παντὶ ἔθνει ὁ φοβούμενος αὐτὸν καὶ
           ἐργαζόμενος δικαιοσύνην δεκτὸς αὐτῷ ἐστιν.
           Truly I receive that God is not a respector of persons, but in
           every nation any one who fears him and does what is right is
           acceptable to him.
    (b) OAV Ek sien waarlik dat God geen aannemer van persoon is nie,
           maar dat in elke nasie die een wat Hom vrees en geregtigheid
           doen, Hom welgevallig is.
           Truly I see that God does not take anybody at face value, but
           that in every nation the one that fear Him and perform right-
           eousness is acceptable to Him.
    (c) NAV Waarlik, ek begryp nou eers dat God nie onderskeid maak nie,
           maar uit enige volk die mense aanneem wat Hom vereer en
           doen wat reg is.
           Truly, I understand now that God makes no distinction but out
           of any nation be accepts those who honour Him and do what
           is right.

(13) Isaiah 58:9 (Kerk 1986: 27)

(a) BH אִם־תָּסִיר מִתּוֹכְךָ מוֹטָה שְׁלַח אֶצְבַּע וְדַבֶּר־אָוֶן

If you take away from the midst of you the yoke, the pointing
of the finger, and the word of harm. . . . . . .

(b) OAV As jy van jou verwyder die verdrukking, die uitsteek van die
vinger en die leuenagtige woord. . .

If you remove from yourself the oppresion, the pointing of the
finger and the mendacious word.

(c) NAV As jy sorg dat mense nie meer by jou verdruk word nie, nie
meer gedreig en vals beskuldig word nie. . .

If you take care that people with you are no longer oppressed
or threatened or accused falsely.

Conclusion

The first translation and its revision had a massive impact on the development,
enrichment and promotion of the Afrikaans language and its recognition as a
national language but negative influence could not be avoided. Pivotal to the
Afrikaner way of thinking was their conviction of being God's chosen people
and thereby merging their own national identity with that of Old Testament Israel — a people separated from the rest of the nations. Quotes from a document
on race relations viewed in the light of the scriptures bear eloquent testimony to
the fact that the nature of the translation encouraged this view. In this translation the strategy of intensification/explication of the ST items is applied in most
cases. The second translation of Afrikaans Bible goes *pari passu* with acquiescent social consciousness among the Afrikaners. This translation introduces a
new vocabulary of reconciliation, clearly apparent from the quotes contained
in a document on church and society. The strategies of substitution, generalization, deletion and paraphrase are applied in the case of the above-mentioned ST
items. This reconciliation vocabulary gave moral support for the Afrikaner to
give consent for a new dispensation. Support for this view is that a small group
of Afrikaners who resists the new dispensation either acknowledges only the
first translation and its revision (the Afrikaner Protestant Church) or opts for a
new source-oriented translation (some members of the Reformed Church).

NAV substitutes offensive terminology of OAV by neutral or general terminology.

	Hebrew/Greek	OAV	NAV
Colossians 3:11 (Ras 1974: 28)	βάρβαρος non-Greek	barbaar barbarian	andertalig speaking a foreign language
	Σκύθης Scythian (regarded by Romans as the absolute example of paganism)	Seith Scythian	onbeskaaf uncivilized
Isaiah 56:6 (Ras 1974: 23)	עֲבָדִים servants	knegte footmen	dienaars servants
Exodus 12:38 (Ras 1974: 23) Nehemiah 13:3 (Ras 1974: 23) Numbers 11:4 (Ras 1974: 23)	עֵרֶב רַב mixed people	mense van gemengde bloed people of mixed blood	mense van ander afkoms people of alien descent
Isaiah 58:3 (Kerk 1986: 27)	עַצְּבֵיכֶם your (heavy) workers	arbeiders labourers	mense wat vir julle werk those working for you
Deuteronomy 15:3; 23:20 (Ras 1974: 23)	נָכְרִי foreigner	uitlander foreigner	nie-Israeliet non-Israelite
Galatians 2:12–21 (Ras 1974: 32)	μετὰ τῶν ἐθνῶν with the nations	Heidene Heathen	nie-Joodse gelowiges non-Jewish believers
	οἱ λοιποὶ Ἰουδαῖοι the remaining Jews	ander Jode other Jews	Joodse gelowiges Jewish believers
	ἐθνικῶς like a Gentile	soos 'n heiden lewe living like a heathen	nie meer aan die Joodse gebruike hou nie no longer observe Jewish custom
	τὰ ἔθνη Gentiles	Heidene Heathen	mense wat nooit Jode was nie people who were never Jews

	Hebrew	OAV	NAV
Isaiah 58:7 (Kerk 1986: 27)	עֲנִיִּים the poor	Ellendiges destitutes	armes the poor
	עֲרוּמִים the homeless	Swerwelinge tramps/vagabonds	dakloses the homeless
	עָרֹם the naked	wat naak is who is nude	iemand sonder klere somebody without clothes
Psalm 140:13 (Kerk 1986: 27)	עָנִי the poor	Ellendige destitute	hulpelose helpless

NAV substitutes the masculine/sexist terminology of OAV by neutral gender/non-sexist terminology.

	Hebre-w/Greek	OAV	NAV
Acts 10:28	ἀνδρὶ Ἰουδαίῳ Jewish man	Joodse man Jewish man	Jood Jew
Galatians 3:28 (Ras 1974: 28)	ἐλεύθερος free man	vry man free man	vry free (person)
Isaiah 56:3, 6 (Ras 1974: 23)	אָחִיךָ your brother	jou broer your brother	mede-Israeliet fellow-Israelite
Deuteronomy 23:7 (Ras 1974: 23)	אָחִיךָ your brother	jou broer your brother	jou bloedverwant your relative

NAV substitutes general relationship terminology of OAV with terminology, which explicates equality.

	Hebrew/Greek	OAV	NAV
Leviticus 19:34 (Kerk 1986: 24)	אֶזְרָח native	'n kind van die land a child of the land	Medeburger fellow citizen
Genesis 42:6	הַשַּׁלִּיט עַל־הָאָרֶץ ruler over the land	maghebber oor die land ruler over the land	beheer van Egipte Egyptian control
Romans 16:7,11 (Ras 1974: 30)	τοὺς συγγενεῖς μου my kinsmen	my stamgenote my tribesmen	my volksgenote my fellow-countryman
John 18:36 (Ras 1974: 32)	οἱ ὑπηρέται attendants	my dienaars my servants	my onderdane my subjects

NAV deletes offensive terminology of OAV

	Hebrew/Greek	OAV	NAV
Ruth 1:1 (Ras 1974: 23) Leviticus 19:34 (Kerk 1986: 24)	לָגוּר to sojourn	om as vreemdeling te vertoef to sojourn as strangers	om 'n heenkome te soek to seek a livelihood
2 Samuel 4:3 (Ras 1974: 23)	וַיִּהְיוּ שָׁם גֵּרִים they stay there as sojourners	was daar vreemdelinge tot vandag toe there were foreigners up to this very day	waar hulle nou asiel het where they now enjoy asylum

Religious terminology of OAV which could be misunderstood as functioning within the political or judicial sphere is explicated by NAV.

	HEBREW/GREEK	OAV	NAV
Deuteronomy 23:8 (23:3) (Ras 1974: 23)	בִּקְהַל יְהוָה in the convocation of the lord	vergadering van die Here congregation of the Lord	lid word van die gemeente become member of the community
Proverbs 14:34 (Ras 1974: 25)	צְדָקָה righteousness	geregtigheid Justice	gehoorsaamheid aan die Here obedience to the Lord
Isaiah 58:8 (Kerk 1986: 27)	צִדְקֶךָ your righteousness	jou geregtigheid your righteousness	hy wat jou red he who saves you
Ephesians 4:24 (Kerk 1986: 26)	ἐν δικαιοσύνῃ in righteousness	in ware geregtigheid in true righteousness	volgens die wil van God According to the will of God
Matthew 5:20 (Kerk 1986: 26)	ἡ δικαιοσύνη righteousness	julle geregtigheid your righteousness	julle getrouheid aan die wet your adherence to the law
1 Corinthians 1:30 (Ras 1974: 34)	δικαιοσύνη righteousness	geregtigheid righteousness	vryspraak acquittal
Luke 10:29 (Kerk 1986: 24)	δικαιῶσαι ἑαυτὸν to show himself to be righteous	homself regverdig to justify himself	homself handhaaf to assert yourself
Psalm 51:8 (Kerk 1986: 30)	אֱמֶת חָפַצְתָּ you took pleasure in the truth	U het welgevalle aan waarheid You take pleasures in truth	U verwag opregtheid You expect honesty

Acknowledgement

(The financial assistance of the National Research Fund to make the attendance possible of the International Conference on Culture and Translation, Beijing, China, where this paper was read, is hereby acknowledged.)

Works Cited

Bax, D.D. 1983. "The Bible and Apartheid 2." *Apartheid is a Heresy*. Eds. J, De Gruchy & C. Villa Vicencio. Cape Town: Citadel Press. 112–143.

Boucher, M. 1986. "Die Kaap onder die Verenigde Oos-Indiese Kompanjie." *Nuwe Geskiedenis van Suid-Afrika in Woord en Beeld*. Eds. T. Cameron & S.B. Spies. Kaapstad: Human & Rousseau. 61–74.

Bredekamp, H.C. 1986. "Die pre-koloniale en koloniale Khoikhoi." *Nuwe Geskiedenis van Suid-Afrika in Woord en Beeld*. Eds. T. Cameron & S.B. Spies. Kaapstad: Human & Rousseau. 102–105.

Burger, D. 1998. ed. *South African Yearbook*. Pretoria: GCIS.

Butler, G. 1986. "Die Verspreiding en Invloed van die 1820-Setlaars." *Nuwe Geskiedenis van Suid-Afrika in Woord en Beeld*. Eds. T. Cameron & S.B. Spies. Kaapstad: Human & Rousseau. 100–101.

Davids, A. 1994. "Afrikaans die Produk van Akkulturasie." *Nuwe Perspektiewe op die Geskiedenis van Afrikaans*. Eds. G. Olivier & A. Coetzee. Pretoria: Southern Publishers. 110–119.

Deist, F. E. 1994. *Ervaring, Rede en Metode in Skrifuitleg*. Pretoria: HRC.

Delisle, J. and J. Woodsworth. 1995. *Translators through History*. Amsterdam: John Benjamins.

Du Plessis, H. 1994. "Taalkontak Variasie in Afrikaans." *Nuwe Perspektiewe op die Geskiedenis van Afrikaans*. Eds. G. Olivier & A. Coetzee. Pretoria: Southern Publishers. 120–129.

Du Toit, A. 1983. "No Chosen People: The Myth of the Calvinist Origins of Afrikaner Nationalism and Racial Ideology." *American Historical Review* 88: 920–952.

Heydenrych, D.H. 1986. "Die Boererepublieke, 1852–1881." *Nuwe Geskiedenis van Suid-Afrika in Woord en Beeld*. Eds. T. Cameron & S.B. Spies. Kaapstad: Human & Rousseau. 143–160.

Hermans, T. 1985. "Translation Studies and a New Paradigm." *The Manipulation of Literature: Studies in Literary Translation*. Ed. T. Hermans. London: Croom Helm. 7–15.

Hofmeyer, I. 1987. "Building a Nation from Words: Afrikaans Language, Literature and Ethnic Identity, 1902–1924." *The Politics of Race Class and Nationalism in 20th Century South Africa*. Eds. S. Marks & S. Trapido. London: Longman. 95–123.

James, C. 1980. *Contrastive Analysis*. London: Longman.

Kerk en Samelewing. 1986. *Report of the General Synod of the Dutch Reformed Church (October 1986)*. Bloemfontein: Pro Christo Publications. (Revised 1990).

Le Cordeur, B.A. 1986. "Die Besettings van die Kaap, 1795–1854." *Nuwe Geskiedenis van Suid-Afrika in Woord en Beeld*. Eds. T. Cameron & S.B. Spies. Kaapstad: Human & Rousseau. 143–160.

Loff. C. 1983. "The History of a Heresy." *Apartheid is a Heresy*. Eds. J. De Gruchy & C. Villa Vicencio. Cape Town: David Philip. Guildford: Lutterworth. 10–23.

Loubser, J. A. 1987. *The Apartheid Bible*. Cape Town: Maskew Miller Longman..

Murray, B. 1986. "Die Tydperk van 1924 tot 1939." *Nuwe Geskiedenis van Suid-Afrika in Woord en Beeld*. Eds. T. Cameron & S.B. Spies. Kaapstad: Human & Rousseau. 249–259.

Nienaber, P.J. 1935. *Die Geskiedenis van die Afrikaanse Bybelvertaling*. Kaapstad: Nasionale Pers.

Pakenham, T. 1986. "Die Tweede Anglo-Boereoorlog, 1899–1902." *Nuwe Geskiedenis van Suid-Afrika in Woord en Beeld*. Eds. T. Cameron & S.B. Spies. Kaapstad: Human & Rousseau. 200–218.

Pale, K. 1988. "The Afrikaans Bible Translation: A Translation for all Afrikaans Speakers?" *NGTT* 39: 122–132.

Ras, Volk en Nasie en Volkereverhoudinge in die Lig van die Skrif. 1974. Report of the General Synod of the Dutch Reformed Church (October 1974). Cape Town: Dutch Reformed Publishers.

Smit, A.P. 1970. *God made it grow. History of the Bible Society Movement in Southern Africa*. Cape Town: The Bible Society of South Africa.

Spies, S.B. 1986. " Unie en Onenigheid, 1910–1924." *Nuwe Geskiedenis van Suid-Afrika in Woord en Beeld*. Eds. T. Cameron & S.B. Spies. Kaapstad: Human & Rousseau. 231–248.

Stadler, A.W. 1986. "Die Tydperk van 1939 tot 1948." *Nuwe Geskiedenis van Suid-Afrika in Woord en Beeld*. Eds. T. Cameron & S.B. Spies. Kaapstad: Human & Rousseau. 260–271.

Terreblanche, S.J. 1980. *Die Wording van die Westerse Ekonomie*. Pretoria: Academica.

Toury, G. 1995. *Descriptive Translation Studies and Beyond*. Amsterdam: John Benjamins.

Van Rensburg, C. 1994. "Die Ontstaan van Afrikaans in 'n Intertaal Konteks". *Nuwe Perspektiewe op die Geskiedenis van Afrikaans*, Eds. G. Olivier & A. Coetzee. Pretoria: Southern Publishers. 166–179.

Wegener, G.S. 1985. *In die Begin was die Woord*. Kaapstad: Human & Rousseau.

CHAPTER 3

Cultural borderlands
in China's translation history

Eva Hung
The Chinese University of Hong Kong

Cultural borderlands: a definition

Chinese translation history is perhaps unique in two ways: (1) it has the longest extant record of continuous activities, covering some three thousand years; (2) it shows that China as host culture was heavily reliant on translators of non-Chinese origins, particularly in terms of culturally-oriented translation activities.[1] The second point means that many of the translation activities which led to new developments and changes in Chinese culture were initiated or undertaken by non-Chinese people. For their work to be effective, they had to have sufficient knowledge of China's contemporary needs to be able to properly place both themselves and their work within this host culture. It therefore does not surprise us that many of these translators came from communities which provided them with the necessary linguistic and cultural background and training to engage in translation work into Chinese. In this paper we refer to such communities as cultural borderlands.

Our purpose here is to clarify the nature of the different types of bicultural or multicultural communities which had an impact on culturally-oriented translation activities in China from the 2nd century to the late 19th century. The term 'cultural borderlands' here refers to two kinds of communities:

1. Communities which were exposed to bicultural or multi-cultural influences because of their location at geographical and/or national boundaries;
2. Communities, large and small, which arose as a result of special social and political arrangements that allowed for the systems and norms of more than one culture to co-exist.

The term 'cultural borderlands' may, superficially at least, suggest a certain resemblance to the idea of "interculture" proposed by Anthony Pym (Pym 1998: 177–192; Pym 2000: 4–5). Pym's "interculture" is represented by the intersection of two overlapping circles. (Pym 1998: 177) While this may be a viable model for translation activities between countries which have the same linguistic and cultural roots, such as some of those in Europe, it does not fit the picture of many other translation traditions. Aside from this, there are other differences. Pym's "interculture" is translator-centred, to the extent that a single translator is considered a micro-interculture. (Pym 1998: 182–183) Cultural borderlands, on the other hand, are not formed exclusively of people who consciously engage in translation activities. Moreover, two elements embodied in the word 'borderlands' are not necessarily present in "interculture". The first is a sense of marginalization. In considering the translation history of a country such as China, where historically the cultural mainstream looked at international translation activities as peripheral at best and treacherous at worst, marginalization is an aspect which is crucial to our understanding of how translators and translated texts functioned. The second is the pressure a 'borderland' constantly experiences from the established cultural norms of its often dominating neighbours. This naturally has an impact both on the translators' self-positioning and on their translation choices and approaches.

In this paper our focus is on cultural borderlands that gave rise to translation communities in China, and on their relationship with the host culture whose

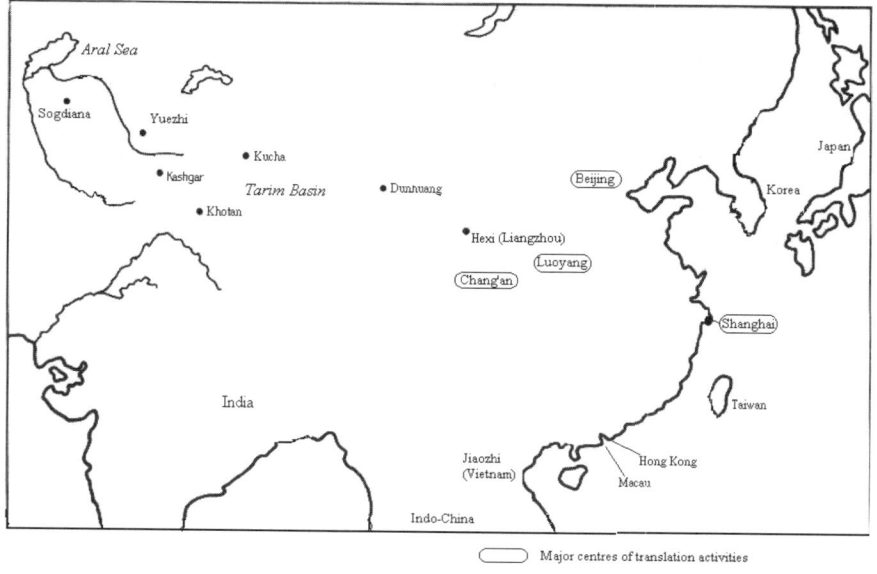

⟨⎯⎯⎯⎯⎯⎯⟩ Major centres of translation activities

• Significant originating places for translators

Map 1.

norms they tried to change. The communities concerned, as well as the major translation centres in which they worked, are shown in Map 1.

These cultural borderlands share some important characteristics: geographical and strategic significance in terms of host culture political/ military/ trade concerns; acceptance or toleration by the host culture establishment; and a certain degree of success in engaging some sections of the host culture in a dialogue. In this paper they are categorized as follows: (1) geo-political borderlands; (2) institution-based borderlands; (3) socio-political borderlands.

The suggested categorization is based on the most prominent feature shown by a borderland. We are mindful of the fact that the cultural shadings within each borderland are much more complex than a simple summary such as this can convey. The family as an institution, for example, played a significant role in the nurturing of translators in many Asian countries. In Japan and Korea, translator posts were often passed from father to son as the required linguistic and related cultural knowledge was kept as a family heritage unavailable to outsiders.[2] The number of translators of Sogdian descent in Tang China (618–907) suggests that even after their relocation from their original borderland, many families from the Western Region retained their multi-lingual skills. Similarly, the role played by Eurasians in the translation activities of Southeast Asia was significant. Bearing factors such as these in mind, our purpose here is to sketch out a ground plan on which future research will build.

Geo-political borderlands

The nature of geo-political borderlands is closely related to their physical location. They can be national or natural border areas. In China's translation history there are two obvious examples. One area, the Western Region, was outside of China proper but was influenced by the proximity and foreign policies of this larger neighbour. The other, Hexi, was China's western frontier which, because of its location, was subject to non-Chinese influences. Both areas were a significant nurturing ground for translators in the Buddhist sutra translation movement from the mid-2nd to the mid-9th centuries.[3]

The Western Region

The Taklamakan oases states (present-day Xinjiang in the PRC; the Western Region in Chinese historical records) and the area immediately to their west

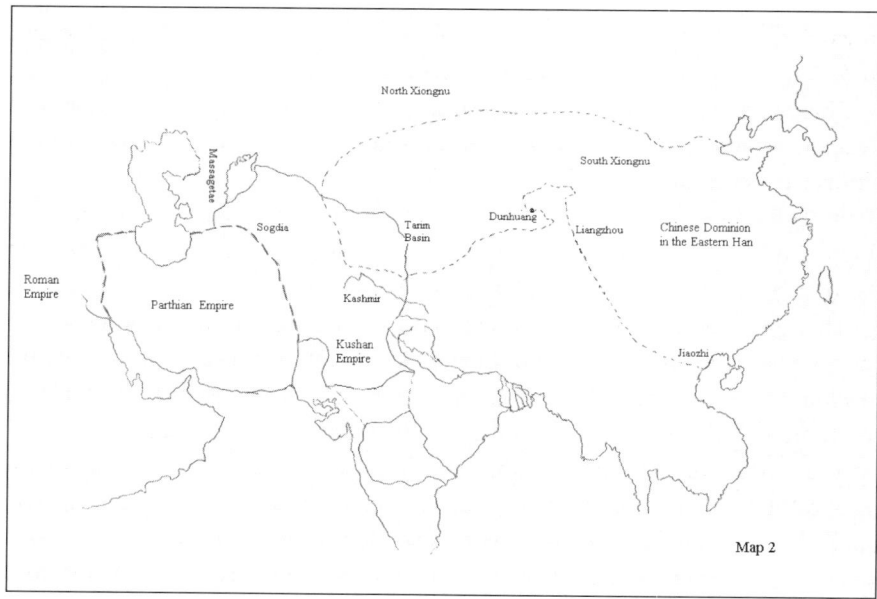

Map 2.

provided the leading sutra translators from the 2nd to the 5th centuries. Here we will focus on the oases states which formed a cultural community highly representative of geo-political borderlands. Dotting the rim of the Tarim Basin, these states were neighbours to two diverse, and often conflicting, modes of civilization — the nomadic as represented by the Xiongnu, and the agricultural as represented by the Chinese.[4] Both modes of production existed in these oases states. Moreover, this area was also important for international trade, for it was situated on the Silk Road which linked East Asia to Europe. There was thus a constant flow of new elements pertaining to the material and spiritual cultures of diverse civilizations. Ethnically the area had a mixed population of Turkish, Iranian, Scythian and Xiongnu descent, the result of population movement and displacement that reflected the rise and fall of individual groups or tribes over centuries. Politically these states had to acknowledge the suzerainty of the Kushan, the Chinese and the Xiongnu empires, sometimes in succession, sometimes simultaneously.[5] (For the political positioning of these oases states at the time when Buddhism spread from Central Asia to China, see Map 2.) Both the population mix and the diverse external influences meant that linguistically this was a melting pot where a combination of different languages and scripts were used over many centuries, with one or more of them adopted as *lingua franca* throughout the region.[6] Archeological finds, including bilingual coins and bilingual texts, bear witness to the linguistic diversity of this relatively small area. It was a borderland with an identity of its own, heavily influenced and sometimes militarily overwhelmed by its bigger neighbours, but still demonstrated characteristics which were distinct from theirs. What distinguished it most from its larger neighbours was cultural plurality and a readiness to embrace foreign ideas. (See Diagram 1).

The proximity and political connection of these oases states to the Kushan Empire, which boasted one of the most devout Buddhist monarchs in history,[7] meant that they had early exposure to Buddhism. Before the Buddhist translation movement started in China, the Inner Central Asian states already had experience in such activities. It was via Central Asia that Buddhist teachings spread to China, and many of the sutras first brought to China were written down in Central Asian languages rather than Sanskrit.

Inner Central Asia was the place of origin of the leading evangelical monks and translators in the first half of China's sutra translation movement, i.e., mid-2nd to early 5th centuries. Starting with the first important translator of the movement, An Shigao 安世高, who came from a dominion state of the Parthian Empire,[8] for three centuries the Chinese sutra translation movement depended heavily on the contribution of monks — and some Buddhist laymen — of Central Asian origins (see Appendix 1). Among them numbered those who gave the movement a new impetus and new directions, such as Zhi Qian 支謙, Dharmaraksa of Dunhuang 竺法護, and most importantly, Kumarajiva 鳩摩羅什, all of whom explored new approaches and set new standards for sutra translation work. It is no exaggeration to say that they laid the foundation on which Chinese Buddhism was built. Rather than the simple result of a numerical superiority compared with monks of Indian or Chinese origin, the truly decisive factors for

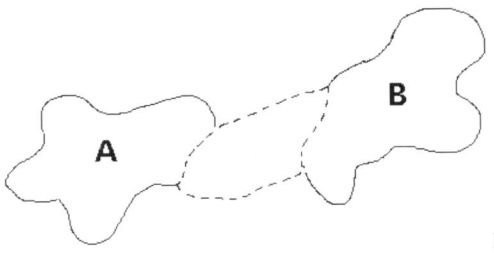

Diagram 1.

the Central Asian monks' dominance were linguistic facility and cultural awareness. While most of the Indian monks preaching in China in this period had little command of Chinese, the leading Central Asian monk-translators managed
to master the Chinese language. In addition, translators of Central Asian origin
who grew up in China (such as Zhi Qian) or in areas bordering on China (such
as Dharmaraksa) received a bi-cultural education: in addition to training in the
Buddhist tradition conducted in Central Asian languages and Sanskrit, they
also studied the Chinese Confucian classics.

For translators to work effectively, an understanding of the host culture
norms was at least as important as bilingual ability. This was particularly true
in the case of China, a country which had always considered herself a superior
culture. Despite the fact that northern China was ruled by invading tribes for
nearly three centuries (317–581), the Chinese sense of cultural superiority was
hardly affected. On the contrary, it was even strengthened by the fact that rulers
of foreign origins decided to adopt Chinese culture as their own: most of the
invading tribes became Sinicized.[9] The sutra translators, who aimed at changing the beliefs and practices of a culture whose sense of superiority was firmly
entrenched, had to be extremely sensitive to Chinese norms and practices in
order for their work to be correctly positioned. The Buddhist monks from the
Western Region, linguistically advantaged, brought up in an environment of
cultural flexibility, and knowledgeable about China's superior material culture,
were thus the ideal intermediaries for this large-scale cultural transfer. Their
success enabled a set of specialist Buddhist norms to be established in China,
thus nurturing local Chinese talent as well as facilitating the work of Indian
monks who came after them. The profound influence Buddhism had on the
subsequent development of Chinese culture thus owed much to the Western
Region, a cultural borderland.

Hexi: a Chinese borderland

Hexi 河西 (Liangzhou 涼洲), or Hexi Corridor, is the narrow strip of territory in
northwestern China which led onto the Silk Road. From the earliest times of
recorded history until the 18th century, it was of strategic importance in terms
of national defence, while in the period under discussion it also had to be pro-
tected for reasons of trade. Of particular relevance to this study was the cultural
and population mix which Hexi experienced, giving its inhabitants unique exposure to non-Chinese languages, customs, and social and economic patterns
which were alien to their inland compatriots. Besides the natural cross-border

contacts common to most national boundaries, Hexi was also an important base for inward migration from the Western Region. In the 1st and 2nd centuries, military conflict in Inner Central Asia drove some of its population to seek refuge in China; subsequently a weak and divided China fell prey to invading tribes which formed the ruling houses that governed northern China for nearly three centuries, creating opportunities for large-scale immigration. China's official histories have recorded that at one point half the population in the area from Hexi to Chang'an was non-Chinese.[10]

Given the unique cultural position of Hexi, it is not surprising that the two Chinese monks who played the most active role in the first half of the sutra translation movement both came from this area. Zhu Fonian 竺佛念, who became the leading interpreter in the translation forums organized by the authoritative Chinese monk Dao'an (4th century), was said to have been conversant with non-Chinese languages since he was young. Baoyun 寶雲, who travelled to the Western Region in search of Buddhist teaching and sutras, was notable as one of the first Chinese monks to serve as chief sutra translator. More importantly, Baoyun was interpreter *par excellence* for foreign monks who were credited as chief translators of sutras they brought to China. In translation forums where the leading monk had little or no command of Chinese, the 'interpreter' was the real translator.[11] The signal position occupied by these two Chinese monks from Liangzhou demonstrates that in the early stages of cultural transfer, critical national borderlands within the host culture play a crucial role as a cradle for translators because they provide unique opportunities for exposure to foreign languages and knowledge.

The two geo-political borderlands described above were not only crucial to the introduction of Buddhism into China, they also played a significant role in nurturing translators for the Chinese government's administrative and diplomatic needs. Historical records show that during periods of active engagement with the outside world, China's government translation work was to a considerable extent dependent on people originating from these geo-political borderlands. The two most notable examples are the expansionist periods of the Han (206 BC–AD 220) and Tang (618–907) dynasties. In the Western Han (206 BC–AD 24), correspondence between the Chinese government and military outposts set up to monitor the Taklamalan oasis states were done in these Inner Central Asian states. In the Tang dynasty, immigrants of Sogdian descent were a major source of Chinese government translators.[12] This is further proof that the significance of geo-political borderlands in intercultural communication is of a broad rather than a specific nature. The crucial role played by Central Asian and Hexi monks in the Buddhist translation movement was thus not a unique phenomenon, but a reflection of the general cultural situation.[13]

The specific importance of a geo-political borderland is, however, highly dependent on the dominant interest and needs of the culture it serves. A shift in interest or need will result in a corresponding shift in its status. This can be seen in how the role of intermediary played by monks from the Western Region was ultimately superseded when a framework for Chinese Buddhism was successfully constructed within China.[14] This framework was constructed largely on the basis of translations done by the groups from geo-political borderlands we have mentioned. But once it gained a firm footing in the host culture, it led inevitably to a preference for direct communication with the source of Buddhism––the Indian subcontinent. Starting from the mid-5th century China showed increasing preference for sutras that had come directly from India; by the 6th century Central Asian texts lost much of their authority. The successful development of China into a major centre of Mahahyana Buddhism also meant a significant enhancement in the status and authority of Chinese monks. We may say that the success of translators from the geo-political borderlands was a major factor leading to their ultimate redundancy.

An institution-based borderland: Jesuit missionaries in China

An institution- or group-based borderland usually has the following characteristics: a comparatively small membership; dependence on host culture institutional toleration and support; limited duration. What the Jesuit missionaries succeeded in constructing in 17th century China is a typical example.

The second wave of culturally significant translation activities in China started in the 16th and early 17th centuries.[15] The Jesuits were the architects of the project as well as its core members. China in the 17th century was far less adventurous than she was in the empire-building period of 1st century BC. She now perceived of herself as self-sufficient and self-contained. The entry and movement of foreigners in the country were strictly controlled; even envoys from recognized tributary states were not always welcome.[16] The activities of Europeans were limited to Macau, and the fact that the Jesuits were thrown out in their early attempts to reach Beijing is evidence enough of the difficulty they had in trying to gain a foothold in China.[17] Under such circumstances, it is hard to envisage the contact point between 17th century China and Europe as the intersecting sections of two circles––the contact was far too sporadic and lim-

ited. The task the Jesuits faced was more similar to that of bridging the gulf between two land masses (see Diagram 2). That they for a time succeeded owed
much to the Jesuit pioneers' willingness to adapt themselves to the host culture,
and to their tireless efforts in persuading the Vatican of the high quality of Chinese culture itself.

The Jesuit project involved laying a foundation of trust in each of the two cultures they set out to bridge. On the Chinese side, the Jesuit policy was acculturation: missionaries learned the Chinese language and adopted local norms. They
also pledged their loyalty to the Chinese emperor and proclaimed themselves
his subjects; some served as court officials.[18] It was in fact their latter function
which won them the permission to carry out missionary activities. The non-religious translation work they did, which has earned them an indelible place in
Chinese history, was done in large part as a response to practical host culture
needs.[19] But there was also an European side to the set-up: the Jesuits were
rooted in the European missionary tradition. Their activities were organized according to the normal overseas mission structure of the Catholic Church, and
missionaries operating in China were answerable both to Papal authority and to
that of the head of the Far East mission. Within the Chinese institution of court
and government they had to establish their credentials and trustworthiness accordingly to a strictly Chinese frame of reference. At the same time, they were
part of the European Catholic institution and had to prove their worth and the
correctness of their way of operation, both by making converts and by adhering
strictly to the accepted principles of Catholicism. As a result of the conflicting
demands from the two sides, the Jesuit enterprise — and the institutional borderland they created — was extremely precarious. In a letter to the deputy superior of the Spanish Jesuits, Father Dominicus Parenin wrote of the Chinese
heir-apparent's[20] warning to them: "You are like people who straddle two boats.
As soon as the boats draw apart, you will fall into the water." (Zhu 1995: 155).

Subsequent events proved the astuteness of the Chinese prince's observation.
But to the Jesuits themselves, an even more appropriate analogy for their enterprise in China would be that of bridge building in extremely strong currents.

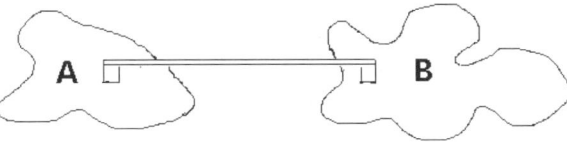

Diagram 2.

Boat journeys are transient, but a bridge, once built, should last, and the Jesuits' cultural bridge was to be constructed with material of the highest calibre. In their selection of working material, the quality they aimed at, and their choice of target audience both in China and in Europe, the Jesuits revealed a clear purpose in establishing a strong and high-calibre--rather than common and broadly based--link between the two cultures. While the ultimate purpose of any missionary is large-scale conversion, the Jesuits were keenly aware of the cultural foundation and logistics that had to be established before their ultimate goal could be fulfilled. To that end, they keenly cultivated scholars and court officials — the Chinese cultural elite.

The translation work done by the Jesuits — the main cables of their cultural bridge — reflects the different agendas and demands of the two cultures they were straddling. Scientific, non-religious work was done to satisfy the practical needs of the Chinese government as well as the intellectual yearnings of scholars and court officials who became converts or friends of the missionaries. Translations of and introductions to Chinese philosophical work were done to convince the Church in Europe of the correctness of Jesuit policy in China.[21] Though the Jesuits' translations of religious material outnumbered their non-religious work, the latter kind was of far greater practical importance in ensuring the survival of their cultural borderland on Chinese soil.

The reason why institution-based cultural borderlands are of limited duration is that they have to be accepted and trusted by their host. If truly successful, their work will create the foundation and the space necessary for the development of a new kind of borderland that is more broadly-based, probably of the socio-political type.[22] If, in the meantime, they should lose the trust of their host, the institution-based borderland is destroyed.

The Jesuits in China represent one of the most difficult positions in terms of group-based borderlands in that they had not one, but two, hosts. Their open-minded acceptance of and engagement with Chinese culture meant that they became culturally different from their Eurocentric colleagues. As a small, distinct and marginal group not only in the Chinese system, but also in the European Catholic Church, they needed to constantly justify their position and choices to the authorities on both sides. Caught between the diverse goals and modes of perception of two authoritative and often arrogant institutions, the Jesuits were finally faced with the ultimate test in the form of the Rites Controversy.[23] The fact that as a last resort they turned to the *Chinese Emperor* for support clearly showed their cultural sympathies and practical concerns, as well as the impossibility of their situation. This was the last straw for the Papacy. In 1773 the Society of Jesus was dissolved — disowned by the institution which sent them to China in the first place. The disintegration of the foundation at one end of the bridge the Jesuits built led to its collapse.

A socio-political borderland: The case of Shanghai

As Anthony Pym suggests, in today's world almost any major city would qualify to a certain degree as an "interculture" (Pym 1998: 188). In the context of this paper they would be socio-political borderlands. However, the degree and extent of cultural mix greatly varies from place to place, as do their history and manifestations of cultural character. In most cases the infusion of foreign cultural elements (mostly through immigration) is a gradual and unplanned process, and it is not always easy to trace the development of such borderlands. If one wants to examine the workings of such a borderland, early 20th century China provides one of the best case studies in the city of Shanghai.

The founding of Shanghai as a major city and a cultural borderland was a direct result of China's national crisis which started in the mid-19th century. The Treaty of Nanjing (1842) which ended the Opium War specified the opening up of five trading ports in China: Guangzhou, Fuzhou, Xiamen, Ningbo and Shanghai. Within twenty years of this event, Shanghai emerged amongst the five as the undisputed leader not only as a trading port, but more importantly as a city with distinctly intercultural characteristics, and in many ways the vanguard of a new Chinese culture. It also became simultaneously the cradle of translators and the centre of an avalanche of translation activities. This despite the fact that Guangzhou had the advantage of being China's only point of contact with the West in the century prior to 1842. What were the constituent elements that favoured Shanghai as a centre of cross-cultural activities?

Shanghai's development as a cultural borderland was dependent first and foremost upon the political and administrative structures built up after the Treaty of Nanjing. Large parts of the city were developed and administered as foreign concession zones,[24] thus bringing in a superstructure as well as infrastructures which were European in origin. However, Shanghai was *not* a regular colony; in the Chinese administered areas the political and legal systems remained Chinese.[25] Even in the concessions, the Chinese population far outnumbered the foreign ones, and Chinese social norms were a part of everyday life. The side-by-side existence of two sets of systems gave Shanghai its intercultural characteristics right from the start.

However, an important factor that cemented Shanghai's position as the centre of translation activities in 19th century China was its location---both geographically and on China's cultural map. Shanghai is located in a region which has traditionally provided China with her scholarly talent, i.e., an area which had had proven influence on Chinese culture. Coincidentally, this area also happened to have been a major centre of Jesuit activities in the 17th and 18th centuries.[26] This combination of excellence in traditional studies and exposure to knowledge of foreign origin made it fertile ground for the nurturing of people with the right outlook and ability to engage in cross-cultural communication.

Like the city itself, translation activities in Shanghai started as Western endeavour on the one hand, and Chinese on the other. The first establishment for translation work in Shanghai, the London Mission Society Press, was founded by Walter Henry Medhurst (1796–1857) in 1844. While the conception and the structure of the Press were European, its personnel included a significant number of Chinese assistants who worked with the missionaries.[27] They were the first generation of 19th century Chinese to come into direct contact with various aspects of Western learning, and to participate in their translation into Chinese. Other missionary-operated publishers were run along the same lines.[28]

The translation work undertaken by Westerners was matched by Chinese government initiatives. By placing the Jiangnan Arsenal in Shanghai, the Qing government of 19th century China played an important part in making the city a major translation centre. Founded in 1865 to replicate Western technology in order to strengthen national defence, the Jiangnan Arsenal set up a Translation Bureau in 1867 to serve the need for the transfer of technological knowledge. For a quarter of a century it was the leading centre for the translation of technological and scientific works, and ranked very highly in terms of influence on China's modernization.[29] The rationale for the Translation Bureau as well as its structure was China-centred, but its leading translators were Western missionaries who should be largely credited with the quality and quantity of the Bureau's work.[30] Thus, although Western- and China-based establishment forces were each building up their own 'hardware' for translation work, the 'software', in terms of human resources, was a common pool.

This pool of talent consisted of Western missionaries who provided the bilingual and Western knowledge, and Chinese assistants who contributed their Chinese linguistic and cultural skills. Had the borderland thus created been limited to these missionary- and government-funded organizations, it would have remained institution-based. However, the amount of new knowledge which was circulated as a result of this, and the impact it had on a reformist generation,

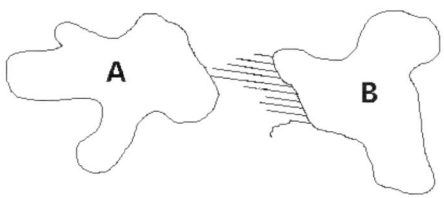

Diagram 3.

caused speedy and exponential changes in the dominant norms within China. In terms of translation activities, the normative changes were as follows: (1) the participation of non-government local forces in translation activities; (2) a rapid increase in the number of Chinese translators; (3) a change in the nature of works chosen for translation.[31] These changes also led to a quantitative explosion in culturally-oriented translation activities. This quantitative change saw the nature of the borderland evolved to that of a socio-political one, where the community included a far larger number of non-translators than translators, and where the audience for reading material transferred from another culture burgeoned. Quantitative changes led to the publication of a wide variety of texts by a growing number of local translators who followed the banners of Westernization and modernization; to them, the new Chinese culture had a lot to learn from the Western models. The resulting landscape of cultural exchange is perhaps most comparable to attempts at reclamation (see Diagram 3).

In the developing Shanghai, the simultaneous existence of two cultural and administrative systems was complemented by the tradition of Chinese as well as Western learning. The convenience of a dual system and the superiority of her pool of talent were, moreover, supported by the city's new-found status as China's publishing centre gave the new intercultural activities the most effective promotion. The confluence of two different traditions built over many centuries, and the introduction of new hardware for the propagation of new cultural norms led to the creation of this socio-political borderland which became the engine for change in turn-of-the-20th-century China.

The relationship between borderlands and the cultural centre

In discussing China's translation history, one phenomenon which should not be overlooked is China's traditional reliance on foreigners for translation talent. Because of China's traditional sense of cultural superiority, translation activities were never the concern of the intellectual mainstream before the mid-19th century. Historical records show that between the mid-1st century and mid-19th century, the talent for culturally-oriented translation work came either from outside of China, or from the small part of the Chinese population which had exposure to foreign languages and cultures due to geographical location or family legacy. These are the cultural borderlands we have examined above. Yet the cultural translation movements throughout Chinese history have all taken place at the cultural centre (see Map 1). In order to understand the relationship between the borderlands and China as host culture, two phenomena deserve our attention: (1) the shift in the borderlands which played a vital part in culturally-oriented translation work; (2) the dominance of the cultural centre in such activities.

The three periods of culturally-oriented translation work under discussion show that both the nature of the borderlands and their physical locations changed. These changes primarily reflect the characteristics and concerns of China, the host culture, at various periods of her history. Translators, as the above cases have shown, all came from the critical borderlands of a specific historical period. From the 2nd to the 5th centuries, the Western Region was a major source of monk-translators. But its importance declined from the 6th century onwards. One of the reasons was the disruptions to traffic on the Silk Road caused by frequent fighting in the region. However, it can also be said that translators from the Western Region were so successful at establishing in the host culture a solid base for the foreign knowledge that they had worked to the diminishment of their own importance.[32] Once Buddhism established firm roots in China, the Chinese became biased in favour of monks and sutras coming directly from the Indian subcontinent. Yet seen from a larger perspective, the gradual growth in importance of the sea route in China's external relations also meant that the Western Region gradually lost its position as China's dominant critical border. The shift in the cultural centre's attention is thus of critical importance in the rise and fall of a cultural borderland.

The nature of the borderland created by the Jesuits was largely conditioned by its contemporary Chinese systems and outlook. In an inward-looking culture, the critical borderland — where change can be initiated most effectively — is paradoxically its centre. Moreover, both in the Ming (1368–1644) and in the Qing dynasties (1644–1911), continued Jesuit presence in China was dependent on the goodwill of the Emperor. Thus the greatest efforts of the missionaries were concentrated in Beijing. The Jesuits had to create a foothold for themselves within Chinese culture in order to carry out their evangelical mission. In that process, their sense of cultural identity and affiliation went through such a dramatic change that it first threatened, and finally destroyed, their link with the Papacy. The reason why it is difficult to envisage a staple and enduring institutional borderland is because institutions and their relations with members and dependents are ever changing. Nor are institutional borderlands, by their very nature, strong and numerous enough to substantially change the dominant strata of their host culture. And so it was that though the Jesuit success at acculturation in China on a personal and group level is impressive, the borderland they created did not have enough critical mass to generate substantial and long-term change within the host culture. The impact of their efforts at knowledge transfer had to wait till the 19th century — when China undertook self-modernization — to be rediscovered. That modernization drive would lead to the development of a new socio-political borderland.

Shanghai was a critical borderland for 19th century China: it had the largest concentration of foreign presence — political, social as well as financial. Though many foreign translators worked within the institutions set up by the Qing government where they operated primarily within a Chinese framework, they simultaneously had their own bases of operation such as periodicals and printing houses. What was of crucial importance to the development of this borderland was the demand for change which came from within Chinese culture, leading to a spectacular quantitative increase in translation activities at the turn of the 20th century. As translation caught the eye of the young reformist generation, attention shifted from the technical and knowledge based texts to works of fiction which were envisaged as a vehicle for national regeneration. This change in the nature of texts to be translated as well as in target readership led to corresponding changes in prioritizing translators' skills and reassessing translation norms. Since translated fiction had to answer the substantial demand for entertaining reading material, the speed of translation became important for the first time in China's cultural translation history. Popular fiction also demanded of the translator the ability to write in the kind of literary Chinese which a foreign translator would find hard to master. This huge and newly emerged demand for translated fiction was therefore fulfilled by *Chinese* translators nurtured in Shanghai. For the first time in China's history, foreign translators were relegated to the sidelines in a cultural translation movement, and the reasons were inextricably bound up with developments within the host culture.[33]

A study of China's culturally-oriented translation movements shows that actual translation activities took place predominantly at the cultural centre: Chang'an and Luoyang during the sutra translation movement, and Beijing in the 17th and 18th centuries. This is perhaps most revealing of the relationship between borderlands and the cultural-cum-administrative centres. While borderlands may be the source of intercultural talent, for translators the heartland of the host culture was where they could most effectively initiate change. On the surface the case of Shanghai may seem like an exception, but on closer examination it conforms to the rule. Unlike Hexi, which remained a borderland, late 19th century Shanghai speedily took over from Beijing as a centre for the development of new cultural norms. While it is true that at no time was Shanghai an administrative centre, the weakness of the Beijing-based Chinese government in the late Qing dynasty significantly reduced that city's political and cultural clout. Thus we see in 19th century Shanghai one of the rare instances when the borderland — where translation talent was most abundant — and the *de facto* cultural centre — where changes to the host culture could most easily be effected — became one.

Appendix 1: Translators from the Western Region (1st–6th centuries)

Name	Origin	Dates	Translation Base	Sutras translated
Late Eastern Han Dynasty (150–220)				
An Shigao 安世高	Parthia 安息	tr. 150–189	Luoyang 洛陽	× 35 volumes + 39 volumes # 95 volumes
An Xuan 安玄	Parthia 安息	tr. 168–189	Luoyang 洛陽	×+ 1 volume # 2 volumes
Lokaksin 支婁迦讖	Yuezhi 月支	tr. 168–189	Luoyang 洛陽	× 10 volumes + over 10 volumes # 23 volumes
Kang Ju 康巨	Sogdia 康居	tr. 168–189	Luoyang 洛陽	+# 1 volume
Zhi Yao 支曜	Yuezhi 月支	tr. 168–220	Luoyang 洛陽	× 1 volume + 2 volumes # 10 volumes
Kang Mengxiang 康孟詳	Sogdia 康居	tr. 194–199	Luoyang 洛陽	× 1 volume + 2 volumes # 6 volumes
Three Kingdoms and Western Jin Dynasty (220–316)				
Zhi Qian 支謙	Yuezhi 月支 (Born in China)	tr. 222–228	Wu 吳	× 27 volumes + 49 volumes # 88 volumes

Kang Senghui 康僧會	Sogdia 康居 (Born in Jiaozhi 交趾)	tr. 247–280 Died in 280	Wu 吳	× 6 volumes +# 7 volumes
Samghavarman 康僧鎧	Sogdia 康居	tr. 249–253	Luoyang 洛陽	+ 4 volumes # 3 volumes
Dharmatrata 曇諦	Parthia 安息	tr. 254	Luoyang 洛陽	+# 1 volume
Kalasivi 支彊梁接	Yuezhi 月支	tr. 256	Jiaozhou 交州	# 1 volume
Bai Yan 白延	Kucha 龜茲	tr. 258	Wei 魏	× 3 volumes + 6 volumes # 5 volumes
Dharmabhadra 安法賢	Parthia 安息	tr. 265	Unknown	# 2 volumes
Dharmaraksa of Dunhaung 竺法護	Yuezhi 月支 (family settled in Dunhuang)	tr. starting 267; died c.290–306, aged 78	Dunhuang and Chang'an 敦煌、長安	× 149 volumes + 165 volumes # 175 volumes
Moraksa 無羅叉	Western Region 西域	tr. 291	Henan 河南	#+ 1 volume
Srimitra 帛尸梨蜜	Kucha 龜茲	tr. 307–312; died c.335–342, aged about 80	Luoyang 洛陽	× 2 volumes + 1 volume # 3 volumes

Northern Dynasties and Eastern Jin Dynasty (317–420)

Zhi Daogan 支道根	Unknown	tr. 335	Unknown	# 2 volumes
Zhi Shilun 支施崙	Yuezhi 月支	tr. 373	Liangzhou 涼州	×# 4 volumes
Samghabhata 僧伽跋澄/僧伽跋橙	Kashmir 罽賓	tr. 381–385	Chang'an 長安	×+ 2 volumes # 3 volumes
Buddharaksa 佛圖羅剎	Unknown	Unknown	Chang'an 長安	×+# 1 volume
Dharmanandi 曇摩難提	Doufale 兜法勒	tr. 384–391	Chang'an 長安	× 2 volumes + 4 volumes # 5 volumes
Samghadeva 僧伽提婆/僧伽提和	Kashmir 罽賓	tr. 391–397	Chang'an 長安 Luoyang 洛陽 Lushan 盧山	×+ millions of words
Kang Daohe 康道和	Sogdia 康居	tr. 396	Unknown	# 1 volume
Samgharaksa 僧伽羅叉	Kashmir 罽賓/ Western Region 西域	tr. 397–398	Chang'an 長安	×+ 1 volume
Dharmayasas 曇摩耶舍	Kashmir 罽賓	tr. 397–418	Unknown	+ 2 volumes # 3 volumes
Fazhong 法眾	Kocha 高昌	tr. 401	Unknown	×# 1 volume
Samghata 僧伽陀	Western Region 西域	tr. 402–412	Zhangye 張掖	# 1 volume
Kumarajiva 鳩摩羅什	Born in Kucha 龜茲	tr. 401–413 Died in 413 aged 70	Chang'an 長安	× 33 volumes + more than 300 *juan* # 74 volumes

Name	Origin	Dates	Translation Base	Sutras translated
Punyatara 弗若多羅	Kashmir 罽賓	tr. 404 Died in 405	Chang'an 長安	+# 1 volume (unfinished)
Dharmarucci 曇摩流支	Western Region 西域	Unknown	Guanzhong 關中	+# 1 volume (finished the untranslated part)
Vimalaksas 毗摩羅叉/ 卑摩羅叉	Kashmir 罽賓	tr. 404–418 Aged 77	Jiangling 江陵	# 3 volumes
Buddhayasas 佛陀耶舍	Kashmir 罽賓	tr. 408–413	Chang'an長安	×+ 2 volumes # 4 volumes
Gitamitra 竺祇蜜多	Western Region 西域	tr. 420	Unknown	× 1 volume # 23 volumes

× *Chu sanzang ji*出三藏記 [Records of the transmission of the Tripitaka]
+ *Gaoseng zhuan*高僧傳 [Biographies of eminent monks]
# *Kaiyuan lu*開元錄 [Sutra catalogue compiled in the Kaiyuan period of the Tang dynasty]

Notes

1. Culturally-oriented translation activities refer to large-scale and continuous translation work which aimed at introducing new knowledge and new norms into China. China also has a long history of administrative and commercial translation activities which will not be dealt with in this paper. For a brief discussion of the differences between cultural and career translation activities in Chinese history, see Hung 2001b. For information about the latter in dynastic China, see Hung, forthcoming.

2. See Yang 2000 and Kondo and Wakabayashi 1998.

3. A drastic decree from the Tang Emperor Wuzong in the year 845 led to the dissolution of Buddhist monasteries. This marked the rapid decline of sutra translation. Later attempts at a revival failed to bring back its vitality and momentum.

4. For an account of how these two major forces contested for domination in Inner Central Asia, see Lattimore 1940.

5. For an example of simultaneous acknowledgement of Han and Xiongnu domination, see records in *Han Shu* 'Xiyu zhuan' on the kingdom of Loulan.

6. See Lin 1995 for details about languages used in the Western Region. The combination of different spoken languages and different written scripts was also true of the Indian sub-continent.

7. Asoka (r. 272/273 BC to 232 BC), who sent Buddhist preachers to spread Buddhism to the areas north and east of his empire.

8. The identification of An Shigao as a key member of the Parthian royal house has now been rejected by most scholars of Chinese Buddhism. Yet traces of this mistaken identifica-

tion remain in many lists of monk-translators in which An Shigao is listed as Parthamasiris. For details about An Shigao's life and his translation work, see Hung 2001a.

9. One outstanding example was the Northern Wei Dynasty (386–534), whose rulers issued a decree forbidding the use of 'barbarian' languages, including their own, in the year 495, and changed their family name from Toba to Yuan the next year.

10. *Jin shu*: 'Jiangtong zhuan'. Immigration from Central Asia was also notable in the Tang dynasty. See, for example, Xiang 1957.

11. In the normal set-up of a Buddhist translation forum the highest authority was the monk who handed down the teachings of the sutra. He was thus the *yi zhu* 譯主, or chief of the translation forum, a term which later evolved into *zhu yi*, commonly rendered as 'chief translator'. In fact bilingual skills were not an essential qualification for a chief of translation forum. The most important qualification was expert knowledge of the sutra concerned.

12. Xiang 1957: 5, 21.

13. Because China's official histories tend to concentrate on the ruling classes, little detail remains of cross cultural activities which took place away from the political and cultural centre. Meanwhile, Buddhist sources have been handed down as part of a new––and separate––tradition, one which aimed at establishing its own legitimacy and authority. Gathering information from these sources to form a true picture of translation activities therefore requires careful contextualization and discrimination.

14. The vulnerability of Central Asian states to external attack also meant that they faced constant pressure in terms of religious practices if their potential or actual conquerors were non-Buddhist. By the time the Chinese monk Xuanzang 玄奘 travelled via the Western Region to India in the years 627/629–644, for example, many of the formerly prominent Buddhist states, such as Kucha (the home state of Kumarajiva), had become Zoroastrian. The whole area was later conquered by Muslims, and has since remained predominantly Muslim to this date.

15. Though some of the activities of cultural transfer were carried on until the late 18th century, the work which had the greatest cultural impact was done in the 17th century.

16. There are records in the *Ming shilu* detailing the visits of kings and envoys from Southeast Asia, and comments saying that the visits were too frequent and should be limited.

17. For details of the difficulties Matteo Ricci had in establishing a foothold in China proper, see Ricci: 1953.

18. At least twenty-three Jesuits served as regular officials in the Chinese court. See Dehergne 1973: 771–773.

19. The Jesuits played a significant role in revamping the Chinese calendar both in the late Ming and early Qing dynasties. Their translations of works of astrology and mathematics were closely related to this endeavour.

20. This was the future Qianlong Emperor (r.1736–1795) under whose reign the Society of Jesus was dissolved by Papal order.

21. The Jesuit community in China did not all subscribe to the same views. See Gernet 1985. Father Longobardo, for example, warned against confusing Chinese and Christian ideas. The dominant trend, however, was cultural compromise. Phillippe Couplet was among the first to explain the Chinese philosophical tradition to a European audience.

22. Please see next section.

23. This concerns the acceptability for Chinese converts to continue Confucian practices such as honouring their ancestors. Given the importance of such rites in Chinese society, a negation of the practices would have made conversion quite impossible. The Jesuits in China sent various missions to the Vatican, hoping to convince the Pope that Chinese rites were civil rather than religious. Their attempts were undermined by harsh Dominican criticism of their position. See Minamiki 1985 for an overview of the Rites Controversy.

24. i.e., zones which were administered by the personnel of foreign countries, and in which foreign laws, rather than Chinese ones, applied. There were two main concession zones: the smaller, French one, and the larger, international one which was in fact run by the British. A Japanese one was added in 1895 and expanded in the 1920s. Foreign concessions became the ideal hideout for Chinese political dissidents until 1949, when the Chinese Communist Party took over China.

25. In contrast, Hong Kong, ceded to the British in the same Nanjing Treaty, was run along completely British lines. Although Chinese ways of operation remained alive, it was largely a part of the software rather than the hardware.

26. Paul Xu 徐光啓, China's leading Catholic convert in the Ming dynasty, was a native of Shanghai, while Leo Li 李之藻, another 'pillar' of the early Catholic Church in China, was a native of Hangzhou. A significant number of Jesuits spent their working lives in Zhejiang province and died there. See Xu 1949.

27. The best known among the Chinese personnel were: Xu Shou 徐壽, Hua Hengfang 華衡芳, Shu Gaodi 舒高第, Zhao Yuanyi 趙元益, Xu Jianyin 徐建寅, Zheng Changyan 鄭昌棪, Zhong Tianwei 鍾天緯, Qu Anglai 瞿昂來, Li Fengbao 李鳳苞 and Jia Buwei 賈步緯. All of them hailed from the provinces of Zhejiang and Jiangsu. For brief biographical information, see Xiong 1994.

28. For a comprehensive description of these establishments, see Xiong 1994.

29. According to extant records the last book translated by the Bureau was published in 1903. As more and more of the young Chinese intellectuals gained direct exposure to Western languages and learning, the reputation of the Bureau declined drastically in the 20th century.

30. A total of nine Westerners were employed by the Bureau. John Fryer, who spent twenty-eight years there, made the most significant contribution.

31. This change became a tidal wave at the end of the 19th century, and was pushed to a zenith of Liang Qichao's launching of the New Fiction Movement which steered translation towards popularization. For details, see Pollard 1998.

32. If one looks only at the number of foreign translators active in China from the 6th century onwards, this would appear to be the case. But if one looks at the overall development of different schools of Chinese Mahayana Buddhism, the significance of Central Asian monks remained strong throughout the movement. The difference is that in the later stages, they had become so deeply integrated into Chinese culture that they worked from within, not as translators but as leading teachers, commentators and founders of different schools.

33. For background information on the fiction translation movement and detailed discussion of certain fiction genres, see Pollard 1998.

Works cited

Dehergne, Joseph. 1973. *Zai Hua Yesu huishi liezhuan ji shumu bubian* (*Repertoire des Jesuites de Chine de 1552–1800*). Trans. Di Sheng. Beijing: Zhonghua shuju, 1995.

Gernet, Jacques. 1985. *China and the Christian Impact*. Trans. Janet Lloyd. Cambridge: Cambridge University Press.

Han shu [History of the Han dynasty]. 1975 edition. Beijing: Zhonghua.

Hung, Eva. 2001a. "Cong An Shigao de beijing kan zaoqi fojing hanyi" [An Shigao and early sutra translation], *Chinese Translators' Journal* 22:3. 52–58.

Hung, Eva. 2001b. "Rewriting Chinese Translation History". Plenary paper for V International Conference on Translation and Interpreting: Translation and Interculturality: Less Translated Languages. Universitat Autonoma de Barcelona, 29–31 October 2001.

Hung, Eva. Forthcoming. 'Government Translators in Dynastic China'. *De Gruyter International Encyclopedia of Translation Studies*. Berlin: De Gruyter.

Jin shu [History of the Jin dynasty]. 1975 edition. Beijing: Zhonghua.

Kondo, Masaomi, and Wakabayashi, Judy. 1998. 'The Japanese Tradition', *Routledge Encyclopedia of Translation Studies*. London and New York: Routledge. 485–493.

Lattimore, Owen. 1940. *Inner Asian Frontiers of China*. New York: American Geographical Society.

Lin, Meicun. 1995. *Xiyu wenming* [The civilization of the Western Region]. Beijing: Dongfang.

Minamiki, George. 1985. *The Chinese Rites Controversy: from its Beginning to Modern Times*. Chicago: Loyola University Press.

Pollard, David. 1998. *Translation and Creation: Readings of Western Literature in Early Modern China, 1840–1918*. Amsterdam & Philadelphia: John Benjamins.

Pym, Anthony. 1998. *Method in Translation History*. Manchester: St. Jerome.

Pym, Anthony. 2000. *Negotiating the Frontier: Translators and Intercultures in Hispanic Society*. Manchester: St. Jerome.

Ricci, Matteo. 1953. *China in the Sixteenth Century: the Journals of Matthew Ricci*. Trans. Louis J. Gallagher. New York: Random House.

Seng You. 516. 1995 edition. *Chu sanzang ji* [Records of the transmission of the Tripitaka]. Beijing: Zhonghua shuju.

Shi, Huijiao. 619. 1992 edition. *Gaoseng zhuan* [Biographies of emminent monks]. Beijing: Zhonghua shuju.

Tang, Yongtong. 1982. *Siu Tang fojiao shigao* [Preliminary history of Buddhism in the Siu and Tang dynasties]. Beijing: Zhonghua shuju.

Tang, Yongtong. 1996 edition. *Han Wei liang Jin Nanbeichao fojiao shi* [Buddhist history in the Han, Wei, Jin, and North and South Dynasties]. Taipei: Luotuo chubanshe.

Xiang, Da. 1957. *Tangdai Chang'an yu xiyu wenming* [Chang'an of the Tang dynasty and the civilization of the Western Region]. Beijing: Sanlian chubanshe.

Xiong, Yuezhi. 1994. *Xixue dongjian yu wan Qing shehui* [The introduction of Western learning and late Qing society]. Shanghai: Shanghai renmin chubanshe.

Xu, Zongse. 1949 edition. *Ming Qing jian Yesuhuishi yizhu tiyao* [An annotated bibliography of Jesuit translations in the Ming and Qing dynasties]. Beijing: Zhonghua Bookstore.

Yang, Xiuzhi. 2000. 'Chaoxian shidai zhi Hanyu yiguan', [Chinese-language translators of the Chosan dynasty]. In *Yazhou fanyi chuantong yu xiandai dongxiang* (*Translation in Asia: Past and Present*). Ed. Eva Hung and Yang Chengshu. Beijing: Peking University Press. 38–53.

Zanning. 1987 edition. Fan Xiangyong ed. *Song gaoseng zhuan* [Song dynasty biographies of eminent monks]. Beijing: Zhonghua shuju.

Zhang, Zhongli, ed. 1994. *Chengshi jinbu, qiye fazhan he Zhongguo xiandaihua (Urban Progress, Business Development and China's Modernization)*. Shanghai: Shanghai Academy of Social Sciences.

Zhu, Jing (ed. and trans.) 1995. *Yang jiaoshi kan Zhongguo chaoting* [Foreign missionaries on the Chinese imperial court]. Shanghai: Shanghai Renmin chubanshe.

Cultural perception and translation

Translating China to the American South

Baptist missionaries and Imperial China, 1845–1911

Ray Granade and Tom Greer
Ouachita Baptist University

The origins of Baptists and their missionary impulse

In 1517, a young German monk posted ninety-five propositions for debate on the door of the Wittenberg, Germany, church. By his action, but without that intent, Martin Luther initiated what came to be called the Protestant Reformation, which divided European Christianity into two major groups: the Roman Catholic inheritors of the early Italian expression of the Christian faith and the protesting reformers. What originated as an attempt to cleanse the Catholic Church of particular abuses quickly radicalized. Thus began a process of division within the faith that has accelerated rather than abated since that time.

One Christian group organized after the Protestant Reformation was known as Baptists. Dissenters from the state Church of England, Baptists emphasized freedom, both through congregational polity and belief in soul competency. Organizing between 1610 and 1641, these direct forebears of American Baptists suffered persecution for their theological differences and refusal to conform to Anglican Church practices. Baptists suffered internal division as well as external persecution. Dissension arose quickly between Armenians and Calvinists. The tension between these two competing theologies has remained a persistent theme in Baptist life, influencing the degree of interest in evangelism. Calvinists see no need of evangelism, for all is God's action; Armenians believe that God uses human agency and requires human activity to establish His kingdom.

Historical accident mandated that, in order to compete successfully with Spanish and French for colonies in the Western Hemisphere, the English populate as well as claim the land. The Spanish and French sent garrisons and traders; the English, settlers. Among those settlers were some adherents to Baptist tenets. Baptists in the British colonies organized first in Rhode Island about 1640.

State-authorized churches in Massachusetts and the Southern colonies curtailed Baptist freedom to worship in their own way and simultaneously taxed them for support of the state church, so Baptists grew most in the Middle Colonies, especially Pennsylvania and New Jersey.

Both in Britain and in the colonies, Baptists emphasized freedom (particularly separation of church and state), evangelism (especially through preaching and distributing tracts and copies of the Bible), and education. This last emphasis reflected Baptist pragmatic interest in having a literate society in which to distribute literature as well as Baptist idealistic interest in social reform. American Baptists grew spectacularly as a result of the First (1726–1742) and Second (1796–1820) Great Awakenings, times of great religious interest and activity in the United States. Their increase in numbers and their emphasis upon evangelism awaited only the right impetus to turn the denomination's interest to the world beyond its own shores. That impetus came from an English Baptist minister named William Carey.

In England in 1792, Carey had organized The Particular Baptist Society for the Propagation of the Gospel Amongst the Heathen. Under its auspices, he went to India as preacher and translator. Baptist clergyman William Staughton, who had been present at the Society's initiation, journeyed to Philadelphia by way of South Carolina and New Jersey. His spoken and written advocacy of Baptist foreign missionary enterprises encouraged American Baptist participation in such efforts. When Congregationalists organized the American Board of Commissioners for Foreign Missions in 1812, Baptists contributed heavily to send Luther Rice and Ann and Adoniram Judson to India as missionaries.

On the long ocean voyage to India, Rice and the Judsons became Baptists and resigned their Congregationalist commission. They agreed that the Judsons would proceed to Burma (now Myanmar) while Rice returned to seek support from American Baptists. An organizational visionary, Rice succeeded admirably. Traveling through the country, Rice stirred enough local interest to produce a general meeting in Philadelphia during May, 1814, which created a national missionary organization — The General Missionary Convention of the Baptist Denomination in the United States for Foreign Missions, generally called the Triennial Convention because of its meetings every three years — with a managing board, called The Baptist Board of Foreign Missions for the United States, to provide continuity between Convention meetings.

Under the Convention's direction, Baptists opened missionary work in Liberia in 1819 and sent their first medical missionary abroad in 1821. In 1826, the Board's headquarters relocated to Boston. From that locus, Baptists began missions in Siam (Thailand) in 1832, France and Germany in 1833, and Greece, Haiti and China in 1835 (Torbet 1950: 103–106, 226–228, 350–353).

Baptist interest in China had been evident for several years before action occurred. When Baptists in Burma converted a Chinese in 1828, the Board considered sending a missionary there to learn the language in preparation for entering China. When Baptists did begin their work in China, they sent Revd and Mrs J. Lewis Shuck into the south (Macao and Hong Kong) and the work progressed toward the north over the course of a quarter-century (Torbet 1950: 351, 361–362).

Baptist evangelism, in China as elsewhere, carried in it the seeds of destruction. Baptists continued to argue violently over the theological implications of Arminianism and Calvinism — whether they should engage in mission activities, and if so, how and by whom those activities should be undertaken and supported. As the nineteenth century progressed, Baptist arguments over what happened outside the country became wrapped up in the great debate that increasingly consumed America's reform fervor — the debate over slavery.

Southern Baptist missions

The division between Northern and Southern Baptists occurred when the Foreign Mission Board (FMB) admitted unwillingness to appoint a slave-owner as a missionary. On May 8, 1845, Baptists from the Southern states — a majority of American Baptists — organized the Southern Baptist Convention (SBC) in Augusta, Georgia. Its constitution established two missionary boards, with the one for foreign missions being headquartered in Richmond, Virginia.

Spurred at least in part by the Emperor's decree of toleration, which gave Protestant missionaries equal footing with Catholic ones, the new Convention's first missionary undertaking was in South China. Revd and Mrs J. Lewis Shuck, Virginians who had been Baptist appointees to China in 1835, had served there between 1836 and her death in 1844. Revd Shuck had returned to the US, transferred his allegiance to the new Convention, and thrown himself into its efforts. By the beginning of the American Civil War, the SBC had established mission stations in South (Canton, Samuel C. Clopton and George Pearcy, 1845, then Revds Shuck, 1846, and Rosewell H. Graves, 1856), Central (Shanghai, Matthew T. Yates, 1847) and North (Chefoo, Shantung Province, Mr & Mrs J.L. Holmes, and Tengchow, Dr & Mrs J.B. Hartwell, 1860) China. Eventually, they established two other stations: in the Interior (Chengchow, Honan Province, W.W.

Lawton and Mr. & Mrs. Eugene Sallee, 1904) and in Manchuria (the C.A. Leon-ards and the C.E. Jameses, 1924) (Torbet 1950: 361–354, 404, 418–425).

Because of their early and continuing interest, Southern Baptists found in China the touchstone of their missionary endeavors. Prior to 1951, the FMB ap-pointed more missionaries to China (over 625) than to any other country — in-deed, more than to any other continent. The Orient offered as much as it re-quired, but the offering was often difficult for those sent to explain to those who had sent them. Missionaries to Western countries had numerous familiar points of reference to use in describing their work to "the folks back home". Missionar-ies to China struggled to explain such an alien culture and make it come alive for hearers and readers whose world view differed so radically from the one in which the missionaries now lived.

The people the missionaries had left behind inhabited a culture hallmarked by individualism, Protestantism, capitalism, and the optimism of a young cul-ture that majored on pragmatism and the present, if not the future. When the SBC commissioned its first missionaries in 1845, the US had existed as a nation for less than a century and English settlers had inhabited the land for less than 250 years. As one historian has observed, the country's major articles of faith were evangelical religion and dynamic democracy — both of which Baptists epitomized (Tyler 1944: 1–45). The country epitomized the certainty that a na-tion could reform itself as necessary on the road to progressively better times until it reached perfection. SBC missionaries carried this cultural heritage with them and viewed Chinese life through its lens. Consequently, the words they meant for mass consumption through the printed word in the United States fol-lowed certain conventions.

This study's assumptions

This paper's conclusions are based on certain assumptions about missionary attempts to translate their experiences in one culture to interested parties in a totally different one. First, the authors assumed that the best picture of this at-tempt at translation would emerge from published and therefore public sources instead of private ones like letters, journals, or reports to superiors. While these latter might provide a factual look at Chinese life from the missionaries' per-spective, they would not reveal what we sought to study. Second, we assumed that a broad survey of published accounts would allow patterns to unfold and reveal generalities that might remain hidden if the investigation were limited to a narrower sampling or even to the output, however prolific, of a single individual. Third, we assumed that we should look most closely at what those in China said about their experience rather than relying exclusively on what others said about them or their experiences. Fourth, we assumed that the most complete picture would be best, so we encompassed both publications of a general nature and those aimed at a religious, specifically at a Baptist, audience. We hoped to discover what differences, if any, existed between the two in the way SBC missionaries presented China. Fifth, we assumed that different eras would produce different pictures, so we limited our research to a specific time period — from the advent of SBC missionaries in 1845 to the initiation of the Republic in 1911. This provided a convenient cut-off date, but it also provided a benchmark era against which another, later study could be juxtaposed.

General discoveries

Certain generalities quickly emerged from our study. First, we discovered that few missionaries published extensively — at least few published items that showed up in the traditional sources that one uses to discover such writings. We perused *Reader's Guide, Nineteenth Century Reader's Guide, Poole's Index to Periodical Literature, Religion Index One*, and the *National Union Catalogue* in our attempt to produce an exhaustive bibliography from which to work.

Perhaps the work done translating English works into Chinese (which did take a prodigious amount of time for not only Scriptures but also hymnals, commentaries, and even dictionaries) left little time for writing for home consumption. Certainly, given the nature of their work, such writing was a leisure activity in a setting that afforded little leisure time, and could rarely be done while missionaries were home on furlough, when speaking to the folks at home and raising support for missionary endeavours provided rigorous respite from the mission field.

In addition to the issue of time for composition, the time on which the study focused made a difference in the pool from which authors might be drawn. Between 1845 and 1911, the SBC appointed 256 missionaries to China (the remaining 372 were appointed between 1912 and 1950). Twenty, or roughly 8% of the SBC missionaries appointed to China during the target period, wrote the sorts of public reports we hoped to find. Of those, only four wrote more than one item, and those four wrote two each, so none were especially prolific. The result was a total of twenty-four published items.

The time of publication was likewise significant for this study, and that timing reflected the other aspects of time as well. The first item published by a Southern Baptist missionary who served in China between 1845 and 1911 was published in 1895. Only four more items were published during the target period: in 1903, 1906, 1909 and 1911.

The timing of publication exhibits a reality of missionary publications. It is no surprise that most of the writing was done by those who survived missionary work until retirement, that the writers' gender was divided almost equally (eleven males, one with multiple items, and ten females, three with multiple items), or that several were career missionaries who wished to record the history of their contemporaries' work. The first publication, for example, was Rosewell Hobart Graves' *Forty Years in China*, a recounting of his experiences that began in 1856. Later autobiographies by China missionaries tell a similar story: see John Burder Hipps' *Fifty Years in Christian Missions* or J. Roscoe Saunders' *67 Years a Pioneer for Christ* as good examples.

Such a timing of publication means, of course, that SBC missionaries were, in most instances, translating to their culture the image of a culture which had been greatly altered, if not completely destroyed, by the time the translation had been made and was ready to be read. The missionaries presented observation as artifact, translation as history lesson rather than current event. Since several of the books (Anna Seward Pruitt's *Up From Zero* is a good example) were designed as study books, heedless generations of US Baptists continued to think of China in terms of its Imperial manifestation. Baptist parents who told their children stories of "the starving children of China" assumed that the Middle Kingdom remained in the mid-to-late twentieth century what it had been at the end of the nineteenth, a half-century earlier. Without new translations of new conditions to compare with the old, these original translations of one culture to another continued to be presented as accurate representations of the present long after their accuracy had vanished.

Two other aspects of timing merit mention. As the above titles indicate, those who translated Chinese culture to Southern Baptists did so on the basis of long tenure rather than brief acquaintance. During the early years, cost and difficulty of transportation and missions theory conspired to produce tenures that would be unimaginable today. The authors of the twenty-four published items we perused accounted for a total of 614 years of service in China — an average of thirty-four years each in tenures ranging from eight to fifty-seven years, eight of which were over forty and two over fifty years. This long-term basis for cultural translations allowed missionaries to account for changes they might observe over time. Unfortunately, few missionary comments indicate such changes. Either they were nonexistent or ignored — or discarded because of the requirements of the inspirational genre in which missionaries wrote.

Second, we discovered that few of those who did so wrote much for general audiences. Only seven of the twenty who wrote published items obviously prepared with a general audience in mind (two of those marginally designed for a general audience). The task of those who wrote for a general audience would have been much more difficult than that of those writing for a religious one. "Generalists" would require greater analytical and descriptive powers in their compositions to enable them to appeal to a more general audience. "Religious" writers would be able to fall back on a particular vocabulary and set of expectations shared by those accustomed to the genre broadly described as "religious literature".

Third, we discovered — as the second generality implies — that all the missionaries' writings can fairly easily be placed into two convenient categories: general (history, sociology, education, travel, or commentary) or religious (theological, hagiographical, or inspirational). Also as the second generality notes, most of the writings fall into the latter category. Autobiographies and biographies by missionaries of their colleagues would certainly be hagiographical. Few missionary writings are theological. The majority, even the autobiographical ones, are inspirational in nature.

The writings by SBC missionaries to China published for home consumption conform to the inspirational genre in several important ways. First, the writings conform to the genre in their use of a certain vocabulary. That vocabulary utilizes words from the general vocabulary in specialized ways that have particular connotations not shared by readers outside religious circles. They form the kind of jargon, or code, familiar to any academic discipline. As former US President Jimmy Carter discovered during his presidency, words like "salvation", "sin", "lost", "heathen", or "born again" have great meaning to religious people that is lost on the general populace (*Playboy* 1976: 63–86).

The second conformation of missionary writings to the inspirational genre lies in their format, or style. Inspirational literature stresses the universality of religious experience rather than the particularity of time and/or place. In stressing God's universality and timelessness, inspirational stories lose their sense of the temporal. The encounter of any person — regardless of age or gender — with God could as easily be set in ancient Rome as in modern China without alteration. Thus, when missionaries wrote of a child running to her room to pray before meals as a means of escaping her mother's prohibition of praying at the table, time and place were inconsequential details sub-ordinated to the main point — faithfulness in the face of adversity. Thus, too, missionary writings are not argumentative in nature, but are generally anec-dotally-based, using a specific event to illustrate the larger points they wish to make.

The missionaries' choice of format in their writing relied heavily, as does all inspirational literature, on a pre-literate form of communication. Central to the Christian religion is a reliance on the spoken as well as the written word. Proclamation of "the word" by a minister is the focal point of weekly congre-gational worship. Ministerial choice of anecdotes to illustrate universal truths, or points, in the sermon is designed to make those points memorable. Since all male missionaries were trained as preachers, it is certainly logical — if not provable — that their training in sermonizing carried over to their writing as a bridge between the two forms of communication, and a style that would be familiar to their audience.

This universality of format allows the writer to transform the exotic into the mundane and emphasize a common humanity as a way to connect the reader with the subject. It also generates an automatic suspension of disbe-lief, so that no part of the story is questionable — the reader accepts it all on faith without analysis. The major consequence of this format is that the reader sees the locale anecdotally, as one might view a show of vaguely familiar slides projected in random order. One lacks the immediacy and continuity of story conveyed by history or travelogue. This consequence forces the reader to look more carefully at the writing to discover nuggets of information while avoid-ing being swept up in religious sentimentality.

The third conformation of most missionary writings to the inspirational genre lies in the formulaic nature of the plot and predictability of focus. Read-ers were never disappointed when they picked up missionary writings expect-ing to discover a tale of human frailty or heroism in the face of peril encoun-tered because of religious conviction. The focus invariably was on God and His action in human life rather than on some facet of human nature, and the outcome was always uplifting. Readers could rest assured that if humanity suffered, even to the point of death, the result would vindicate that suffering. Christians who endured persecution faithfully would be rewarded with the as-surance of God's presence through every trial and everlasting life after death. In short, like all inspirational literature, missionary stories focused on God and his action in the human arena through their language, format, and plot, rather than focusing on real life in some real locale.

The fourth and final generality is that, in their attempt to translate the culture in which they lived to the culture they had left, missionaries relied on formulas familiar to both American culture in general and its Southern subset in particular. Like President Woodrow Wilson would so famously do with Germany in World War I, the missionaries carefully distinguished between the Chinese people and the Chinese government, for example. The former they lauded on a number of counts, and generally praised; the latter they often questioned in action, though rarely in intent, presenting it as ineffectual or misguided rather than evil or malicious.

As to the formulae familiar to their fellow Southerners, none would have been more so than the missionaries' observations about rigid social divisions and carefully-scripted social interactions in their new world. The Confucian system of relationships, though more extensive and precise in nomenclature than those in the American South until about World War II, was comfortably familiar to Southern Baptist readers whose world picture more closely resembled that of Elizabethan England than that of the urban, industrial settings familiar in the north.

Other equally-strong and equally-evocative formulae for Southern readers lay in other social relationships. The Oriental concept of "face" the missionaries likened to their own culture's preoccupation with honor and the resulting exaggerated politeness and extreme remedies when honor was questioned or compromised (like the illegal but highly popular *code duello*). Sectional antagonism between north and south played out in China just as it did in the US. And a rural, agricultural society and its attempts to come to terms with urban and industrial forces would certainly have resonated with Southern readers. So while they did not make explicit references to these formulae, Southern Baptist missionaries were careful to provide their readers back home with signposts to the familiar that those readers could use for comparisons and to make the exotic familiar.

Five major areas of missionary observation

Although missionaries generally used an anecdotal approach to their writing, as noted in the discussion of the works' inspirational approach, we chose to categorize observations to make them more coherent for this paper. To that end, we have tried to generalize about the missionaries' specific representations of particular aspects of China: government, education, health care, sociology, and religion/philosophy.

Government

Because of their doctrinal concern with the separation of church and state, Baptists have always been particularly interested in government, and especially its relations with religion. Missionary observations about Chinese government involved largely the extent to which the government helped or hindered missionary efforts, and secondarily the extent to which the government was progressive in its outlook. They postulated all comments on a certain philosophy of government that overarched their interest in governmental relations with religion. In that philosophy, government's prime requisite was to provide order and stability as the framework within which all activities occurred, whether those activities were social, economic, or religious in nature. The corollary to that prime requisite was that government provide order and stability while ensuring maximum personal freedom for its citizens. In short, missionaries judged any government by its ability to secure its citizens' pursuits of life, liberty and property.

Missionaries exhibited the greatest respect for governmental authority as embodied in the Emperor. Never did they hint otherwise. When governmental relations deteriorated, missionaries generally noted that the poor relations resulted from bad advisers rather than a mistaken policy on the Emperor's part. While they went out of their way on occasion to portray central authority in the best light, they did, regardless of which mission station they inhabited, find the pre-Republic central government cumbersome and ineffectual. Their assessment was that the country's size and poor transportation and communication systems exacerbated those characteristics.

Missionaries noted the central government's inability to provide economic order when they commented on the lack of a universal system of weights and measures and of a dependable regulated circulating medium with which to conduct business transactions in the kingdom. Their writings represented a business system which would be familiar to some of their readers, for the lack of a dependable regulated circulating medium plagued the agriculturally-based South throughout the target era.

While the government's lack of control over economic interchange elicited observations from missionaries, they did not find it the most significant example of central governmental failure. Missionaries viewed with great alarm the central government's reliance on local officials over whom it exercised little control and among whom solicitation of bribery was rampant. It was the lack of social rather than economic order resulting from this lack of central authority which concerned missionaries most. Beyond the matters of wide-spread governmental graft and corruption, two facets of this lack of social order repeatedly appeared in missionary writings: the prevalence of violence, particularly banditry, and the prevalence of vice.

The missionary view of social order was influenced in part by the change in social order at home in the whole country, but especially in the South, between 1850 and 1900. Much of America was still frontier, and the violence associated with a less-settled society was familiar to both missionaries and their readers. America also experienced its great civil war (1861–5), during which roving bands of bandits were a fixture in much of the South and alternated with representatives of contending armies to lay waste the populace. Many names immortalized by the dime novels of the post-War years — names like Younger and James and Quantrill — belonged to men whose war-time activities epitomized their lawless careers. The ruthless Wild West era, which lasted until the new century, merely extended the field of operation for the bandits the press called "outlaws".

When SBC missionaries to China wrote for those at home of the need to enforce treaty rights, which local officials often ignored, or of the death of a missionary at the hands of bandits while trying to protect his friends from their rampages, like that of J. Landrum Holmes in 1861, their readers could immediately conjure up and identify with such a picture. Missionary experiences during the Taiping Rebellion, Tientsin Massacre, and Boxer Rebellion — and even wars with France and Japan — would have reminded American readers of their own tumultuous experiences during the Civil War, Indian Wars, and Mexican and Spanish-American wars. Both writers and readers, each half a world away from the other, would have found each others' stories resonating in their ears and hearts. The major difference would have been that the violence of the American experience was based on the issue of central governmental authority being exercised, while in China it originated in the lack of central governmental authority rather than in its exercise.

The prevalence of vice was a substantially different picture between the two countries, for what the missionaries viewed as vice was outlawed in the US but not in China. In China, the missionary view of the government's relation to vice was bound up in China's tolerance for, and lack of interest in criminalizing, social ills. The most common examples cited by the missionaries in their writings were the practices of binding women's feet, of gambling, and of opium use.

Missionaries decried gambling as pernicious, and in this judgment they could rest assured that readers at home would heartily agree. Gambling was universally criminalized in all parts of the US, though it was never unpopular with a certain portion of the population. Missionary concern over opium was a different story. At home, their hostility to opium was tangled with an ongoing American debate over the broad category of drug use. American readers found missionary discussions of opium couched in terms almost identical to those used by the temperance movement at home. But unlike gambling, drug use had not been criminalized in the US. Use of alcohol had been regulated for the purposes of taxation, and use to excess which interfered with civil order was illegal. Throughout the target era, a segment of the American population attempted to criminalize the sale of beverage alcohol at first the national, then the local, level. The series of organizations that represented the prohibition forces — the Washingtonian Society, Sons of Temperance, and Women's Christian Temperance Union — succeeded in the effort shortly after the target era and demonstrated the strength of an impulse with which the missionaries would have been in great sympathy.

Missionaries reserved their darkest tones for the maltreatment and mistreatment of the female segment of China's population. While they would decry gambling as pernicious and opium use as a terrible and destructive vice, missionaries reserved their gravest concern for the government's systematic failure to elevate women's status from object to equal. Jesse Coleman Owen, who served near the end of the target era, penned *The Old Story in Tsin, or a Portrayal of China's Struggle for Freedom and Reform*, which focused on all the evils flowing from binding women's feet and the greater evil of which it was a symbol, in 1937. As much as any other writing, this book attempted to depict evocatively the social problems which a beneficent government could have prevented.

Missionaries thought that the government's persistent use of an antiquated system of civil service examinations, based on ancient but useless learning, epitomized the need for educational reform, especially as it related to females. Missionary writings on the issue of education, perhaps better than any others, displayed what one historian called the Baptist "genius of ministering to the disinherited peoples of society". American culture exhibited an abiding faith in the efficacy of education to elevate an individual's status and an assumption that universal education provided the most secure foundation for progressive governments. Unlike the European cultures from which it originally derived, American culture assumed that educating women was not only valuable to, but also a fundamental requirement for, society. A vast array of schools at all levels (elementary through college) grew out of the philosophy that educated women enriched society in their own right, then enriched it again by in turn educating their own children as good citizens.

Education

When missionaries arrived in China, they found an educational philosophy completely at odds with that of their homeland. Education in China was a scholarly one, based solely on the great classics of Chinese literature and designed to produce functionaries who could serve the Emperor. Women, who could not serve in official capacities because of their status, were barred from being educated. Without exception, the missionaries commented on this difference in philosophy and sought to make it intelligible to a culture at home which had long before passed the point of questioning whether women should be educated and was deep in the throes of ascertaining what direct political and economic role they should play in national life.

Missionary attitudes concerning education were perhaps best explained by their reports about their own efforts to provide education for women as well as for prospective pastors. Lottie Moon's efforts in Pingtu would have been the most familiar to their readers. Baptists believed in education as a means to end ignorance, produce social progress, and improve the lot of Chinese. They were sure that it could, as Anna Pruitt wrote in *Up From Zero*, reveal attractive and cultured men and women who could work with unselfish heroism "for the betterment of the people" (Pruitt 1938:3). And it was an SBC missionary who, in 1911, wrote to the American masses of the first step in the desired direction when the Emperor changed the educational basis of the civil service examinations (Provence 1906:214–216; see also Annual 1911:184).

Though Chinese government and education required translation to be intelligible to American readers, no aspect of Chinese culture required more effort at translation than that of health care. Varieties of governmental and educational theory and practice were familiar enough to their readers to allow missionaries security in their allusions and explanations. While their readers lacked experiential exposure to some of what the missionaries described in their writing about China, none of them found the stories alien. Such was not the case with health care because of radically different medical traditions.

Health Care

Western — and by extension, American — medical theory and practice originated in the Greek scientific tradition. Galen's classification of illnesses and separation of anatomy from physiology laid the foundation upon which all further western medical thought rested. That edifice emerged more with the addition of Avicenna's compilation of Arabic advances, and then the focused attention on the workings of the human body during and immediately after the Renaissance.

The Renaissance spirit flowered in the fledgling US, thanks in large part to Thomas Jefferson's careful tending. During the second quarter of the 19th century, American medical practice standardized because medical education became available on a large scale and because state and local governments codified a licensure procedure. Although the germ theory would not dominate American medical practice until after the work of Pasteur and Lister shortly following mid-century, the tenets of scientific medicine upon which it was based were the foundation of most educated individuals' medical understanding when the SBC sent its first medical missionaries to China: J. Sexton James and George Washington Burton in 1846 and 1851 respectively.

In writing about health care in China, missionaries noted two fundamental differences between the cultures. First, Chinese health care was highly individualized and solely a family responsibility. During the target era, China had no conception, much less system, of public health care. Lack of a public health system would not have surprised readers in a country that would not begin governmentally-sponsored and -funded public health programs until the end of the target era. The concept of absolute personal or family responsibility was a shock. While Americans during the target era were individualistic in their outlook, they were conditioned, some would say by the frontier heritage, to think of community assistance in many areas, including health care. They found it difficult to comprehend how friends or employers could turn away someone in need of medical attention. Missionaries explained the phenomenon by noting that China lacked exposure to that which they viewed as the underpinning of America's outlook: the Biblical story of the Good Samaritan and the Christian teaching of an individual's responsibility for others.

Second, Chinese health care was rooted in a totally different philosophy than that of the West. Western medical practice was grounded in science and empiricism (Enlightenment Rationalism); that in China was supernaturally-based. As presented in missionary writings, Chinese medicine was based on superstition and spirits. Illness resulted from evil spirits, either accidentally encountered or actively promoted by enemies, rather than from natural causes. A person's illness might result from harming an animal (like a weasel), from the improper location of a building or openings in its walls, or even from unfortunate contact with the elements. For missionaries' readers, the concept of malevolent spiritual forces producing human physical illness was a superstition which they dismissed as belonging to the Middle Ages and a belief in witches. They found such thinking incomprehensible, despite the best missionary efforts at translation.

No matter how alien the medical philosophy might be, the diseases mentioned by the missionaries ranged from the common (scarlet fever, cholera, typhoid, yellow fever) to the rare (bubonic plague), but none of those mentioned would have been unfamiliar to their readers. Nor would most Chinese methods of treatment have been unknown to American readers. When missionaries wrote of herbal remedies, most readers were familiar with "home remedies" of the same variety. The Chinese practice of acupuncture (or "needle therapy") was another matter. To readers accustomed to cures effected through drugs, or surgery performed with the patient anesthetized, such a procedure sounded unsanitary at best and superstitious at worst.

The everyday aspect of health care that struck most missionaries most forcefully, and the one upon which all seized as representative of the gulf between the two cultures' general attitudes toward health care, was that of sanitation. Western medical practice, being based upon scientific principles, touted the efficacy of proper sanitation as the greatest single contribution to public health.

Less than two decades after the SBC's first medical missionary went to China, America's Civil War gave the American medical community its first large-scale chance at practical medical experimentation and training. Large numbers of young men suffered from a variety of diseases and injuries, and doctors discovered much from their experience in that war. Among their discoveries was the efficacy of proper sanitation. While they did not yet understand the germ theory of medicine, they were on its cusp. Sanitation Commissions grew up on both sides of the fighting, and the publicity behind that experience had Americans conscious as never before that cleanliness was not only next to godliness, it was healthy to boot.

When missionaries wrote about Chinese health care, all of them fastened upon the deplorable attitudes toward proper sanitation which, for them, epitomized its greatest weakness. Inadequate sanitation might characterize rural areas, they admitted, but surely in cities, where most mission stations were, proper sanitation should be the norm.

Social Relationships

In translating the fourth major area, social relationships, missionaries exhibited the greatest respect for the Chinese and their culture. They wrote sympathetically of shortcomings in health care, government, and education, laying most problems in each area at the feet of ignorance rather than malice or inability. Missionary observations about Chinese society mixed appreciation with concern over ignorance, as when D.H. Herring recalled seeing two chickens killed during a boat trip and "their blood sprinkled fore and aft to propitiate the gods of the river for the dangerous voyage ahead" without offering criticism (Jeffries 1963: 25). T.P. Crawford's approach to the other end of the social spectrum reflected the same outlook. When his wife criticized the Empress as a jealous woman who caused most of China's trouble, he replied that the Empress neither knew nor wanted to know about things outside the Middle Kingdom and would be happy if other nations would let her alone. Her ignorance and weakness produced fear rather than jealousy. As he noted, "when you're afraid — well, you know what that does to people! She fears the predatory instincts of the Western nations only slightly less than those of Japan". (Crawford 1903: 127).

This respect for the Chinese and their culture produced a quandary over whether to follow the old customs or maintain Western traditions. Chinese dress designated official rank in a manner unfamiliar to a "classless" American culture. Gordon Poteat vividly described the use of hooks, sashes, and tassels to represent merits and badges to encourage virtue (Poteat 1924: 37). The traditional long robe of a classical Chinese scholar and the accompanying queue assured a particular place in Chinese society. Some missionaries advocated wearing native dress, living in modified Chinese dwellings rather than western style houses, and even reducing missionary salaries to align them with those of the Chinese. That respect also led them to find facets of Chinese society compatible with Christianity. They recorded "many instances of kind consideration", among them the appreciation of one Chinese woman for the "hard work you are doing for us" and another who expressed "great respect for those who are spending their lives teaching others to be good" like "our own sage, Confucius, who went in his cart from village to village exhorting the people to morality" (Foster 1909: 131). After reading the *Book of Changes*, D.H. Herring told his readers that some of the material he found in classical Chinese literature mirrored the New Testament.

Another attempt at such correlation concerned the two countries' changing political scene. Herring's lively curiosity about China's political turmoil reflected his having grown to manhood in the turbulence of the Reconstruction South. His observation that America and China had suffered civil war simultaneously preceded his comment that Richmond, Virginia, center of foreign missions for Southern Baptists and capitol of the former Confederacy, "represented all that was gallant in a dead, but not forgotten confederacy [sic]". (Jeffries 1963: 68).

Few cultural similarities would have been more familiar to Southerners than observations about rigid social divisions and carefully-scripted social interactions in the missionaries' new world. The Confucian system of relationships, though more extensive and precise in nomenclature than those in the American South, was comfortably familiar to Southern Baptist readers whose world picture more closely resembled that of Elizabethan England than that of the more urban, industrial North. The Asian concept of "face" the missionaries equated with their own culture's preoccupation with honor and the resulting exaggerated politeness and extreme remedies for even imagined slights. With these formulae, Southern Baptist missionaries carefully provided signposts to the familiar so that their readers back home could make the exotic comfortable.

In part a result of their use of the inspirational genre of writings, in part because they thought it would further their cause, missionaries generally sought a translation that stressed similarities rather than differences. Stressing similarities in their translations of Chinese culture was the missionaries' way of encouraging American interest in foreign missionary work that did not rest on "stories of remarkable conversions that stand out so brightly from their surroundings, but in the belief that the leaven of the gospel has power to work its way into the life of the nation as a whole, as it has worked its way into the life of other nations" (Poteat 1924: 38). Gordon Poteat called differences between China and America "temporal and superficial" and similarities "eternal and fundamental", and noted that China offered "the opportunity to live for Christ the same kind of life that we should live in any country, planting the seed in the hearts of people very much like the people of America, the difference being largely in the fact that there is so much unplowed ground here" (Poteat 1924: 38). Besides, stressing similarities would minimize what D. H. Herring called "this everlasting feeling of superiority, one country for the other." (Jefferies 1963: 171).

Despite the similarities, missionary tension at living between two cultures emerged clearly. As Anna Pruitt noted, it was as necessary for the missionaries to translate themselves to the Chinese as it was to translate their words. Ignorance of the outside world prompted most Chinese to see missionaries as tools of a foreign government, subversives teaching attitudes and activities injurious to the sovereign state; individuals seeking to earn merit through good works; or merely "foreign devils."

This necessity for personal translation played out in several ways. Missionaries angrily criticized representatives of American tobacco and oil companies in China, who lacked interest in the Chinese and respect for their culture and heritage. These westerners, missionaries wrote, were pernicious in their attitudes and activities, unchecked by conscience and unmotivated by understanding or altruism. Missionaries felt that these westerners presented a mistranslation to the Chinese and caused social problems for inoffensive missionaries.

Religion/philosophy

Chinese and American ignorance of the other's world played their parts in philosophy, as well as in the other four major areas of missionary comment. Missionaries, all college graduates who generally had trained in a Southern Baptist theological seminary, had little, if any, training in Eastern thought. The conflict between expectation and reality laid the foundation for examining Eastern philosophy, the theoretical framework for personal and institutional endeavours. The focus of attention was the distinction between Eastern and Western methods of reasoning.

R. H. Graves, after forty years in China, concluded that the difference between East and West involved philosophy. China's conservatism, by which he meant traditionalism as opposed to progressivism, satisfied them with the present. Living in "squalor and poverty", their attachment to ancestral villages equalled that of "men of more favored lands" for "their more comfortable and elegant dwellings on country farms". Graves concluded that this "most striking characteristic of the Chinese", this "colossal conservatism", originated in excessive national pride, which blinded the Chinese to reality: "men of narrow minds, filled with utter ignorance of other lands, as most of the Chinese are, are inclined to think that all excellences belong to their own race" (Graves 1895: 37).

Finally, with regards to philosophy, missionaries distinguished between Western inductive and Eastern deductive reasoning. Graves observed that the Chinese venerate the past because they "do not employ the Inductive method of reasoning in their philosophy", but instead always looked backward to a Golden Age while inductive reasoning looked toward one in the future. The Chinese had moved from a healthy respect to a reverence for the past. As a result, Confucian respect for the individual, especially the elderly (which was "very commendable" and worthy of emulation in "more favored lands") had been transferred to their country's history (Graves 1895: 44–45). The Confucian belief in filial piety had degenerated into hypocrisy, with the end result a worship of ancestors. This debate regarding cultural reasoning helped missionary justification of Western culture's superiority. Positive characteristics of Western culture — industry, conscientiousness, love of truth, accuracy, an enlarged view, breadth of mind, obedience to law, perseverance, enterprise and practical common sense — were all Anglo-Saxon traits and the result of right reasoning. To introduce Western ideas into Chinese culture would reduce Chinese self-conceit.

Missionaries were aware of China's transition, which they called an awakening, during the target era. A successful awakening, according to Graves, must come from two sources — free intercourse with the rest of the world and Christianity "permeating every part of the Empire, leavening and remolding its institutions". Missionaries believed that nothing more ensured success in the modernization process than Christianity's presence. "If Eastern philosophy and science come to China divorced from Christianity", Graves observed, "Confucian scholars will accept the new learning with proud self-complacency, and will find it only a confirmation, and a more elaborate illustration of the teachings of Confucian scholars for the last two thousand years". Western science and philosophy, taught by Christian men, would provide "the most convincing testimony to God in nature, in history and in providence" (Graves 1895: 199). Only Christianity, the missionaries argued, could offer the Chinese a true philosophy of the physical universe. This message to readers in the American South confirmed the superiority of Western civilization and linked that civilization to Christianity as its most important ingredient.

While such a belief might appear arrogant and self-centered, missionaries were attempting to give China their own culture because they believed that it had produced a better life, materially and spiritually, and they wanted others to participate in and enjoy that comfort. As Michael Schaller noted, "Christianity represented not just a spiritual belief but a complex set of values intimately related to Western cultural heritage. Spreading religion, then, meant spreading an entirely new way of life in China" (Schaller 1990: 15). To the missionaries, that new life was good, one which supporters in the American South already enjoyed. These dedicated men and women sought to convert the Chinese, but also built schools, hospitals and orphanages. They pioneered Chinese language study and often praised China's heritage. They were trapped between their belief that Western culture was superior due to Christianity's influence and their love and respect for Chinese heritage.

David Bonavia pointed out this paradox in his appraisal of the success and failure of Christianity in China:

The most important religious influence on modern China has been Christianity, not principally through conversions but through the scientific and political ideas which were brought to China by the missionaries. Western medicine, Western ethical concepts, Western music, sports and ideas of democracy — all were useful tools in winning Chinese souls for Christ. Certainly all these aspects of Western civilization would have been absorbed by China sooner or later, but they would have taken much longer to spread from the accessible coastal areas into the hinterland had it not been for missionary zeal. (Bonavia 1987:71).

Conclusion

As missionaries tried to translate Chinese culture to supporters in the American South, they were conscious of conflicts between East and West. They tried to respect Chinese traditions while offering Christianity and Western culture as a better way of life. Just as they translated themselves and their religion to the Chinese as Anna Pruitt stated, they translated what they found in China to American readers as R. H. Graves' 1895 memoir, *Forty Years in China: Or China in Translation*, illustrates. In both instances, their translation work was faithful to the original, a faithfulness prompted in each instance by love, appreciation, and respect for the original text.

The balanced, thoughtful, and appreciative account of China relayed to home folks by missionaries bred in their readers an abiding affinity for the Middle Kingdom. Even though they often presented observation as artifact, translation as history lesson rather than current event, missionaries conjured up in their readers an affection undimmed by time and enhanced rather than obscured by the inspirational genre they adopted. Certainly the choice of Miss Charlotte Diggs "Lottie" Moon, missionary to Shandong Province, as the namesake for the annual Southern Baptist offering to missions encouraged that affection.

Another aspect of these writings aided that affection's longevity. Four of the missionary writings were released in the target era, the rest over the years that followed. Three emerged within the next decade, three in the following decade, five during the 1930s, two in the 1940s, and five more than a half-century later. Though the images portrayed a bygone era, their consistent appearances kept those images fresh in readers' minds. Without contradictory images from other sources, missionary translations of Imperial Chinese culture to Americans remained their unquestioned picture of the Middle Kingdom, and missionary prescriptions for its betterment their unquestioned assumptions. In addition, as post-Imperial governments discovered, effecting changes in Chinese culture was a slow and arduous process that kept the picture from being outdated too quickly.

Measuring response to missionary translation efforts would require a careful perusal of denominational publications to track reader responses in letters sent for publication. One could even, perhaps, seek sermon allusions to China. Perhaps the best gauge of reader response is an indirect one. Missionaries carefully promoted the Chinese cause by distinctly separating government from governed. When Southern Baptist mission work in China ended with the expulsion of their missionaries in 1950–1, Southern Baptists reacted against that government while retaining their love and concern for the governed. There was a qualitative difference in Southern Baptists reactions toward the regimes of the Union of Soviet Socialist Republics and the People's Republic of China. Certainly a good part of that difference can be laid to what readers found in the pages of the missionaries' translations of their adopted land to the one of their nativity.

Works cited

Adams, Daniel J. 1987. *Cross Cultural Theology: Western Reflections in Asia*. Atlanta: John Knox Press.

Anderson, Park Harris. c1936. *"He Knoweth Not How", a Story of Chinese Baptist Initiative . . . for the Information of Baptists and Others*. Nashville: Broadman Press.

Annual of the Southern Baptist Convention 1911. 1911. Nashville, TN: Marshall & Bruce Co.

Bausum, Robert L. c1975–1977. *Pass It On: Four Generations of Missionary Service*. New York: Vantage Press.

Bostick, Lena Stover. 1961. *An Ambassador for Christ, George Pleasant Bostick*. Luray, VA: Lauck.

Bostick, Wade D. and Abbie T. 1911. "Famine Scenes in China". *Missionary Review of the World* 34: 449–450.

Bonavia, David. 1987. *The Chinese*. New York: Penguin Books.

Bryan, F. Catharine. c1949. *At the Gates; Life Story of Matthew Tyson and Eliza Moring Yates of China*. Nashville: Broadman Press.

Bryan, F. Catharine. 1938. *His Golden Cycle: The Life Story of Robert Thomas Bryan*. Richmond: Rice Press.

Bryan, Robert Thomas. c1927. *Christianity's China Creations*. Richmond: Foreign Mission Board, Southern Baptist Convention.

Cauthen, Eloise Glass. c1978. *Higher Ground: Biography of Wiley B. Glass, Missionary to China*. Nashville: Broadman Press.

Chambers, Christine Coffee. c1939. *Builder of Dreams; The Life of Robert Edward Chambers*. Nashville: Broadman Press.

Cohen, Paul A. 1963. *China and Christianity: The Missionary Movement and the Growth of Chinese Antiforeignism*. Cambridge: Harvard University Press.

Coleman, Inabelle Graves. 1959 edition. *One of Us : The Story of the Life of Willie Hayes Kelly*. Durham, NC: I. G. Coleman.

Coleman, Inabelle Graves. 1938. *For This Cause*. Nashville: Broadman Press.

Crawford, Tarlton Perry. 1903. *Evolution in My Mission Views; or Growth of Gospel Mission Principles in My Own Mind*. Chicago: Regan Printing House.

Fairbank, John K., ed. 1974. *The Missionary Enterprise in China and America*. Cambridge: Harvard University Press.

Fairbank, John K. and Edwin O. Reischauer. 1989. *China: Tradition and Transformation.* Boston: Houghton Mifflin Co.

Foster, L. S. 1909. *Fifty Years in China; an Eventful Memoir of Tarleton Perry Crawford, D. D.* Nashville: Bayless-Pullen Company.

Gaston, Annie Bunn. 1916. *The Legend of Lai-Chou.* New York: Fleming H. Revell.

Graves, Rosewell Hobart. 1895. *Forty Years in China: or China in Translation.* Baltimore: R. H. Woodward.

Harris, Florence Powell. 1968. *How Beautiful the Feet.* Hongkong: Luen Shing Printing Co.

Hearn, Lizzie P. 1912. "Dining with Chopsticks". *Delineator* 80: 265.

Herring, James Alexander. 1969. *The Foursquare Dictionary in Chinese and English.* Taipei: Mei Ya Publishers.

Hipps, John Burder. 1966. *Fifty Years in Christian Missions: An Autobiography.* Raleigh: Edwards and Broughton.

Hipps, Margaret Stroh. 1945. *Neighbors Half a World Away.* Nashville: Broadman Press.

Hudgins, Francis E. 1958. *Temples of the Dawn.* Nashville: Southern Baptist Convention Press.

Hundley, Lillie Mae. 1983. *While It Is Yet Day.* Canyon, TX: Staked Plains Press.

Jackson, John Edward. 1942. *A Criticism of the Clergy.* Barnesboro, PA: Criterion Press.

Jefferies, Susan Herring. 1963. *Papa Wore No Halo.* Winston-Salem: John F. Blair.

Latourette, Kenneth Scott. 1929. *A History of Christian Missions in China.* New York: Macmillan.

Leavell, Charlotte (Henry). 1957. *Genealogy of the Nine Leavell Brothers of Oxford, Miss.* Charlottesville, VA: np.

Leavell, George W. c1928. *Some Fruits of the Gospel : Experiences of a Medical Missionary.* Nashville: Sunday School Board, Southern Baptist Convention.

Leonard, Charles A. 1969. *Repaid a Hundredfold.* Grand Rapids, MI: Eerdmans.

Little, Laura Nance. 1938. *Darings in the Dawn.* Richmond: Rice Press.

Nevius, Helen S. C. 1869. *Our Life in China.* New York: Robert Carter and Brothers.

Nichols, Buford L. c1948. *It Happened in China : Random Glimpses of Life in China.* Nashville: Broadman Press.

Owen, Jesse Coleman. 1937. *The Old Story in Tsin, or a Portrayal of China's Struggle for Freedom and Reform.* Boston: The Christopher Publishing House.

Playboy. 1976. "*Playboy* Interview: Jimmy Carter". *Playboy* 23 (November 1976): 63–86.

Poteat, Gordon. c1921. *A Greatheart of the South, John T. Anderson, Medical Missionary.* New York: George H. Doran Co.

Poteat, Gordon. c1924. *Home Letters from China : The Story of How a Missionary Found and Began His Life Work in the Heart of China.* New York: G. H. Doran.

Poteat, Gordon. 1940. *Stand By for China.* New York: Friendship Press.

Provence, H. W. 1906. "Imperial Decree Abolishing Examinations". *World To-Day* 10: 214–6.

Pruitt, Anna Seward. 1929. *The Day of Small Things.* Richmond: Foreign Mission Board, Southern Baptist Convention.

Pruitt, Anna Seward. 1938. *Up from Zero.* Richmond: Rice Press.

Reynolds, Cosa Elizabeth. 197? *My Walk with God : Even in War-Time China.* [Roanoke, VA]: C. E. Reynolds.

Riddell, Olive. 1969. *The Wheels Kept Rolling.* Richmond: Woman's Missionary Union of Virginia.

Routh, E. C. c1950. *Evening and Morning in China.* Nashville: Broadman Press.

Sallee, Annie Jenkins. c1948. *Torchbearers in Honan*. Nashville: Broadman Press. Edition used: Freeport, N.Y.: Books for Libraries Press, 1972.

Sallee, Annie Jenkins. c1933. *W. Eugene Sallee, Christ's Ambassador*. Nashville: Sunday School Board, Southern Baptist Convention.

Saunders, J. R. c1969. *67 Years a Pioneer for Christ*. Manila: Baptist Press.

Schaller, Michael. 1990. *The United States and China in the Twentieth Century*. New York: Oxford University Press.

Smith, Bertha. c1965; 1995. *Go Home and Tell*. Nashville: Broadman Press.

Stamps, Elizabeth Belk. 1972? *To China with Love*. Ormond Beach, FL: np.

Starr, John Bryan. 1997. *Understanding China: A Guide to China's Economy, History and Political Structure*. New York: Hill and Wang.

Teal, Edna Earle. 1973? *My Walk with God in China: An Autobiography of Edna Earle Teal*. Orlando, FL: Christ for the World Publishers.

Torbet, Robert G. c1950. *A History of the Baptists*. Philadelphia: Judson Press.

Tupper, H. A. 1891. *A Decade of Foreign Missions. 1880–1890*. Richmond, VA: Foreign Mission Board of the Southern Baptist Convention.

Tupper, H. A. 1880. *The Foreign Missions of the Southern Baptist Convention*. Richmond, VA: Southern Baptist Convention Foreign Mission Board.

Tyler, Alice Felt. c1944. *Freedom's Ferment: Phases of American Social History to 1860*. Minneapolis: University of Minnesota Press.

Watson, Lila. 1958. *Grace McBride, Missionary Nurse*. Nashville: Southern Baptist Convention Press.

Webster, James Benjamin. 1923. *Christian Education and the National Consciousness in China*. New York: E. P. Dutton and Company.

Webster, James Benjamin. 1932. *Interests of Chinese Students*. Shanghai: Bureau of Publications, University of Shanghai.

Whilden, Lula F. 1917. *Life Sketches from a Heathen Land*. Greenville, SC: Woman's Missionary Union of South Carolina.

Whitehead, James D., Yu-Ming Shaw, and N. J. Girardot, eds. 1979. *China and Christianity: Historical and Future Encounters*. Notre Dame: Center for Pastoral and Social Ministries, University of Notre Dame.

Chapter 5

Translating the concept of 'identity'

Eva Richter and Bailin Song
City University of New York

Introduction

In 1987 author Eva Richter was teaching at Hebei Teacher's University in Shi-jiazhuang, China, and reading a somewhat abstruse work on Dickens with one of her graduate students. The critic claimed that Dickens had projected his own identity into the characters of his novels and proceeded to analyze the ways in which he had done so. The student became increasingly frustrated, till finally he slammed the book shut and exclaimed: "How am I supposed to understand what this author is saying when I don't even understand some of the underlying concepts here? Tell me, what is 'identity'?" The question had the effect of an illuminating shock. We suddenly found ourselves standing on the edge of a great cultural divide between East and West.

Much of Western, and particularly American, literature rests on the assumption that every individual has an 'identity' distinct from that of every other. In order that the message of the original be understood and the impact of the work be felt, therefore, it is extremely important that the concept of identity and its related terms 'self', 'soul', 'person' be fully understood and properly translated so as to convey as much as possible of the original idea and its nexus of intellectual and emotional connotations. In order to do this, we must first understand how the terms in question operate in literary contexts. Only then can we hope to find equivalent translations in Chinese, where 'self' has different connotations and where individualism is frequently seen as negative.

In this paper, therefore, we will explore the meaning of the term 'identity' and its operation in three literary works, Walt Whitman's "Song of Myself", Kate Chopin's *The Awakening*, and Chaim Potok's *My Name Is Asher Lev*. The first two works have received several translations, which we will examine. In addition, we will present alternative translations offered by several respondents of Chinese origin living in the U.S. and discuss the adequacy and/or limitations of all these versions in conveying a cultural and intellectual construct that does not seem to have a clear counterpart in Chinese thought. Out of this discussion we hope will come both clearer understanding of the difficulties in translating this concept and constructive suggestions for future work.

Part I: The Concept of Personal Identity

A Western perspective

The very Western concept of personal identity rests on the foundation of the idea of a 'person' as distinct from the generic 'man'. Its related construct is the 'self', a conscious, thinking, reflexive and autonomous entity — individual, distinct from others, but sharing common characteristics with them. This construct is an integral part of Western and particularly of American philosophy and literature, but it has long roots in Western philosophy since the Greeks. (See, for example, Boethius, *Contra Eutychen et Nestorium*.)

For the English philosopher John Locke (1632–1704), the terms 'person' and 'self' were nearly synonymous. In Book II of *An Essay Concerning Human Understanding*, Locke defined 'person' as "a thinking, intelligent being, that has reason and reflection, and can consider itself as itself, the same thinking thing, in different times and places" (1975: 335). He distinguished between physical identity or identification and personal identity, basing the latter upon consciousness, a concept intended to embrace both awareness and memory. Thus the identity of an individual person, according to Locke, depends upon his/her awareness of what s/he has done and the ability to remember having done it. The memory integrates the person that I was yesterday, who experienced events and acted or did not act on them, with the person that I am today, who experiences and acts on different events and thinks different thoughts. The concept of 'identity', then, is a concept that seeks out sameness and constancy, a core of continuity in the face of change. To quote a more contemporary philosopher, E.S. Brightman defined a 'person' as "a complex unity of consciousness, which identifies itself with its past self in memory, determines itself by its freedom, is purposive and value-seeking, private yet communicating, and potentially rational" (Ferm 1950: 341).

The existence and actions of such a 'person' as a self-reflexive, self-conscious, autonomous and purposive individual with a distinct 'identity' are subsumed and guaranteed in the American Declaration of Independence with its insistence on personal freedom to pursue individual happiness. The concept is a characteristic of American life on which the French author, Alexis de Toc-queville, in his classic work *Democracy in America,* comments. In the chapter entitled "Of Individualism in Democratic Countries", De Tocqueville says that to be a self, to be independent, to become self-conscious and self-created are important elements of the dream of America. He identifies the concept as the motivating force behind both individual actions and important social move-ments in America, including the abolition movement, the drive for women's suffrage, the waves of European immigration, and even the exploration of the western frontier with its credo of rugged individualism. He sees these all as shaped by the ideal of autonomy inherent in the creation and recognition of a 'self' — an 'identity' distinct, different from the 'identity' of others — creating its own personal destiny (98–99). R.W.B. Lewis in *The American Adam* com-ments on the same ideal of the self-created man as an important element of the American dream.

The term 'identity' has great currency in colloquial American parlance. Na-tionally, culturally, racially and indeed in every way, America is an incredibly diverse and complex society. In fact, many would today deny that it is *a* soci-ety; Walt Whitman's statement "I contain multitudes" is literally correct applied to America. The country's diversity, pluralism, and complexity are alternately a source of strength and pride — and of despair. What, indeed, is America? What is the famous (or infamous?) "American Dream"? What do we mean when we call ourselves "Americans" when we all bear with us the fragmented memo-ries of the vastly different nationalities, cultures, histories, and languages from which we originally came? Third and fourth generation men and women born in America still identify themselves as Chinese, Greek, Italian, Irish. It is only when they get a US passport and travel outside the country that they begin to think of themselves as 'Americans'. And then to what extent is an Irish-Ameri-can, an African-American, a Chinese-American, a Jewish-American, an Arab-American the same as or different from other 'Americans'? To what extent do we even want to be the same as others?

The prevailing metaphor for America until the 1960s was the 'melting pot'. The image was of a large crucible into which everyone was immersed, our sub-stance to be melted by the fires of American life and mingled fluidly together into a new amalgam. It would be hard in such an amalgam to recover one's ori-ginal, individual nature. That would be lost, transmuted into something new and different, something common to the entire pot. The melting pot image empha-sized the importance of society over the individual, the common destiny over the personal, the national over the ethnic, and predictably, it fell into disrepute.

What replaced it was the image of the salad bowl, in which each ingredient, each separate vegetable maintains its nature, flavour and integrity while enhanced by the other salad ingredients. The salad is a single dish, but it comprehends many entities. In this metaphor the concepts of individualism, cultural difference and integrity, national origin and history are maintained, existing happily within the framework of a single overarching concept. Each vegetable in the salad is separate and distinct, its nature identifiable, its separate attributes clearly perceptible. Each contributes equally to the nature and enjoyment of the whole. Each is equally important.

America is a society in constant flux — we mean that literally: the only social constant is flux. We do not have the foundation of thousands of years of a continuous history, a continuous linguistic, philosophical, religious, and social tradition such as China and India have. And it is because we are constantly defining the society and defining ourselves within the society that the concept of 'identity' takes on such crucial importance. It is not enough for us to claim a public 'identity', a set of external labels like 'woman', 'wife', 'mother', 'Jewish', 'New Yorker', 'teacher', 'middle class', 'American citizen'. These are important attributes that help locate us within the society, but they do not allow us the expression of an interior reality and existence distinct from that of all the others who share these external characteristics with us. We are not even sure what these characteristics mean for the society at large. What does it really mean to be a woman? To be a wife? A mother? And so on. We talk constantly about *who we are* as a nation and a society, and *who we are* as individuals. And when we say of someone (as we frequently do), "She does not know who she is", that is a very critical statement. Highest praise is conveyed by saying of someone, "She knows exactly who she is." The expression generally is meant to convey the idea that a person has discovered her individual 'identity', that she is in harmony with her 'self', that the way in which she functions and integrates her experiences within the society is in harmony and consistent with the way she conceives her individual nature as distinct from her general nature or public persona, which she may share with everyone else in her general category.

Thus, in the American scheme of things the discovery and subsequent affirmation of one's 'identity', one's 'inner truth', one's 'self' or 'personhood', (as distinct from the merely externally defined term 'personality') is the highest good and proof of an individual's moral commitment and integrity. The search for and development of this 'identity' is the subject of much of American literature. In such works, the author or the main character embarks on a quest to identify him or herself in terms of an individual nature that is both the sum total of external experiences and definitions, and the experience of an inner 'self' distinct from other individuals. The 'inner identity' is constituted of the subject's individual nature, sensibility and personal history and is at the same time a determinant of how the individual sees and reacts to surrounding social, historical, and physical forces. Personal integrity in such works derives not from adherence to social norms or conventional notions of right and wrong but from consistency of action in terms of a perceived personal quest for an individual 'identity'.

Identity in Whitman's "Song of Myself"

Described as the quintessential American poet, in "Song of Myself", Walt Whitman sings and celebrates himself with passionate commitment, "with original energy", and without the slightest trace of embarrassment at his self-glorification. This uninhibited feeling, we would venture to say, given the conventions of modesty inherent in Chinese culture, is already difficult to translate into a Chinese version consistent with the original connotations, although as we shall see, it is not impossible. John Updike comments on "the exultant egotism which only an American could have voiced" (1978: 33). "Song of Myself" has been described as, "Probably the finest enactment in all literature of the adventure of self-making" (Zweig 1984: 18), "overtly a celebration, ... [of] the American Sublime of influx, of Emersonian self-recognition and consequent self-reliance" (Bloom 1976: 250), and a "profound and lovely comic drama of the self" which unfolds Whitman's "drama of identity" (Chase 1955: 58; Carlisle 1973: 177–178). According to Bloom, Whitman's most original invention is the "psychic cartography" in "Song of Myself" "of three components in each of us: soul, self, and real me or me myself" (1994: 270).

Whitman opens the poem by introducing himself with the line, "I celebrate myself, and sing myself .../For every atom belonging to me as good belongs to you" (I, 1–3). In the fourth line he says, "I loafe and invite my soul...". After a catalogue of meetings, historical events, social and personal contacts and their attendant emotions, Whitman repudiates them all by saying, "But they are not the Me myself./ Apart from the pulling and hauling stands what I am/Stands amused, complacent, compassionating, idle, unitary..." (IV, 9–11).

The 'self' in this representation seems to refer to the man as physical being and personality, affecting and being affected in turn by all with which he comes into contact. It is the entity we mean when we utter the word "I"; it is Walt Whitman, the American, the active man we observe going through the experiences and consequent emotions and actions of his life. In this form, Whitman is a representative man, one who includes all of America's social conditions and heritage of experience and history. The second component of Whitman's being, the "soul", is the agent of consciousness which the "I" must invite to bear upon the catalogue of events, actions and objects in order to make harmonious sense of them. It is the "soul" that creates the perceptual, emotional and intellectual connections between the poet and all other beings.

Finally, the "Me, myself" is an unchanging inner core of being, a fundamental nature which exists *ab initio*, that is, prior to experience and knowledge and which, though enlarged by experiences and perceptions, is fundamentally unchanged by them. Significantly, the word "Me" in this phrase "the Me, myself", is capitalized, because it names the fundamental attribute of Whitman's being; it is his basic 'identity' — the poet who subsumes all others and simultaneously transcends them. After an extended catalogue of Americans with whom he identifies, he says, "I resist anything better than my own diversity" (XVI, 20). "(I am large, I contain multitudes)", (LI, 8) he exults. He refers to himself as "a kosmos" (XXIV, 1); "Encompass worlds, but never try to encompass me" (XXV, 17), he says, thus claiming his independence and his autonomy. He is generous, however: "When I give I give myself" (XL, 9); "And nothing, not God, is greater to one than one's self is"(XLVIII, 3). "Nor do I understand who there can be more wonderful than myself" (XLVIII, 14). There is an insistence here by Whitman on his own, highly individual, unchanging nature, his *self*. The soul and the body are equal partners to Whitman (XLVIII, 1–2), but the self underlies, subsumes and transcends their operation. It is frequently contradictory, and it refuses to be tamed: "I too am not a bit tamed" (LII, 2). Finally, and perhaps this will be a caveat to us who are trying so hard to find linguistic equivalents where none may exist, Whitman claims that he is "untranslatable" (LII, 2).

Identity in Chopin's *The Awakening*

The concepts of individual identity, the self, and the quest to understand these underlie the actions of the heroine of the novel *The Awakening*, by Kate Chopin (1851–1904). This novel, written in 1899, has become very popular in the United States, especially among feminist critics. Set in 19th century Louisiana, the novel traces changes in the life and perceptions of Edna Pontellier, a young, socially prominent matron with two children, married well but without love to a banker, and living in a very restrictive society whose social expectations are highly codified. Edna goes to a seaside resort with her family during a summer vacation and falls in love with Robert Lebrun. He loves her too, but in order not to compromise her reputation and his own, he leaves. Edna's love for Robert has awakened her to the needs of her own nature. She is not a "mother-woman" like her friend Adele Ratignolle and recognizes different desires in herself that cannot be satisfied by the round of social obligations and everyday routines required by her status and the traditions of Creole society. Even as a child "she had apprehended instinctively the dual life — that outward existence which conforms, the inner life which questions" (26). She now begins to define her *self* in terms of an existence separate from her identification and roles as daughter, wife, mother. In a conversation with her friend Adele she says, "I would give up the unessential; I would give my money, I would give my life for my children, but I wouldn't give myself" (80).

She discovers a creative streak in herself, starts to paint, refuses to hostess the required and boring round of parties that would advance her husband's position, and finally, when her husband is out of town and her children are staying with their grandmother, she leaves her grand house, which she finds oppressive and stifling, for a small, unpretentious cottage in which she can do as she pleases. "Whatever came", Chopin writes, "she had decided never again to belong to another than herself" (133). Her husband, of course, cannot understand her at all and wonders whether she is losing her mind. "He could see plainly that she was not herself. That is, he could not see that she was becoming herself and daily casting aside that fictitious self which we assume like a garment with which to appear before the world" (96). "Herself" and not "herself" — here is the core dilemma. Edna is not the person her society identifies her as being, an identity conferred on her from the outside by the social norms and conventions which heretofore have structured her life. She is, however, beginning to recognize her real self, her inner identity as an individual whose integrity as a human being demands that she recognize and act in accordance with her newly discovered self-knowledge (Seyersted 1969: 139). The move to the cottage gives her,

> a feeling of having descended in the social scale, with a corresponding sense of having risen in the spiritual. She began to look with her own eyes; to see and to apprehend the deeper currents of life. No longer was she content to 'feed upon opinion' when her own soul had invited her.   (p. 156)

Note here the anti-bourgeois sentiment, Edna's desire for independence, and her assumption of autonomy and responsibility for her own actions. She has exchanged social approval for spiritual integrity, advancing in the spiritual scale to which, in a clear echo of Whitman, "her own soul had invited her". Again, as in

Whitman, the soul is the agent of self-recognition, the perception of her fundamental 'identity'. The path to full self-discovery is not easy, but Edna resolutely
follows it. To her sympathetic doctor, she says, "Perhaps it is better to wake up
after all, even to suffer, rather than to remain a dupe to illusion all one's life" (184).
It is certainly significant that before she leaves, Edna has been reading Emerson and falls asleep over her book. For Emerson the highest goal of human consciousness is to define oneself as a subject with an independent inner life. In his
essay "Self-reliance", he writes, "Nothing is at last sacred but the integrity of your
own mind" (1971: 139).

Driven by a passionate nature newly awakened by her love for Robert, Edna
takes a man of questionable reputation, Alcée Arobin, as her lover. Robert returns; they declare their love for one another, but Robert, ever the honorable
man, renounces Edna. She returns to the scene of their first meeting at the seaside. She thinks of her children and understands clearly what she meant by saying "she would give up the unessential, but she would never sacrifice herself for
her children" (188). Then she strips naked by the shore and walks into the waves.
One last time she considers her husband and children and thinks, "But they
need not have thought they could possess her, body and soul" (190). And then
"it was too late; the shore was far behind her, and her strength was gone" (190).

For Edna "the essential" is her core identity, that part of each individual "for
which each human being is responsible and without which no human being is
possible" (Ewell, 162). She recognizes, however, that she will not be able finally
to escape the strictures of her society, far as she has come along that road. She
walks into the waves, giving up her life (the unessential) to preserve her own (essential) self and her children's peace and safety.

From the very beginning Whitman exudes a sense of supreme confidence.
Far from being the alienated soul commonly depicted in twentieth century literature, he has a clear sense of his own identity, and his poem incorporates
each succeeding discovery of another aspect of himself in a whooping "bar-
baric yawp" of joyful, uninhibited song. *The Awakening* strikes a different tone;
the strength and integrity of the woman in a male-dominated, restrictive society
lead to a final act of renunciation, in contrast to the public assertiveness available to Whitman, the dominant American male.

Identity in Potok's *My Name Is Asher Lev*

Since the United States is fundamentally a country of immigrants, one profoundly American experience is that of a first generation child of immigrant

parents, standing between his immigrant heritage on the one hand and the demands of a new country and language on the other. All the questions about identity, the nature of the self, and personal integrity alluded to above coalesce in this experience. The immigrant child is part and yet not part of his parents' culture, part and yet not part of the new country, suspended between two worlds, belonging to neither. He must rely on his perception of who and what he is to create the kind of life that will give him the greatest freedom of expression and best ensure a life of dignity and integrity.

Chaim Potok's novel *My Name Is Asher Lev* proclaims its concern with identity in the title itself, for after all, one's name is what one uses to identify oneself to others. More profoundly, the novel is about the immigrant dilemma, compounded here by the fact that the main character is both an artist and the child of orthodox Jews. That in itself presents a problem. Based on the Second Commandment with its injunction against graven images, orthodox Jews are forbidden (as are strict Moslems) to represent the human figure in any way. How can an artist function within these strictures without repudiating the entire religion and culture and finally the family? Must the artist, then, in order to keep faith with his society repudiate his art and the personal impulse that leads him to create it? Is the creation of art a matter of fairly arbitrary choice on the artist's part, like the choice of a profession — whether to become a doctor, a lawyer, or a salesman? Or is the artistic nature a fundamental attribute of one's 'self', in other words, part of one's essential 'identity'? Can the artist decide not to create art without destroying his 'self', or would such a decision betray his fundamental nature?

Asher Lev's mentor, Jacob Kahn, tells him that art is not a toy. "This is a tradition; it is a religion, Asher Lev. You are entering a religion called painting" (203–204). And he continues: "As an artist you are responsible to no one and nothing, except to yourself and to the truth as you see it. . . . An artist is responsible to his art. . . . I will teach you responsibility to art" (208–209). Asher is an artist; that is his identity. The creation of art is creation out of himself. Clearly, cultivation of that self is a commitment and the artist's highest responsibility. Just as clearly, Asher is charting a collision course with his religion, his social group, and his family.

In proclaiming his name, Asher Lev is identifying himself as a Jewish immigrant belonging not to America as Walt Whitman does but to an outsider group. The name Asher is not 'American', but unlike some immigrants who anglicize their names, Asher Lev holds on at least to this external emblem of his identity. His internal identity as a creative artist represents far more of a problem, how-

ever, and dooms Asher be an outsider, working against the strictures of his society. The most salient characteristic of the Jew in Western culture is that he is
identified as the Outsider, the Alien. And thus, in recognizing and following
his artistic nature, Asher becomes, paradoxically, doubly a Jew — he is an Outsider because he is working against and outside of the Jewish heritage; but as
the Outsider he embodies the most common characteristic ascribed to the Jew
in Western culture.

Little by little, he throws off the external indications of his orthodox Jewish
heritage — the skullcap and hat, the long black coat, the ritual shirt. But he identifies with his Jewish heritage and defines it in terms of its history of suffering,
alienation and exile. He wishes to represent this suffering through his art, but
Judaism has no traditional iconography to convey his artistic perception. To
the horror of his parents he chooses the image of the cross, the pre-eminent
Christian symbol of suffering, to represent his mother's life. In using this image,
Asher Lev has broken faith with his religion, his culture, and his family. But he
has affirmed the independence of his perceptions which grow out of his personal need to express himself as an artist. Jacob Kahn warns him: "... an artist is
a person first. He is an individual. If there is no person there is no art" (244). The
'person' here is the autonomous man who makes decisions about the course of
his life in accordance with his consciousness (not his conscience) and takes responsibility for his decisions. As a 'person' Asher Lev is committed to his art. He
cannot stop creating without betraying his fundamental identity. The paradox
is that in affirming his artistic nature he betrays his society. The "message" of the
novel is ambiguous, and discussion rages as to whether Asher Lev is a tormented
hero or a villainous traitor.

A Chinese perspective

All of the definitions of 'identity' and its related terms presented in this paper
so far are positive. The discovery of the 'self' is seen as a complex undertaking,
a quest which confers dignity and merit on the seeker. The integrated, autonomous self is the highest ideal in a system of thought based upon individualism and self-expression, and the reading and interpretation of the three texts
we have discussed in this paper turns on the term 'identity' and its related con-
structs. Clearly, translation of this concept presents real problems in Chinese
where the society and the dominant political philosophy have traditionally emphasized adherence to community and tend to regard the term 'self' as synonymous with 'selfishness'.[1]

An informal survey of some Chinese respondents in the United States[2] elicited interesting reactions to the following question: "If you (as a Chinese, not an American) are asked to brainstorm on 'self' and 'individual/individualism', what kind of ideas and/or associations do you come up with? What do you have to say about the two concepts"? Almost all of the answers immediately jumped from 'self' to "self-centered", "selfish", "opposed to the collective good". "From a merely Chinese perspective", one person answered, "I have primarily only negative things to say". He went on to say that in both Marxist and Confucian thought the individual self is subordinate to the collective and should be willing to sacrifice itself for the greater good, defined variously as the state, the family, the social unit, etc. Another respondent associated 'self' always with discipline as in the phrases "restrain oneself", and "discipline oneself". Again, he contrasted the negative connotations of "individualism" with the positive ones of "collective/collectivism", commenting that individualism is often associated with "individual heroism", which he equated with "selfishness".

We note that above we considered whether Asher Lev was to be seen as a "tormented hero". In direct opposition to the respondent we just quoted, the term 'hero' had only positive connotations. Also, it is interesting to consider that although self-discipline is positive for Americans, the works we discussed above are ones in which the main characters gained stature and admiration not because of their self-restraint and self-discipline but because of their self-expression — certainly in the case of Whitman, the more uninhibited the better!

Another Chinese respondent made varying associations with the term 'individualism', "ranging from the more noble concepts such as self-sacrifice . . ." to the negative ones of "self-gratification", "self-abuse", and again, "selfishness". Once again we come up against a cultural divide: self-sacrifice is not always seen as noble in American thought. Edna Pontellier in *The Awakening* is a heroine (positive connotations again) to feminists precisely because even though she was willing to give up her life, she would not sacrifice her self.

Differences in cultural attitudes such as we have indicated here will obviously result in different interpretations of a given text, as will differences in manipulating the target language and in appreciating and interpreting the source culture. It might be interesting to contrast Chinese and American interpretations of the works we have examined, but that is somewhat beyond the scope of this paper and could be the subject of future research. We do recognize also that political and cultural developments may result in changes in the connotations carried by key terms and concepts. It is certainly noteworthy that *The Awakening* has received four recent Chinese translations (Cheng 1996; Lü 1990; Wen and Jia 1991; Yang 1996), and that many recent Chinese literary works, especially those by women, turn on the question of self-fulfilment and self-realization. (See, for example, the anthology of short stories entitled *I Wish I Were a Wolf,* [Kingsbury 1994]).

Part II: Translations in the literary context

At this point, however, it would probably be instructive to take key terms and phrases relating to the concepts of 'identity' and 'self' in the context of the three works selected for this paper and examine Chinese equivalents for them, both in published translations and in suggestions offered by native speakers of Chinese living in the US and fully conversant with the nuances of American culture. Our approach is empirical. We will evaluate the adequacy of all these translations, both published and solicited from respondents, in terms of how close they seem to us to come to the intent of the original texts. We are not trying to validate or privilege one or another translation in accordance with an abstract and arbitrary ideal but rather in terms of their fidelity to key concepts of the works under discussion, as delineated in the previous sections of this paper. As we shall see, in a few cases we feel the published translations are adequate, but in others they seem lacking in various ways, while the informally offered translations may more nearly approach the intent of the original.

We have invited the following people to present their versions of the terms under consideration: they are a professional translator, a linguist, an English professor, and several laypersons, all fluent in both Chinese and English. Those who responded are Honggang Ma, Shanshan Xu, Bingfu Lu, Guoqiang Wu, Jianping Yue, and Dequan Yue.[3] Honggang Ma is a translator who owns Mark's Translation and Documents in the US, a firm that provides translation services to Chinese immigrants, visiting delegates, local courts and so on. Shanshan Xu, who has a degree in English, is a business owner in Canada. Bingfu Lu, a linguist, Guoqiang Wu, an English professor, and Jianping Yue, an engineering professor, are all currently living and working in the US. Dequan Yue is a retired physics professor who also worked as a journalist in China. Each of these has had in-depth exposure to Western culture as well as a good command of both English and Chinese. All of them were originally from Mainland China. Their proposed translations are presented here.

Identity

Respondent/translator	Translation
Shanshan Xu	真實自我；標誌；歸屬
Honggang Ma	自我屬性；屬性；文化認同
Jianping Yue	本性；特徵；別於他人的固有個性
Bingfu Lu	歸屬
Guoqiang Wu	通一性；認同

The respondents agreed that 個性, a dictionary translation (A New English–Chinese Dictionary, 1979), is a good rendition of 'identity' that conveys its denotative meaning of 'personality' or 'personal characteristic'. However, it is too limited for connotations associated with expressions such as 'She has found her identity', or 'We know exactly who we are'. In such cases, 真實自我, a rendition offered by one of the respondents, is more accurate. 自我屬 性, another respondent's version, is also close to the core concept of 'identity' being discussed here because it embodies a combined meaning of *self* and an individual's 'uniqueness' (i.e., his or her individuality). 屬性，本性，特徵 are Chinese synonyms, all carrying the meaning of 'characteristic', and 'inherent quality', but like個性, they are too limited for the connotations. On the other hand, 歸屬, 認同, and 通一性 seem to express the idea of 'belonging to', 'identifying with', 'accepting', 'assimilating', 'being the same or universal', all of which indicate the loss of a distinct 'self' and 'his or her uniqueness'. 文化認同 indicates 'cultural identity', which is a different meaning than the one under discussion here. 標誌 might be a far-fetched translation because it usually means 'sign', 'mark', and/or 'symbol'.

Individualism

Respondent/translator	Translation
Honggang Ma	個性至上主義
	個性獨立主義
	本我獨立主義
Bingfu Lu	個性崇拜主義
Jianping Yue	自我主義
	個人奮鬥主義

Lexicographers and translators have long rendered 'individualism' into 個人主義 and/or 利己主義. 個人主義 or 利己主義 may be an acceptable equivalent of a minor sense of *individualism* — "the pursuit of individual rather than common or collective interest; egoism" (the third entry definition of *individualism* in *Webster's Third New International Dictionary*). However, since 個人主義 or 利己主義 has mainly negative connotations, both politically and culturally, these expressions do not lead Chinese readers to associate them with the Western idea of individualism. If we look at the main definition given in *Webster's Third New International Dictionary*, "a social theory advocating the liberty, rights or independent action of the individual, or the principle or habit of or belief in independent thought or action", we find that the concept is at least neutral, if not entirely positive. Therefore, we believe that we need to find other translations which do not transmit negativity as the dictionary renditions, 個人主義 and 利己主義, do.

Honggang Ma's versions, 個性至上主義, 個性獨立主義, 本我獨立主義, and Bingfu Chen's 個性崇拜主義 all seem to reflect an emphasis on the pursuit or development of individuality, independent thinking, or action of the self or individual. They do not allude to the side effects of 個人主義 and 利己主義 — at the expense of or to the detriment of the collective interest. They are, thus, much better translations, although 至上 and 崇拜 seem to carry a slight sense of negativity due to their frequent use in association with negative political contexts, as in 個人崇拜. Perhaps it would be a good idea to replace 崇拜 with 崇尚. It may sound more positive to say 個性崇尚主義 than 個性崇拜主義.

Jianping Yue maintains that both 自我主義 and 個人奮鬥主義 are better translations. He thinks that these translations are devoid of the negativity associated with 個人主義 and 利己主義. They also transmit the character of individualism in Franklin's and Emerson's sense of self-reliance and achievement. In addition, they convey the characteristics of autonomous action rather than psychological well being.

So much for the framing concepts. Now let us turn to specific translations of key terms in passages of the literary works under discussion.

Whitman: "Song of Myself"

Respondent/translator	Translation
Honggang Ma	自我之歌
Guoqiang Wu	自我之歌

Jianping Yue	自我之歌
	我的歌
Dequan Yue	我的暢想曲
Tunan Chu 1988	自己之歌
Luorui Zhao 1991	我自己的歌

The theme of Whitman poem, "*Song of Myself*", is "I celebrate myself". The key word in both the title and the theme is "myself". To Whitman, 'self' is not a dirty word, but, rather a joyous concept. The 'self' in Whitman's representation refers to a man as physical being and personality. The translation versions provided here, both published and solicited, all seem to capture that original joyous mood of singing and celebrating, especially in the phrase, 暢想曲. In treating "myself", the core concept of this poem, some versions have rendered the term in its literal denotation as 自己, 我自己, and 自我. A serious shortcoming of these renditions is that the important connotations of 'self' — fundamental nature, personality, special qualities, or simply identity — are not transmitted, because 自己, 我自己, and 自我 usually refer only to the physical being of "I". Unlike 'self' in English, they do not connote 'personality'. Similarly, the connotations of 'self', as explored in this paper, are also lost in 我的歌 (Jianping Yue) and 我的暢想曲 (Dequan Yue).

Whitman: "But they are not the Me, myself"

Respondent/translator	Translation
Honggang Ma	但這一切也還不能全部代表那有獨特一面的我。
Bingfu Lu	他們是他們，我還是我。
Dequan Yue	但他們並非爲我。
Jianping Yue	沒有什麼人能代替我自己。
Guoqiang Wu	這些都不能代表真正的我。
Sang 1969	那些是那些，與我有何干？
Wu 1979	但這些並不是我自己。
Chu 1988	但這一切都不是我。
Zhao 1991	但這些都並非那個 "我" 自己。

It seems to us that Jianliu Sang's published translation of the sentence, 那些是那些,與我有何干, does not accurately convey what Whitman is trying to say with the sentence. As we have discussed in the first part of this paper, the capitalized word "Me" in the phrase, "the Me, myself", names the fundamental attribute of Whitman's being; it is his basic 'identity' — the poet who subsumes all others and simultaneously transcends them, not the one who has nothing to do with others or is not connected with others, as 與我有何干 expresses.

It is interesting to note that most of these versions, including the three published ones, have "the Me, myself" translated literally as 我 or 我自己. Nevertheless, this literal rendition is insufficient for conveying the American connotation of "myself" as expressed in the context of the poem. To the authors of the paper, the connotations of "myself", i.e., "my identity", are explicitly transmitted and thus highlighted in 這一切也還不能全部代表那有獨特一面的我 (Honggang Ma) and 這些都不能代表真正的我 (Gaoqiang Wu).

Chopin: "I would give my life for my children; but I wouldn't give myself."

Respondent/translator	Translation
Honggang Ma	我能爲我的孩子們犧牲我的生命（一生），但不會爲他們去犧性我獨特的個性。
Bingfu Lu	我會爲孩子獻出我的生命，但是不會獻出我自己。
Jianping Yue	我願爲我的孩子而犧性，但卻不能失去我的本性。
Dequan Yue	我願爲我的孩子而犧性，但不願放棄自己。
Guoqiang Wu	我可以爲孩子獻出生命，但不會爲他們而放棄自我（我只爲我的意思）。
Lü 1990	（我）可以爲孩子犧性生命，但是我決不放棄我自己。
Web and Jia 1991	我會爲孩子們拿出我的生命，但是我決不會貢獻自己來。
Cheng 1996	爲了孩子我會獻出我的生命，但是我不會獻出我自己。
Yang 1996	（我可以）爲孩子放棄生命，但是不可以放棄自我。

Again, all the four published versions have the term "myself" translated literally as 我自己 or 自我, as did three of the respondents' versions. However, such a literal translation will probably mislead the Chinese reader into thinking that the mother is selfish. Such a rendition may confuse the reader, for the first part of the sentence seems to tell the reader otherwise. To a Chinese, a mother who is willing to give up her life for her children is surely not a selfish person. A good translation must, therefore, convey the original idea of "myself" as being her real self, her inner identity. Two versions provided by the respondents seem to have done just that with 但不會爲他們去犧牲我獨特的個性 (Honggang Ma) and 但卻不能失去我的本性 (Jianping Yue). We think that it is also acceptable to translate the sentence as 但不願放棄對自我意識的追求, because the "I" is just beginning her voyage of self-consciousness and will continue to search for her true self and her inner identity.

Potok: "... an artist is a person first. He is an individual. If there is no person, there is no art."

Respondent/translator	Translation
Honggang Ma	藝術家首先是一個有血有肉有情感的人，他同時也應是一個有個性的人。若沒有那有血有肉有情感的一面，便不會有藝術了。
Bingfu Lu	一個藝術家首先是個人。而且是個獨特的人。如果沒有個人的自我，也就沒有藝術。
Jianping Yue	每個藝術家首先是他自己，一個具有獨立個性的人。沒有不同藝術家的特性，也就沒有藝術而言。
Dequan Yue	藝術家首先是成其爲人，是個性的人。如果沒有人格，就沒有真藝術。
Guoqiang Wu	藝術家首先是具有位格的人，是個體，沒有個體的人，就沒有藝術。

As discussed in the first part of the paper, the 'person' here is the autonomous man who makes decisions about the course of his life in accordance with his consciousness (not conscience) and takes responsibility for his decisions. In simple Chinese, the 'person' can be defined as 一個獨立自主，憑感性意識（而非道德心）行事，且對個人行爲負責的人. In light of such a definition, we think that Honggang Ma captures the crucial sense of the original sentences and adequately conveys the connotations of 'person' and "individual" in phrases like 一個有血有肉有情感的人, 一個有個性的人 and 那有血有肉有情感的一面. In Jianping Yue's translation, 他自己, 一個具有獨立個性的人 and 特性 also effectively communicate the idea of 'person' and "individual". The other three versions, however, all render the word 'person' in the first sentence literally as 人, which, we think, is not sufficient for conveying the connotations of "person".

Because Chinese culture does not, historically or politically, emphasize individualism or promote the pursuit of personal identity, it is indeed very difficult to translate accurately into Chinese the Western, especially American, concept of identity and its related terms and phrases consistent with the original connotations. Inadequate and inexact translations cause confusion and misunderstanding. For example, as shown in the analysis of the translations of "individualism", the terms 個人主義 and 利己主義, two prevalent Chinese translations of "individualism" provided by dictionaries, convey a negative meaning — the pursuit of individual interest at the expense of, or to the detriment of, the collective interest, a sense which is not that of the original. Translations like these will often lead to the misunderstanding and misinterpretation of the source culture and should, therefore, be replaced by more accurate ones, such as those offered by the respondents.

Another major concern that we want to raise is the difficulty of transmitting effectively into Chinese the connotations associated with terms such as 'self', 'myself', 'person', and 'individual'. In translating "myself", and "Me, myself" in Whitman's and Chopin's works, almost all the published and some of the solicited versions render the terms literally as 自己, 我自己, and自我, which mean more or less the same thing, referring mainly to the physical being of "self" and leaving out the other connotations. These translations, as a result, do not fully convey the sense and the impact of the original. They will not achieve the same effect and cause the same reactions in the reader as the original. But, as we discussed, some of the solicited versions, albeit not perfect, with the added characters do convey the connotations of the original terms. We believe that they should be used.

Conclusion

Translating concepts and terminology across a cultural divide presents unique challenges, especially when these terms are so central to the original culture and are mutating rapidly in the receiving culture. The discussion we have presented here is by no means intended to provide definitive solutions to a fascinating problem but rather to facilitate an ongoing conversation and create bridges of understanding between two cultures. It is an enterprise Whitman would surely have applauded despite his exclamation "I am untranslatable!"

Notes

1. It is interesting to note that De Tocqueville himself is very leery of American individualism, which he describes as a novel expression embodying a novel idea. He contrasts it with "selfishness", as follows: "Our fathers were only acquainted with *égoïsme* (selfishness). Selfish-

ness is a passionate and exaggerated love of self, which leads a man to connect everything with himself and to prefer himself to everything in the world. Individualism is a mature and calm feeling, which disposes each member of the community to sever himself from the mass of his fellows and to draw apart with his family and his friends, so that after he has thus formed a little circle of his own, he willingly leaves society at large to itself. Selfishness originates in blind instinct; individualism proceeds from erroneous judgment more than from depraved feelings; it originates as much in deficiencies of mind as in perversity of heart" (1990: 98).

2. All the Chinese respondents were originally from Mainland China and lived there from the 1950s to 1980s. Currently they are living and working in the United States. The political, ideological, and economic conditions under which they were brought up may have affected how they perceive and interpret certain fundamental concepts. In other words, Chinese people from other parts, such as Taiwan and Hong Kong where different political systems exist, may have different perceptions.

3. The names are given here in English convention, with family names coming last.

Works cited

Bloom, Harold. 1976. *Poetry and Repression — Revisionism from Blake to Stevens*. New Haven: Yale University Press.

Bloom, Harold. 1994. "Walt Whitman as Center of the American Canon". In *The Western Canon*. New York, San Diego, London: Harcout Brace and Company, 264–290.

Boethius. Edition 1973. "Contra Eutychen et Nestorium". In *The Theological Tractatus*. Trans. H. F. Stewart, E. K. Rand, and J. Tester. Cambridge, MA and London: Harvard University Press.

Boren, Lynda S, and Sara de Saussure Davis (eds). 1992. *Kate Chopin Reconsidered: Beyond the Bayou*. Baton Rouge and London: Louisiana State University Press.

Brightman, E. S. 1950. "Personalism (Including Personal Idealism)". In V. Ferm, ed. *A History of Philosophical Systems*. New York: Philosophical Library. 340–352.

Carlisle, E. Fred. 1973. *The Uncertain Self: Whitman's Drama of Identity*. Ann Arbor: Michigan State University Press.

Chase, Richard. 1955. *Walt Whitman Reconsidered*. New York: William Sloane.

Cheng, Xiling (tr.). 1996. *The Awakening*: Chinese translation. Chengdu: Sichuan renmin chubanshe.

Chopin, Kate. 1972. *The Awakening*. New York: Avon Books.

Chu, Tunan (tr.). 1988. "*Song of Myself*": Chinese translation. In *Caoye ji*. Beijing: Renmin wenxue chubanshe.

De Tocqueville, Alexis. 1990. *Democracy in America. Vols. I and II*. New York: Vintage Classics; Random House, Inc.

Emerson, Ralph Waldo. 1971. *The Collected Works of Ralph Waldo Emerson*. ed. Joseph Slater et al. Cambridge, MA: Harvard University Press.

Ewell, Barbara C. 1992. "Kate Chopin and the Dream of Female Selfhood". In Lynda Boren and Sara de Saussure Davis, *Kate Chopin Reconsidered: Beyond the Bayou*. 157–165.

Ferm, Vergilius Ture Anselm. (ed). 1950. *A History of Philosophical Systems*. New York: Philosophical Library.

Kingsbury, Diana B. (tr.). 1994. *I Wish I Were a Wolf: The New Voice in Chinese Women's Literature*. Beijing: New World Press.

Lewis, R.W.B. 1955. *The American Adam — Innocence, Tragedy, and Tradition in the Nineteenth Century*. Chicago: University of Chicago Press.

Locke, John. 1975. *An Essay Concerning Human Understanding*. Ed. Peter H. Nidditch. Oxford: Clarendon Press.

Lü, Wenbin (tr.). 1990. *The Awakening*: Chinese translation. Heilongjiang: Heilongjiang renmin chubanshe.

Miller, Edwin Haviland. 1989. *Walt Whitman's "Song of Myself" — A Mosaic of Interpretations*. Iowa City: University of Iowa Press.

Miller, Jr. James E. 1964. *Whitman's "Song of Myself" — Origin, Growth, Meaning*. New York: Dodd Mead.

Potok, Chaim. 1983. *My Name Is Asher Lev*. New York: Ballantine Books.

Sang, Jianliu (tr.). 1969. "Song of Myself": Chinese translation. In *Huiteman shiji*. Taipei: Zhengwen chubanshe.

Seyersted, Per. 1969. *Kate Chopin, A Critical Biography*. Oslo and Baton Rouge: Universitetsforlaget and Louisiana State University Press.

Updike, John. 1978. "Walt Whitman: Ego and Art". *The New York Review of Books*, February 9, 1978: 33–36.

Wen, Zhongqiang and Shuqin Jia (tr.). 1991. *The Awakening*: Chinese translation. Sichuan: Lijiang chubanshe.

Whitman, Walt. 1982. *Complete Poetry and Collected Prose*. New York: Penguin Books.

Wu, Qiancheng (tr.). 1979. "Song of Myself": Chinese translation. In *Caoye ji*. Taipei: Yuanjing chubanshe.

Yang, Yingmei (tr.). 1996. *The Awakening*: Chinese translation. Taipei: Nüshu wenhua shiye youxian gongsi.

Zhao, Luorui (tr.). 1991. "Song of Myself": Chinese translation. In *Caoye ji*. Shanghai: Shanghai yiwen chubanshe.

Zweig, Paul. 1984. *Walt Whitman — The Making of the Poet*. New York: Basic Books.

CHAPTER 6

Translation and national cultures

A case study in theatrical translation

Alain Piette
Université de Mons–Hainaut

Introduction

Of the three great Belgian dramatists writing in French who made their mark on Western international drama, Maurice Maeterlinck (1862–1949; winner of the Nobel Prize for Literature in 1911), Michel de Ghelderode (1898–1962), and Fernand Crommelynck (1886–1970), the last has curiously fallen into oblivion. Yet, in the 1920s and 1930s, with the notable exception of the English-speaking countries, there wasn't a single theatre in Europe or Latin America that did not want to produce one of his plays. Crommelynck's plays were not only performed in almost all of the European languages in Western Europe, but also in Eastern Europe and South America.

The climax of the dramatist's theatrical career was no doubt the mythical production that the famous Russian director Vsevolod Meyerhold made of his best-known work, *The Magnanimous Cuckold*. Even today, Meyerhold's production of the play at the Moscow Art Theatre in 1920 is making theatre history and has been at the centre of many a critical essay.[1] However, despite the production's success and significance, Fernand Crommelynck's authorship is usually obliterated, while Meyerhold's brilliant direction is usually remembered as the only major contribution. In this connection, it is worth mentioning that an exhibition entitled *The Art of the Avant-Garde in Russia* held jointly by the Los Angeles County Museum of Art in 1980 and the New York-based Solomon R. Guggenheim Museum in the winter of 1981 was advertised as a reconstruction of Meyerhold's production of *The Magnanimous Cuckold*. The posters and the programmes for the exhibition did not even mention the name of Fernand Crommelynck.[2]

The reasons for the public's loss of interest in Crommelynck are difficult to ascertain. There is a Crommelynck mystery, or rather there are several. How can we account for the loss of popularity in the second half of the 20th century of a dramatist who, in the 1920s and 1930s, was considered the greatest European playwright writing in French and whom the French director Jacques Copeau called "unquestionably the best creative mind of his time?" (Copeau, in Guitard-Auviste 1970: s.p.) Why did Crommelynck, whose artistic career was obviously at a peak, abruptly decide in 1934 to stop publishing works for the stage, at the relatively young age of forty-eight? Why has his theatre elicited so many passionate and contradictory responses among the critics and theatre-goers of the time? But, above all, why did his plays, which were performed in almost all the countries in the world, including Eastern Europe and South America, enjoy so little success in the United States and in Britain? And why were they never translated and published into English, with the exception of two little known translations, one of *The Magnanimous Cuckold*[3] and the second of *The Sculptor of Masks*?[4]

Assessment of the critics

In January 1987, on the occasion of the 100th anniversary of the playwright's birth, an international symposium was organized in Brussels around the theme of the international reception of Crommelynck's plays. Speaking about the reception of the plays in the English-speaking countries, David Grossvogel, an American scholar who had published mostly on Ghelderode, presented a list of the productions of Crommelynck's plays in English. The list was characteristically brief, all the more so since it was incomplete, and Grossvogel concluded that the reason for Crommelynck's unpopularity in the English-speaking world was firstly, that his universe was totally foreign to British and American sensitivities (he made no difference between those), and that secondly, the ornate lyrical language used by the playwright made the plays totally untranslatable into English (Grossvogel 1987: s.p.). For his part, the British critic D. B. Wyndham Lewis believed that Crommelynck's lack of success in English was primarily linguistic and cultural: in his opinion, Crommelynck's lyricism was foreign to British consciousness and was consequently untranslatable. "Probably the play [*The Magnanimous Cuckold*] should never have been translated into or played in English at all [...]", he wrote, "The most gallant translator, even a poet, could make nothing much [of these babblings] in English. The English genius does not lend itself to public cooings and roulades" (Lewis 1941: 24). And David Grossvogel, already mentioned above, pretty much concurred with him when he averred that "In our country [the USA], this lyrical torrent would very quickly overflow the fragile dams between which our language flows, a language that says always less than it suggests" (Grossvogel 1987: s.p.).

Strangely enough, though, another British critic, Roy Walker, held a different opinion about the idiosyncrasies of the English language and culture, although he shared his two colleagues' dislike of Crommelynck's theatre: "We [in the UK] like to be told at once what the mood is to be—not too complex at that and allowed to settle comfortably into it. We must be shown where to put our healthy sympathies and not have them thrown in our faces every few moments" (Walker 1958: 827). And he added that the plays of Cocteau, Ionesco, Ghelderode, and Crommelynck were far too abstract for British audiences!

Even a Belgian critic, Camille Poupeye, somewhat patronizingly ranked the playwright in his series of "exotic dramatists", together with the likes of Barrie, Strindberg, Andreyev, and Wedekind. The French critics for the most part vented their superiority complex toward their Belgian neighbours by dismissing Crommelynck's work as totally foreign to French sensitivity. The great French director Antoine, although he liked Crommelynck's play *The Childish Lovers*, declared that it seemed "to be a wonderful translation into French of a work coming from a country with a different way of thinking and of feeling" (Antoine, in Berger 1946: 6).

Despite these critics' objections to the language of Crommelynck's plays, I daresay that his lyricism, even in translation, is eminently theatrical. Although I do not mean to suggest that a play does not lose any of its effectiveness in a foreign language, I do believe that it can work in translation. What these critics suggest implicitly is that there are some national cultures and languages that are simply not translatable into English. As the official exclusive translator of Crommelynck's complete work for the stage into English,[5] I beg to differ.

Crommelynck's plays *are* difficult to translate—indeed what play is not?— but I do not think that the linguistic and cultural barriers are the major obstacles to a successful staging of Crommelynck's plays in the English-speaking world. Lewis's, Grossvogel's, and Walker's statements strikingly recall the silly, pseudo-patriotic assertions of certain French critics who, at the beginning of the century, dismissed the works of Ibsen, Strindberg, and indeed Crommelynck (who all went on to enjoy a colossal success in Paris) as foreign to French consciousness. The implication was of course that the native drama was by far superior to the alien one. But dramatic history later proved that this jingoism was closely akin to narrow-mindedness, as the tremendous impact of the plays of Ibsen, Strindberg, and indeed Crommelynck, in all the languages and countries in the world eventually demonstrated.

The real issue

The real reason why Crommelynck has largely remained an unknown quantity in the English-speaking countries probably lies in a different approach of the theatrical tradition in these countries. Crommelynck's plays are above all farces, and the American and British repertoires contain fewer farces than those of continental Europe where the farcical tradition is almost as old as theatre itself. As a result, although the essentially non-realistic methods of Meyerhold, Brecht, Antoine, and Copeau are also taught in drama schools, the modern actor's training—perhaps more so in America than Britain—is primarily based on Stanislavski's theories of psychological realism and affective memory. The late Italian filmmaker Sergio Leone was fond of telling the anecdote of an American film star under his direction who constantly wanted to delve deeper into the psychology and motivation of his character, thus incessantly holding back the shooting of the film, whereas the role he had to play was that of a larger-than-life caricature spaghetti western figure with no pretence whatsoever at verisimilitude. As the actor asked him for the umpteenth time "What's my motivation here?" Sergio Leone finally retorted one day: "Your pay check!" The anecdote is probably apocryphal, but it shows quite well the incompleteness of this actor's training. Crommelynck's farces, as Meyerhold established, require the actor to continually jump in and out of character: "To assume somebody else's personality and to reject it at will: that is the miracle, the manifestation of a quasi-divine power", says a character in Crommelynck's only detective novel, *Is Mister Larose the Murderer?* (Crommelynck 1981: 196). That is how Crommelynck regarded the work of his actors, and that is also why *The Magnanimous Cuckold* fitted so perfectly into the Meyerhold model. Therefore, just as Meyerhold's theories are invalid outside symbolist drama and farce, Stanislavski's Method proves ineffectual outside stage realism. And it is that difference in the theatrical tradition of the English-speaking world that is responsible for the relative lack of success of Crommelynck there.

The problem for Crommelynck, and indeed for his translator, is that naturalism still prevails on the stage of many theatres. When we read some of the negative reviews that Crommelynck's plays have elicited all along the years, we immediately realize that the criterion of verisimilitude emerged as the absolute value by which to judge the quality of a performance. "In the theatre," Paul Souday wrote in 1911 in his review of a production of Crommelynck's *The Sculptor of Masks*, "psychology ought to matter more than anything else" (Souday 1911: s.p.). Gabriel Marcel was puzzled by Crommelynck's theatre, for he admitted that he had been wondering since 1920 "whether the playwright hadn't forsaken realism that year to branch into new paths and explore a new realm of pure invention" (Marcel 1946: s.p.). And that was in 1946! Crommelynck himself confirmed in an interview with a bewildered critic that his "is first and foremost an absolutely subjective theatre: no realism" (Crommelynck, in A.1925: s.p.).

Conversely, the reading of the positive reviews leads us to believe that the most successful productions of Crommelynck's plays were staged in the non-realistic mode. In 1933 in Rome, the most prominent element of the set of *The Magnanimous Cuckold* was a slide, probably inspired from the Meyerhold production. Moreover, the inscription of the word "CUCKOLD" on some parts of the scenery made any realistic staging impossible. In 1969, the *Teatro Nacional Cervantès* of Buenos Aires decided to introduce masks in its acclaimed production of the play in order to stress its grotesque aspect.

Theatre has come a long way since 1920. Pirandello, Crommelynck, Meyerhold, Brecht, Beckett, Ionesco, and many others have opened new doors and broken new ground. However, the overwhelming influence of Stanislavski's Method on world theatre in general, and on the American and British theatres in particular, as well as the reluctance of many directors, actors, critics, and indeed theatre-goers to leave the realistic realm, makes the staging of a-psychological works often difficult and confusing. To be effective on the stage in its conjunction of form and content, farce requires a carefully constructed stylised design, such as the Meyerhold and Brecht models offer. Crommelynck's characters are by nature paroxystic. The naturalistic staging approach leads to a little credible or one-note performance in which the protagonist is simply a madman. The slapstick approach, on the other hand, only makes for an empty superficial spectacle in which pace and rhythm are often confused with frenzy and precipitation. Neither approach has any human relevance in a non-representational theatrical genre.

As every theatre buff knows, theatre is meant to be performed first, and many new plays (and *a fortiori* their translations) are often not published in book form until after the play has enjoyed a successful run on stage. Indeed, some plays (and *a fortiori* their translations) never get to the publication stage at all due to their commercial failure on stage. If you add to this phenomenon the fact that plays *and* translations are costly to put into print and do not sell very well, you would understand why most publishers, who are for the most part conservative, shy away from theatrical translations unless the latter are preceded by a blockbuster run on the stages of the most prominent playhouses. On top of it all, theatres have long since adopted the practice of commissioning their resident directors or dramaturgs to translate the works they want to stage in order to avoid paying copyright or translation fees for existing translations. These commissioned translations, which are usually and somewhat euphemistically called 'adaptations', are extremely short-lived, for they disappear when the production at which they are exclusively aimed ultimately closes. They are for the most part disposable translations, as it were.

There is, then, absolutely no reason why Crommelynck's universe should be foreign to English or American consciousness, when it is not to Russian, Polish, Czech, Bulgarian, German, Dutch, Flemish, Italian, and Spanish consciousness, to mention only a few of the cultures and languages in which Crommelynck's plays did enjoy unmitigated success. And Crommelynck's plays were translated into and performed in English, too. Except for the two plays I mentioned earlier, they were simply not published because of unsuccessful staging concepts. I have been able to find, in Los Angeles of all places, an unpublished English translation of what is probably Crommelynck's most complex play to translate, *Carine, or the Young Woman in Love with Her Soul.*

In its caricaturization of human passions or the dramatic exacerbation of the most human feelings (jealousy, avarice, greed, misanthropy, lust, selfishness), Crommelynck's theatre is closely akin not only to pantomime, but also to the farces, *sotties*, and morality plays of the 14th, 15th, and 16th centuries. It thus finds its roots in some of the oldest forms of popular theatre. "Torn between its physical appetites and its need to go beyond the immediate significance of its actions in order to get nearer to the mysteries of creation", Paul-Louis Mignon wrote, "it is the heir to the greatest medieval theatrical tradition, of which it has at the same time the popular naivety, the religious fervour, and the impious obscenity" (Mignon 1956: 2). François Mauriac perfectly saw the vastness of Crommelynck's dramatic universe when he defined the playwright also as "an image-maker from the days of the great cathedral builders" (Mauriac 1926: 82).

Unlike Ghelderode's theatre, which never completely realized the fusion of all its sources of inspiration and ultimately remained a gaudy, though brilliant, junk shop, Crommelynck's theatre managed to solve its apparent paradox, which is also that of Belgian drama as a whole: although it has its roots in both the medieval and the classical traditions, although it is fraught with so many influences from a glorious past, it succeeds in being profoundly modern and in moving us through its deeply original approach to the greatest universal and eternal human myths.

Conclusion

The complete work for the stage of Fernand Crommelynck had until now never been published in an English translation, unlike those of his illustrious compatriots, Maeterlinck and Ghelderode. All things considered, my translations did not so much fill a gap as establish that there is no such thing as one culture 'foreign' to another if one is willing to try and understand it. "After all," Crommelynck himself declared in one of his many interviews on French radio, "has anyone ever dreamt of calling Jean-Jacques Rousseau a Swiss writer?" (Crommelynck, *O.R.T.F.* 1955). No, of course not. Literary or dramatic genius knows no borders. "The most beautiful pages on Belgium were written by Stefan Zweig, an Austrian Jew, who was writing about Emile Verhaeren, a Fleming, who wrote in French," recently declared Gérard Mortier, the former artistic director of the Belgian National Opera to a journalist of the French newspaper *Le Monde*, who asked him to describe the specificity of Belgian culture (Mortier 1987: 11). And no measure of insularity or jingoism will convince me that the human genius is not universal. Denying this would indeed be tantamount to denying the basic humanity in each and every one of us regardless of race, sex, nationality, creed, language, or indeed culture.

Notes

1. See Piette and Cardullo 1997 and Piette 1996 for a complete bibliography.

2. *Los Angeles County Museum of Art*, 1980: "The Avant-Garde in Russia, 1910–1930: New Perspectives"; *Solomon R. Guggenheim Museum*, 10–13 December 1980, 15 October 1981, 3 January 1982.

3. Jan-Albert Goris (a.k.a. Marnix Gijsen), *Two Great Belgian Plays, About Love: The Magnificent Cuckold by Fernand Crommelynck. The Burlador by Suzanne Lilar*, New York: Heinemann, 1966.

4. Alba Amola, Bettina L. Knapp, and Nadine Dormoy-Savage, *An Anthology of Modern Belgian Theatre: Maurice Maeterlinck, Fernand Crommelynck, and Michel de Ghelderode*, Troy, New York: The Whitston Publishing Company, 1982.

5. Alain Piette and Bert Cardullo, eds. and trans. *The Theater of Fernand Crommelynck - Eight Plays*, Selinsgrove, NJ: Susquehanna University Press; London: Associated University Presses, 1998. Fernand Crommelynck, "The Knight of the Moon, or Sir John Falstaff", in Alain Piette and Bert Cardullo, eds. and trans. - *The Fallen Staff: An Anthology of Falstaff Plays from Shakespeare to the Twentieth Century*, University of Delaware Press, forthcoming.

Works Cited

A. [*sic*], Paul. 1925. Interview with Fernand Crommelynck. In *Paris-Midi*, 19 April 1925. My translation.

Alain, Piette and Bert, Cardullo. 1997. *The Crommelynck Mystery - The Life and Work of a Belgian Playwright*. Selinsgrove, New Jersey: Susquehanna University Press; London: Associated University Presses.

Alain, Piette. "Crommelynck and Meyerhold: Two Geniuses Meet on the Stage". In *Modern Drama*, XXXIX, No. 3 (Fall 1996): 436–447.

Berger, André. 1946. *A la Rencontre de Fernand Crommelynck*. Brussels: La Sixaine. My translation.

Crommelynck, Fernand. 1981. *Monsieur Larose est-il l'assassin?* Brussels: Jacques Antoine, Passé Présent. My translation.

Crommerlynck, Fernand. 1955. "Théâtre français et théâtre flamand de nationalité belge". Interview given on French radio (*O.R.T.F.*, 25 June 1955). My translation.

Grossvogel, David. 1987. "Ghelderode and Crommelynck" (Unpublished paper). In *Conférence Internationale Fernand Crommelynck à la scène*. Brussels: Archives et Musée de la Littérature, Palais des Beaux-Arts, 23–24 January 1987.

Guitard-Auviste, Ginette. 1970. "Crommelynck, traditionnaliste d'avant-garde". In *Les Nouvelles Littéraires*, 26 March 1970. My translation.

Lewis, D.B. Wyndham. 1941. "The Theatre of Crommelynck". In *Message*, No. 2 (December 1941): 23–25.

Marcel, Gabriel. 1946. In *Les Nouvelles Littéraires*, 31 January 1946. My translation.

Mauriac, François. 1926. In *Les Cahiers d'Occident*—2ème série, No. 5 (15 January 1926): 78–82. My translation.

Mignon, Paul-Louis. 1956. "Fernand Crommelynck ou le sculpteur de masques". In *L'Avant-Scène*, No. 132 (1956): 2. My translation.

Mortier, Gérard. 1987. In *Le Monde*, 27 November 1987:11. My translation.

Poupeye, Camille 1924. *Dramaturges exotiques*—1ère série. Brussels: Renaissance d'Occident. My translation.

Souday, Paul. 1911. In *L'Eclair*, 2 February 1911. My translation.

Walker, Roy. 1958. In *The Listener*, LIX, No. 1520 (15 May 1958): 827.

The Japanese experience

The reconceptionization of translation from Chinese in 18th-century Japan

Judy Wakabayashi
Kent State University

The traditional encounter with Chinese texts

Japan had no written script until the adoption of Chinese characters in the 4th century, although it was not until the 6th or 7th century that their use became widespread. Individual Chinese characters represent both sound and meaning, and this latter characteristic meant they could be borrowed to represent the same meaning in Japanese, regardless of the pronunciation.[1] Based on this shared use of Chinese characters, by the early Heian period (794–1185) a unique practice known as *kambun kundoku* 漢文訓読 (Chinese read in the Japanese manner) had evolved. This took the form of giving the Chinese characters their Japanese reading and adding reading marks known as *kunten* 訓点 to indicate the order in which the Chinese words should be read in accordance with Japanese syntax. As Rabinovitch (1996: 108–9) observes, this "enabled the reader to quickly assimilate a piece of Chinese as Japanese, albeit Japanese of a special kind". It is not known for certain who devised this method, although Kibi no Makibi 吉備真備 (693–775) has been credited with its invention. Whatever its origin, without doubt its impact has been enormous, reaching right down to the 20th century.

There were two forms of *kambun kundoku*. In the first form reading marks and the occasional gloss showing the Japanese pronunciation were added directly to the Chinese text. With the second form the text was written out separately in Japanese word order in a version (known as *kambun yomikudashi* 漢文読み下し—i.e., Chinese written out as Japanese)[2] that was obviously no longer Chinese—although nor was it 'proper' Japanese. Four different types of reading marks were used in the non-written-out form:

1. *kaeriten* 返り点: Various transposition marks were placed at the lower left of the character to indicate the order in which the Chinese words should be

read in accordance with Japanese syntax and how they should be grouped together. These included the following:

- The mark レ: indicates that this and the following characters should be read in reverse of the Chinese order.
- 一, 二, 三 (the numbers 1, 2, 3 and so on): indicate inversions involving more than two characters.
- 上 (upper), 中 (middle), 下 (lower): direct the reader to return to an earlier character, passing a numbered inversion on the way.
- 甲, 乙, 丙, 丁 etc. (a sequence corresponding to A, B, C, D etc.): direct the reader to return to an earlier character, passing on the way an inversion marked by 上中下.
- 天 (heaven), 地 (earth), 人 (man): used if further categories were required.

2. *Okototen* (ヲコト点 or 乎古止点) diacritics consisted of *katakana* 片仮名 (one of the two phonetic syllabaries developed in Japan around the 9th century; the other was *hiragana* 平仮名) and lines added to the corners of Chinese characters to indicate the inflectional ending or particle, which depended on the shape and position of the diacritics. For instance, under the widely-used *hakaseketen* 博士点 system, if the character 引 had a mark at the bottom left corner it was read as *hikite* 引きて, and if the mark was in the top left corner it was read as *hikuni* 引くに. *Okototen* were used from the Heian period to the Muromachi period (1336–1573), and were the forerunner of the following category.

3. *Katakana* glosses were sometimes added to the lower right of a character to indicate the Japanese inflectional suffixes and grammatical particles.

4. *kutôten* 句読点: punctuation, which was applied in accordance with Chinese conventions, not how the words appeared in the Japanese rendering.

The example from Crawcour (1965: xviii) shows an annotated *kambun* text on the right and its written-out version on the left (see Fig. 1). These reading marks were used in combination with the *kun* 訓 glosses (i.e. Japanese pronunciations) of the Chinese characters. Initially the choice of reading for particular characters was not standardized, but still it was not entirely up to the individual reader's discretion, and by about the 10th century the readings had become largely fixed. Nevertheless, private schools taught different forms of *kundoku*, so *kambun kundoku* cannot be treated as a single entity. Different approaches were also adopted over time, varying from ones that emphasized staying close to 'real' Chinese to ones that attempted to draw closer to 'real' Japanese. Satô argues that "some kundoku in the earliest periods was more like what we normally think of

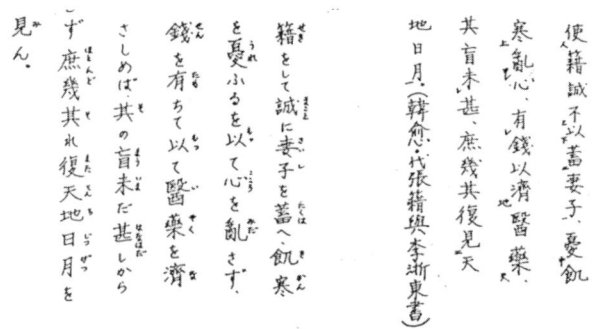

Figure 1.

as 'translation,' as the 'readers' made efforts to find indigenous words for Chinese expressions [. . .]. What we normally think of as *yomikudashi* developed later, and it is a way of reading Chinese in Japanese, staying as close to each character as possible (without glosses), mostly retaining the Chinese (though Japanized) pronunciation, often introducing unknown words and phrases as a result, and frequently employing unnatural syntax." (1996b: 11).

Sakai points out the two-stage transformation involved with *wakun* 和訓 (another name for *kundoku*):

> there must be two stages of transformation or translation before the understanding of the text is attained. The original is given as a visual text, which Japanese readers … are normally incapable of vocalizing. Thus the first stage of transformation is concerned with reorganizing the syntactical order and supplementing the text with the Japanese particles *te, ni, o ha*. Since this process entails transforming the linear order of words and ascribing voice to ideographs, the visual and oral aspects of the text cannot be treated independently. *Yomikudashi* (vocalized wakun text …) makes sense only as an operation on the graphic text. […] the focal point of reading has to shift back and forth among ideographs to follow the directions provided by the marks, and thus, the given linear order of the original is destroyed. One should note, however, that the text resulting from this transformation is also linear if it is vocalized (1992: 226–227).

Sakai (1992: 227) gives the following example of a Chinese sentence, its vocalization in Chinese, the reading marks and particles that are added and the way this was vocalized in Japanese:

Original Chinese: 譯之一字。爲讀書眞訣。蓋書皆文字。文字即華人語言。

Present-day Beijing pronunciation: Yi zhi yizi, wei dushu zhenjue, gai shu jie wenzi, wenzi ji huaren yuyan.

Kundoku version: 譯ハ一字、他、書籍ハ逆讀、↓撰゛御逆文字゛゛文字ハ言構ク゛假言゛゛

Vocalized version: Yaku no ichiji, dokusho no tame ni shinketsu tari, kedashi sho wa mina monji ni shite, monji wa sunawachi kajin no gogen nari.

It is this vocalization that represents the second stage of transformation.

By enabling Japanese readers to construe Chinese texts as if they were written according to Japanese syntax and pronunciation, *kambun kundoku* represented a unique short-cut to Chinese texts and circumvented the need for translation in the conventional sense. What made this possible was the two languages' shared use of ideographs, and Tsukishima has a point when he argues that if another writing system had already existed in Japan no doubt conventional translation would have occurred instead (1965: 45). Nevertheless, the syntactical differences between Chinese and Japanese meant there were inevitable limitations as to how well Japanese readers could understand Chinese texts annotated in this way.

Studies of Chinese texts tapered off from around the end of the 9th century when official contacts ceased, and the ability to read Chinese works in their original pronunciation also declined and Chinese came to be read only in its Japanese (*kun*) reading. Nevertheless, Chinese continued to occupy its position as the language of official business at the court and it remained popular amongst the elite, who continued to study the Chinese classics, even if they could no longer pronounce what they were reading.

Meanwhile, this method of *reading* Chinese texts in a Japanese manner had been adopted also for *writing* original Japanese texts, and this Chinese-based method became not only accepted but also the most prestigious mode of writing in Japan. By this time two phonetic scripts had been developed that enabled Japanese to be written without the use of Chinese characters, but the prestige of the Chinese language meant that it continued to occupy centre stage. Chinese as written in Japan included various features not used in indigenous Japanese writing, such as first-person pronouns, rhetorical devices such as the double negative, and certain expressions of Chinese origin, but it was not totally different from indigenous writing—in fact, in terms of grammar the language used was classical Japanese.

Kambun 漢文 (the Chinese way of writing) and *wabun* 和文 (classical Japanese) were used with very different functions—i.e., *kambun* was the language of scholarship and *wabun* was the language of "poetry and other creative or popular literature" (Bedell 1983: 31). The interaction between these parallel traditions enriched the Japanese language and literature, introducing new genres and giving the lexicon a greater richness—or 'polluting' it, depending on one's views on linguistic purity. The result of this blending of Chinese and Japanese was a multilingual environment in which various styles of writing or language co-existed:

1. Pure *kambun* consisted solely of Chinese characters and followed Chinese word order.
2. *Hentai kambun* 変体漢文 (also known as variant Chinese, naturalized Chinese, pseudo-Chinese, 'bastardized' Chinese or sinicized Japanese). This term covers a broad range of hybrid practices that differed in the extent to which the Japanese syllabaries were included (sometimes not at all) and the extent to which the text followed Chinese syntax and used vocabulary of Chinese origin. From the outset it was written with Japanese readers in mind, and Chinese readers would have found it difficult to understand. Rabinovitch comments that variant Chinese became "so intertwined with the Japanese idiom that its users were probably not conscious of which elements were 'Chinese' and which were 'native'. . ." (1996: 101). As variant Chinese became more and more assimilated, fewer syntactic changes were necessary to read the text as Japanese, few reading marks were required, and common words no longer required glosses. Official materials and texts in many other genres were written using variant Chinese, which reached maturity around the late Heian and early Kamakura (1185–1333) periods and remained in use until the early decades of the 20th century.
3. Imperial decree style (*semmyôtai* 宣命体) used both Chinese characters and *manyôgana* characters,[3] which were written in smaller print and a little to the right of the characters. Edicts in this style were intended to be read as Japanese, even though Chinese characters were used.
4. Texts using the indigenous *katakana* script: *Katakana* were added to the characters to indicate the Japanese reading, or the text was written solely in *katakana*. Twine writes that "*Katakana-majiribun* [mixed *katakana*-Chinese character orthography] developed in the Heian period. ... While this was originally written as Chinese, with many reverse marks to indicate Japanese word-order and tiny *katakana* diacritics to show syntax, it came with the passage of time to be written out in Japanese word-order with, eventually, full-size *katakana* interspersed among Chinese characters. In appearance it resembled *kambun kundoku*, but whereas that style strove for fidelity to the Chinese original, this offshoot developed a hybrid, more homegrown aspect with native Japanese expressions interwoven among Chinese words and

phrases. Later *hiragana-kanji* combinations were also seen." (1991:61–62)

5. *Hiragana* texts: These were written nearly entirely in the phonetic *hiragana* script, although on rare occasions some *kambun* was included. Female members of the aristocracy wrote their diaries in *hiragana* prose, although there is evidence (e.g. indirect references to this practice in *The Diary of Murasaki Shikibu*) that at least some Heian women also used Chinese to a limited extent.

6. *Wabun* 和文 (classical Japanese) originated in the Heian period and was also used in some translations. It was written almost exclusively in *hiragana* and consisted mostly of native Japanese words, although later works written in this style used more vocabulary of Chinese origin. Not only the script but also the style differed from Chinese-influenced writing styles—Twine observes that "Compared to the stiffer, more concise Chinese, *wabun* gave an impression of soft, melodious elegance and grace inherited from *waka* (Japanese poetry), preferring circumlocution and euphemism to bluntness and brevity." (1991:57). Nowadays, however, it is rarely used except for composing classical poetry.

This hybrid regime was a feature of the writing scene in Japan, with each different style carving out its own particular niche. As Sakai points out, "In eighteenth-century Japan . . . there was no single standardized language to which the majority of the population had immediate access. Instead, there were many language styles . . . which the same individual had to employ according to the occasion." (1992:217). Thus he argues that "to be able to read and write was to be able to operate in more than one linguistic medium in some parts of Japan at least until the eighteenth century. [. . .] Moreover, literacy was not regulated by the demand that the primary function of writing should be to transcribe what is suggested by 'mother tongue.' Therefore, it often meant a capacity to read and write in a rather 'macaronic' medium that was rather different from the language of familiarity" (1997:20). This multilingual environment was highly influential in shaping views on language and translation.[4]

The ambiguous status of *kambun kundoku*

Given that this unique practice of *kambun kundoku* sidestepped the need for translation in the conventional sense of the word, it is worth considering its status in Japan and its perceived relationship to prototypical translation. This am-

bivalent practice gives rise to the question of whether *kambun kundoku* constitutes translation, and examining it might throw some light on the parameters of
translation in Japan (see also Wakabayashi 1998). As Hermans observes, "conflicts over borderline cases ... tend to lay bare the constitutive norms of translation, and hence what is taken to be the difference between translation and adja-
cent fields ..." (1999: 86).

There seems to be no clear consensus in the literature as to the status of *kambun kundoku*, with some writers using the term 'translation' (often in quotation
marks to indicate its atypical nature), while others argue that it is not translation but a way of reading. Based on the non-prescriptive premise put forward by
Toury that translation is whatever is accepted as translation in a particular target
culture (1995), let us first survey the views of some Japanese writers who regard
kambun kundoku as translation or a 'kind' of translation or covert translation.
Discussing the period when Japan imitated China and was culturally very 'Chinese' (about AD 650–1000), Ishikawa says *kambun kundoku* was used to translate (*honyaku* 翻訳) Chinese into Japanese (1998: 290). Yoshikawa (1973: 633)
likewise uses the term *honyaku* when discussing *kundoku*, and Tsukishima
uses the related term *wayaku* 和訳—"translation into Japanese"—and argues
that *kundoku* was an extreme word-for-word translation, although the resulting
Japanese was far removed from pure indigenous Japanese (1965: 44–45). Saitô
not only regards *kambun kundoku* as translation, but also explicitly views the
end product as Japanese (1996b: 146). Katô states clearly that the first period of
translation was the written-out versions of Chinese classics (1982: 274).

Elsewhere, however, Katô is somewhat more cautious, maintaining that *kundoku* "is in effect translation with the important qualification that it is translation into a language that the translator would not speak or write under any
other circumstances." (1983: 64). Katô and Maruyama state that *yomikudashi*
is a "type" of translation in which the gist is conveyed, but not the tone, and
there are meaning discrepancies in the minor details (1991: 351). Satô contends
that this process of interpreting Chinese texts constituted "mental translation",
and that "*Kundoku* arises from this interpretation and records the results of it"
(1983: 195). Engels, who is Japanese, notes some similarity between *kambun
kundoku* and the contemporary practice of sight translation (i.e. the immediate
oral rendering of a written text), saying that "the Japanese read the Chinese text
and translate it into Japanese simultaneously. But there is a crucial difference;
when the Japanese read classical Chinese, they do not translate the text into
what they consider to be the equivalent Japanese sentences. They first decipher
the ideas or things represented by each kanji, then, following the word order

rules they have learned, construct the meaning of the whole sentence. Finally they transfer what they have comprehended into the correct style for reading classical Chinese, which they have also acquired as part of their learning. [...] This final process is only made explicit when the translated sentence is vocalised and it does not affect the writing" (1998: 15).

Other writers, however, regard *kambun kundoku* simply as a system of *reading* Chinese. The authoritative *Kojien* 広辞苑 dictionary defines *kundoku* as a form of reading, without mentioning translation in any way, as does the *Nihon Kokugo Daijiten* 日本国語大辞典, although the more recent *Daijirin* 大辞林 does call it 'a kind of translation', but one that differs from ordinary translation in that it is completely literal and tries to retain the original *kambun* as much as possible. Kitamura explicitly takes the view that *kambun kundoku* is *not* translation, but a japanized reading, and he argues that the use of reading marks to convert the syntax to Japanese order "does away with the need, in the true sense, of translating the Chinese; it is rather a process of technical assimilation." (1993: 13). Satô, however, opposes such a view of *yomikudashi* as a process of reading Chinese in Japanese, describing it instead as "an ultimate form of translatesee [sic] that tolerates a range of truncated locution while presuming, on the reader's part, substantial knowledge of the language to be translated" (1994: 11).

Like their Japanese counterparts, non-Japanese writers are uncertain as to how to classify this practice. Backus describes it as "a partial as well as a literal translation", and states that "Although the *kundoku* method of reading *kambun* results in a translation, its purpose is not so much to convert Chinese into Japanese as to provide the Japanese reader with minimum clues through his own language sufficient to enable him to make a basic sense of the text." (1983: 124). Kornicki describes *yomikudashi* as "a conventional instant rendering of Chinese into Japanese" (1998: 254), while Dore describes it as "...'reading off' Chinese texts in bastard Japanese" (1965: 143). Bedell describes *kambun kundoku* as providing "simultaneous translation", adding that "The adoption of Chinese by the Japanese thus follows the pattern evident in other areas of influence: extensive assimilation and adaptation to Japanese needs and capacities." (1983: 31). The following statement by Miller suggests that he too views *kambun kundoku* as a form of translation: "in this ... variety of writing, where the use of Chinese characters in writing Japanese is ultimately based on translation, there is always the quite real possibility that when a text, once having been written, must now be read, a considerable degree of ambiguity will be inherent in its orthography— ambiguity arising out of the inevitably ambiguous nature of all inter-lingual translation." (1986: 23–24). Commenting on an article by Kondô and Wakabayashi in the *Routledge Encyclopedia of Translation Studies*, Baker observes that *kambun kundoku* "seems to be something in between intralingual and interlingual translation, and I do not believe we have any theories that can account for this type of practice" (1998: xvii).

Even more telling than the debate over the translational status or otherwise of *kambun kundoku* is the fact that many Japanese have simply not considered this mode in relation to translation at all, regarding them as completely separate practices and not making any mental link at all between the two. Saitô—who believes that *kambun kundoku* is a 'kind' of translation method—cites the lack of interaction between people studying translation and those studying *kambun kundoku* as one possible cause for this neglect, and emphasizes that any discussion of the history of translation in Japan cannot ignore this practice because:

1. The subsequent study of European languages adopted the methods of *kambun kundoku* (i.e. the decoding-based reordering aspect, since with these languages there was no shared use of ideographs).
2. Many translations in the Edo and Meiji periods were written in *kambun kundoku* style. (Saitô does not distinguish between *kambun kundoku* as a method of making Chinese texts understandable for Japanese readers and *kambun kundoku* as a particular style of writing Japanese.)
3. The result was that *kambun kundoku* wording influenced original texts written in the 'literal translation style' that was popular at certain times in Japanese translation history. (1996a)

When the word *honyaku* (translation) later came into widespread use in relation to languages other than Chinese, the prior existence of a specific term—*kundoku*—in relation to Chinese texts acted to prevent the perception of a link between *kundoku* and translation. (Nowadays the term *honyaku* is also used to refer to conventional translations from Chinese into 'proper' Japanese, not *kundoku*.) As Table 1 shows, this anomalous practice challenges certain widely accepted notions of translation, yet it has led to surprisingly little theoretical discussion even within Japan. With *kambun*, there are no translator's prefaces or afterwords discussing the 'translation' process itself, just commentaries on the meaning of the text, so there is no body of theoretical writing by the 'translators' of Chinese works rendered in *kambun kundoku*. In my view this lack is also largely due to the simple fact that different labels have always been used to refer to *kambun kundoku* and translation, which belong to separate scholarly traditions in Japan, thereby hindering scholars from associating the two and gaining further insights into the nature and parameters of translation in Japan.

Despite the considerable differences between the end product of this process and authentic Japanese texts, it does seem to have been widely regarded as part of the Japanese language. Describing *kundoku* as a "process of translation and explication" and a "method of simultaneous reading and translating", Satô remarks that "Reading by this method directly alters a text in the Chinese language into Japanese." (1983:194). Similarly, Miyoshi (1974: 8) argues that "A *kambun* text, as read by a Japanese, sounds Japanese and is Japanese, although it could also be read by a Chinese and pronounced in Chinese." Kamei argues that when *kambun* is viewed in relation to *wabun* it appears to be a foreign language—and hence an object of translation—but for intellectuals it was an essential "native language" that was their means of communicating with each other, and the written-out style in particular undoubtedly had full Japanese "citizenship" (1991:71). Kamei concludes, therefore, that *kambun* is a bivalent language (1991:72). Over the centuries *kambun kundoku* became so widespread that people had no hesitation in accepting its products as Japanese, despite the obvious differences between it and indigenous writing. It is not that no alternatives existed—there *were* indigenous ways of writing the Japanese language, and the fact that these forms were not used to translate Chinese is noteworthy. Is it conceivable that the use of *kambun kundoku* enabled a more accurate rendering of the meaning of Chinese texts than would have been the case if the same texts had been translated into classical Japanese, for instance? Or has Keene pinpointed the reason when he writes that "This method of translation...is popular with readers who feel that it enables them to come close to the original Chinese texts, even if they do not understand what precisely is meant." (1987:57)—and even if the Chinese has become quite japanized?

Inasmuch as *kambun kundoku* ostensibly transforms texts written in Chinese into a form understandable by Japanese readers, it cannot be rejected out of hand as translation. The question of whether *kambun kundoku* constitutes translation boils down to one's concept or definition of translation, and we have seen that there seems to be no consensus on this issue, either within Japan or amongst non-Japanese writers on the subject. It is obvious, however, that *kambun kundoku* differs from conventional translation in several important respects, as Table 1 shows.

What is of particular interest to contemporary translation scholars is this concept of a hybrid language—something that is receiving increasing attention today (e.g. Robinson 1997; Bassnett and Trivedi 1999) as a potentially creative new 'middle' between the traditional source/target language dichotomy. In a non-Japanese context, Woodsworth links such liminality to postcolonial

Table 1. *Kambun kundoku* compared with prototypical translation

Prototypical translation	*Kambun kundoku*
The source text is written in a foreign language.	The source text is written in Chinese. *Kambun kundoku* cannot be used with other source languages because it is premised on the shared use of Chinese characters (although some aspects of this practice had a powerful influence on translation from other source languages).
The target text is a physically *separate* product from the source text, which is usually not directly available to readers of the translation.	The source text is *retained*, so that "the written text appears exactly the same before and after the mental translation" (Engels 1998: 15), or it is *annotated directly*, again remaining available to readers. The result was a blurring of the traditional source text/target text distinction, so that the target text was continuous with the source. As Kamei observes, theoretically it seems impossible for one and the same text to be both the source text and its own translation, but that was indeed the case with *kambun kundoku* (1991: 65). In later years the annotated text was often rewritten in Japanese order as a separate text—*yomikudashi*—but the end product still resembled the source text far more than with conventional translations. Genette defines 'intertextuality' (his first type of 'transtextuality') restrictively as "a relationship of copresence between two texts or among several texts: that is to say, eidetically and typically as the actual presence of one text within another." (1997: 1–2). What he has in mind is such practices as quoting, plagiarism and allusions, but perhaps this category could also be extended to include *kambun kundoku*, where the "intertextuality" exists not on the level of extracts included in the target text but at the level of the whole text.
The target text is written down.	The 'target text' is only partly written down—much of it exists only as a *mental* operation undertaken by the reader (except with written-out versions).
In very broad terms, all of the source words are converted into the target language.	The bulk of the words are left in their original written form—i.e., the shared use of ideographs meant that the nouns and verbs remained exactly the same without being translated into a different visual form (even if they were now pronounced in Japanese), and only the word order, particles and inflections differed. Full conversion occurs only when the text is vocalized.
The source text is usually not translated exactly word for word, even with literal translations.	*Kundoku* involves an extreme form of word-for-word translation. Tsukishima claims that its literality is due to two things: (1) it was a scholastically complex task, and (2) *kambun* source texts were regarded as being written in very worthy language. (1965: 75).
The translation is written in the target language and reads	The annotated or written-out text consists of a *hybrid language* or 'interlanguage' that is very different from

Table 1. (*cont.*)

as a target-language product (despite varying degrees of "translationese" that may be present).	indigenous Japanese – differences that go well beyond the 'translationese' that sometimes occurs in conventional translations. This Sino-Japanese meant there was no clear demarcation between the source and target languages. The end product is not 'proper' Japanese (or Chinese), and retains strong overtones of Chinese. Tsukishima writes that the language used in *kambun kundoku* is a special language that operates within the constraints of *kambun* and has peculiar distortions not occurring elsewhere (1965:10). The written-out versions of *kambun* did, however, penetrate Japanese writing to create a new style that became a more integrated part of the Japanese language. If the practice of *kundoku* had not existed and conventional translation had occurred instead, it is more than likely that the Japanese language would not have been influenced by Chinese to such a great extent. Sakai observes that "wakun is ... a rather parasitic and foreign language within Japanese and constantly disturbs the possible constitution of an interior." (1992: 225) In a different context Mehrez writes that "because of the culturo-linguistic layering which exists within them", hybrid texts "have succeeded in forging a new language that defies the very notion of a 'foreign' text that can be readily translated into another language. [...] we can no longer merely concern ourselves with conventional notions of linguistic equivalence, or ideas of loss and gain which have long been a consideration in translation theory. For these texts ... create a language 'in between' and therefore come to occupy a space 'in between.'" (1992: 121). Whereas Mehrez's focus was on "culturo-linguistic layering" in the *source* text, *kundoku* challenges conventional notions of the *target* text.
Readers usually have little or no knowledge of the source language.	*Kundoku* demands familiarity with the written form of the source language (as well as the conventions of reading it in the Japanese manner).
The source language is usually not used widely in the target community as a means of writing.	*Kambun* was also used widely to write original texts in Japan—in fact, in certain genres it was the preferred language for writing—thereby further invalidating the source language/target language dichotomy.
A *translator* expresses the meaning of the source text in the target language.	The 'translator' is, firstly, the *annotator* or *author* who added the reading marks in a largely mechanical linguistic operation that requires little or no interpretation of the meaning. All that was necessary to position the reading marks was a knowledge of Chinese grammar, so this person took over the role of the translator to some extent. The second 'translator' is the *reader*, who is required to vocalize the Chinese text in a Japanese

way. The result is a blurring of the traditional author/ translator/reader distinction. In a different context Adejunmobi has commented on "texts where the ability to translate as languages intersect becomes a prerequisite for comprehension. The multilingual world of their texts imposes translation as a mode of reading, since both ... languages actually figure in the text." (1998:174). Similarly, Mehrez writes that readers are "...'in between', at once capable of reading and translating, where translating becomes an integral part of the reading experience" (1992:122). Both of these comments are applicable to *kambun kundoku.*

The translator attempts to convey not just the meaning but also the style and other aspects of the source text in a way that is compatible with the target language.	The style of the Chinese text remains dominant, with little or no attempt to reproduce an equivalent style in Japanese, and the focus is on the denotative content.
Translators have some freedom to bring their own individuality and expressive techniques into the choice of words and phraseology.	The Japanese words used to vocalize each character of the Chinese text are predetermined, and the 'translator' (in the form of the annotators and readers) has virtually no freedom of choice either at the lexical level or in terms of the grammatical arrangement of sentences. Although different scholastic traditions did use different readings for particular Chinese characters, within these traditions annotators/readers had no autonomy. (Kojima, however, argues that adding reading marks to a text does involve an act of interpretation, as does the act of reading a text written in this way [1966:181].)
The translation is non-exclusive in that it is understandable to all readers of the target language.	*Kundoku* texts are elitist in that they are only understandable to those trained in this technique of deciphering Chinese. Notably, women and children could generally not read such texts, and for many centuries neither could people other than samurai, priests and bureaucrats.
Distinction between the visual and aural aspects of the text.	Blurring of the visual and aural aspects of the text. Sakai points out that this practice "cannot be thought of as ... either verbal or nonverbal. The visibility of Wakun scripts ceaselessly interferes with the possible determination of a text as purely verbal." (1992:217). He adds that "The status of the language into which a Chinese text is transformed is obviously ambiguous and unstable.... the major portion of this transformation has to be undertaken visually, or at least with reference to visual signs." (225). Sakai also notes that "In the early eighteenth century, it was a general rule not to vocalize the original ... The original text was given primarily as something to look at. Only if it were transformed could it be vocalized according to the Japanese way of reading Chinese." (227–228). Moreover,

Table 1. (*cont.*)

	he points out that the resulting vocalized version is "far from immediately comprehensible, since [some words] are phonetic imitations of the Chinese original and cannot be understood by the general readership unless the visual text [the original Chinese text or the version with *wakun* added] is referred to." (227)
The source text can be vocalized as is.	*Kambun kundoku* involves a two-stage process of vocalization : 1. Reordering the text and adding Japanese particles so that the text can be vocalized as Japanese, albeit not readily comprehensible Japanese. 2. Transforming the text vocalized in this manner into 'proper' vernacular Japanese. (226–227)
The translation is read linearly, without interruption.	There is a back-and-forth interrupted movement as the reader follows the word-order indicators (although the 'translation' becomes linear if vocalized).
The target text is generally "familiar".	The target text is a mixture of the familiar and the foreign. Even after readers had become accustomed to this practice, it is likely that such texts aroused "feelings of disjunction and unease" (Mezei 1998: 238) in Japanese readers. The written-out version was a technique for minimizing the foreignness and degree of incomprehension entailed in *kambun*. Thus the Chinese was domesticated in a way that projected a 'transnational' identity at once both Chinese and Japanese but fully neither.
The translation is usually not annotated, except for the occasional translator's note or in the case of scholarly translations.	Commentaries and notes are often appended, "either in the form of doubled columns of smaller characters or they made use of the space outside the margins of the text" (Kornicki 1998: 138).
Abridged translations are possible.	Abridged translations are virtually non-existent.

issues, observing that "The emergence of [minority] literatures is often characterized by a certain plurilingualism or code-mixing. Postcolonial writers ... may write in the language of the ex-colonizer and, at the same time, include traces of the native tongue in the text, thereby creating a language 'in between' [Mehrez 1992]." (1994: 60). Although she was not referring to *kambun kundoku* and there was never a formal relationship of colonization between China and Japan, her comments are in some ways applicable to this practice, with Japanese writers using the Chinese language but incorporating indigenous elements to create a hybrid interlanguage. Yet unlike postcolonial writers who attempt to challenge the dominant language of the colonizer, subverting the Chinese language was not the aim of practitioners of *kambun kundoku*—instead, their attitude was one of acquiescence and deference to this ostensibly superior model. A primary reason that *kambun kundoku* was carried out for so long, even after the development of a Japanese writing system, was the immense prestige accorded *kambun* in Japanese society as the language of China, the 'centre' to Japan's 'periphery'. This is another instance in which the political and cultural dominance of a nation imparts a prestigious cachet to its language. Yet despite the commanding position of the written Chinese language in Japan, the outcome of the practice of *kambun kundoku* was that over time the Chinese language in Japan was indeed subverted or 'bastardized'.

Ogyû Sorai: advocate of "real" translation

Ogyû Sorai 荻生徂徠[5] (1666–1728) is best known as one of Japan's first modern thinkers and as a leading Edo period Confucianist, but he also had an interest in translation that led him to criticize the prevailing practice of *kambun kundoku* and resulted in a reconceptualization of translation in 18th-century Japan.

Perhaps somewhat ironically, Sorai's interest in translation was sparked by his encounters with the *spoken* form of the Chinese language. Although all intellectuals of his day could read Chinese to which reading marks had been added, very few understood the spoken language or undoctored texts in contemporary Chinese. Despite the fact that Japan had been in contact with China for over a thousand years, it was only toward the end of the 17th century that knowledge of the spoken language began to have any impact. McEwan notes that "In the earlier stages of this process the chief bearers of the new knowledge were members of the newly introduced Ôbaku sect of Zen Buddhism, and a number of natives of Nagasaki who had been in contact with Chinese residents from childhood." (1960/61: 199). These two elements came together when Sorai's patron, Lord Yanagisawa Yoshiyasu 柳沢吉保 (1658–1714), who had studied colloquial Chinese because of his interest in Zen, employed a native of Nagasaki under whom Sorai took up the study of the spoken language. His more important teacher, however, was Okajima Kanzan 岡島冠山 (1674–1728), who was formerly a Chinese interpreter at the Nagasaki custom house. In 1711 Sorai and two colleagues founded the Ken-en tôwa (The Chinese conversation group of the Ken'en school,[6] also called Yakusha 訳社 or Translation Society) and invited Okajima to teach them translation. The group met four or five times a month and the society functioned at least up until 1725, when it had twelve members. Thus there were now two approaches to studying Chinese—the *kundoku* method of the past, which focused on deciphering written texts, and the method introduced by Chinese interpreters in Nagasaki, which emphasized spoken Chinese. Sorai's ability to speak Chinese and read works that had no reading marks made him stand out amongst his peers.

Sakai has suggested that in Japan at that time Chinese was not viewed as an explicitly foreign language — i.e., "the figuration of a foreign language, in clear contrast to the language of familiarity or 'mother tongue', had yet to be inaugurated." (1997: 20). In other words, the long years of reading and writing in Chinese and variant Chinese had made this written language so assimilated that the boundaries between written Chinese and written Japanese had been erased. In the context of translation this meant a blurring of the distinction between the source and target languages, and as Sakai points out, "Translation implicitly requires that two language unities be clearly delineated; where it is impossible to demarcate them, translation is also impossible." (1992: 216).

Sorai led the way in arguing against this conflation of the two languages, and was adamant in viewing Chinese as a distinct entity rather than as an assimilated part of Japanese. Thus he criticized the practice of *kundoku*, on the grounds that it involved explaining the meaning of the characters as pronounced in Japanese rather than understanding the original Chinese. In his *Gakusoku* 学則 (*Instructions for Students*), which he composed between 1711 and 1717, he criticized the *kundoku* method allegedly devised by Kibi no Makibi, who changed the pronunciation and

> reversed the word order and mixed the words and then gathered them together, thus bringing the wills of the two countries into communication. As a result, what we considered until that time to be gibberish we came to think of in the same fashion we regard the Japanese language. [...] Kibi's achievement was a great one for Japan, and the people have placed their reliance on it down to the present./ However, ... when we came to consider those words as our own, the ancient literature, records, proprieties, and music were no longer Chinese words. That is, had Confucius boarded a raft and come with Tzu-lu to Japan, had he *seen* the words there would have been no problem; but had he *heard* them he would not have understood them. [...] The ancient literature, records, proprieties, and music are Chinese words. If we treat them like Japanese words, the ultimate result is bound to be that we turn the literature and records into barbarian dances ... (tr. Minear 1976: 12–13) .

Sorai also said that

We always follow Kibi's method. The sentences have whiskers, and toads have tails.[7] The markings are strung together and as numerous as stars, chaotic as a swarm of mayflies. Only afterward can we grasp the meaning of the texts. These are the ancient literature, records, proprieties, and music of Kibi. They are not the ancient literature, records, proprieties, and music of the Middle Kingdom. The damage is probably worse than that which occurred when we considered them to be gibberish./ What, then, shall we do? It is the languages which are different. With the aid of Kibi's achievement, we can parse Chinese texts and get their meaning, but we cannot recite them and thus cannot hand them down reliably. We can get by for the present, but over the long run the teachings will become murky.... treat China as China, and Japan as Japan ... (tr. in Minear 1976:14 from Sorai's *Instructions for Students, Instruction One*)

In other words, Sorai was opposed to viewing domesticated *kundoku* texts as Japanese, and he wished to retain an awareness of their foreignness. As Sakai emphasizes, with *wakun* "language unities were constantly eroded and put into question. Wakun confuses those categories we take for granted today: it cannot be thought of as either Japanese or Chinese [...] Wakun prevents readers from directly facing the original Chinese writings because the Japanese annotations partially translate and interpret these writings. As long as the reader encounters Chinese writings in Japanese annotation, the foreignness of the Chinese language is disguised by being familiarized into the already established mode of conceptualization." (1992:217). Sakai also comments that "Translation is understood as the transference of speech from one interior to another. Since the unity of an interior is defined in terms of immediate and direct comprehension, the kind of verbal expression that seemingly belongs to the interior but does not facilitate easy and straightforward communication is to be rejected and denounced" (1992:220) – as *kundoku* was by Sorai. Sorai wanted to demarcate the two languages more clearly, to expose their disjunction. Thus in *Daigen jûsoku* 題言十則, the first volume of *Yakubun sentei* 訳分筌蹄 (A Guide to Translation; 1711),[8] Sorai advocated abolishing *kundoku* and construing Chinese texts directly in their Chinese pronunciation and as a foreign language. Sakai observes that Sorai regarded *kundoku* as "an obstacle that stood between the originary speech and the readers, and he implicitly assumed that authentic reading should give readers immediate and direct access to the original" (1992:225). He believed that the *kun* reading might provide the meaning but not the wording of Chinese texts.[9] Sorai explicitly discussed the problematic relationship between translation and the practice of *kundoku*. In *Yakubun sentei* he wrote that Japanese scholars claim that *kundoku* is a "recitation of the writings. In fact, it is nothing but translation. Nonetheless people do not realize that it is translation." (tr Sakai 1992:224–225).

Yet Sorai's views on these two languages were not without internal contradiction. In the preface of the *Yakubun sentei* he wrote that "the object of my theory of translation is to bring together the Chinese and Japanese languages in unity." (tr. McEwan 1960/61: 202), which seems to gainsay his argument about demarcating the boundary between the two languages.[10] According to Yamashita, the goal of Sorai's "science of translation" was to merge and unify China and Japan— "Although he may have been suggesting that more exact Japanese translations of Chinese words would bring the two peoples closer together, it appears that he did envision the merger of the two peoples and cultures." (1985: 171–172).

Another fundamental distinction introduced by Sorai was that between speech and writing, a distinction that had been blurred by the mixture of verbal and visual processing involved in *kundoku*. Sakai comments that "Ogyu's method, therefore, signifies a twofold endeavour, first, to identify the level of voice as distinct from the graphic inscription in the process of reading and, then, to eliminate the visual factor from it." (1992: 228). Sorai believed that "the less visible is the presence of writing, the more transparent the text ought to be." Thus Sorai regarded reading marks as "additional and excessive" and "taught his students to approach Chinese books not as visual but as aural.... this new method... called for transforming Chinese writings into colloquial Japanese" (1992: 225). Sorai argued that the language used in *kun* readings made texts seem unnecessarily difficult and ostentatious, since it consisted of "refined words chosen by nobles of the Heian period from the Japanese language used in those days" (Yoshikawa 1983: 112). Similarly, Dore points out that "Sorai was chiefly concerned with the inaccurate comprehension which resulted from tying to individual Chinese words a conventional translation which may have been the nearest approximation to the sense of the Chinese a thousand years ago (when Chinese characters were first used to write Japanese) but often was so no longer." (1965: 134).

Hence Sorai advocated the use of the vernacular when translating, believing that only then could the meaning be properly understood, and his own translations were rendered into free and vernacular Japanese. In this respect he was influenced by the Nagasaki interpreters, who used the vernacular, so Sorai called his approach *kiyô no gaku* 崎陽之学, the "learning of Nagasaki translators". This Nagasaki method consisted of studying Chinese as a modern language, something regarded at the time as the work of the Nagasaki interpreters, not scholars. The vernacular had none of the authority or prestige accorded to *kambun*, but Sorai's aim in adopting it was to ensure ease of understanding, without the need for commentaries or a further stage of 'translation'. Yoshikawa comments that Sorai advocated the use of the plain colloquial tongue "because the matters described in Chinese classics, though written in Chinese, are nothing special but simply affairs concerning man, essentially the same as what we, the Japanese, casually express in our own language." (1983:110–111). Using commentaries gives the false impression that Chinese texts are much more difficult and profound than they really are. Hence Sorai presented three options, with the third being his ultimate objective:

1. *Yakubun no gaku* (also known as *yaku* 訳): This consisted of translating Chinese works into authentic and colloquial Japanese, and was a compromise interim measure. In *Kunyaku shimô* 訓訳示蒙[11] Sorai suggested *yaku* as a new method of reading, recommending that people who were unfamiliar with Chinese pronunciation or not yet capable of the next stage should at least adopt this approach instead of the *kundoku* method. Yoshikawa gives the example of reading the Chinese sentence 過則勿憚改 (meaning "When you have faults, do not fear to abandon them"; *The Analects* I.8) as "Shikujittara yarinaoshi ni enryo suruna" or "Shikujiri wa enryo naku yarinaose", which are authentic Japanese utterances, not Japanized readings of Chinese (1983:110). Sorai argued that the original Chinese sounded ordinary and colloquial to Chinese readers, so the Japanese should sound equally normal to Japanese readers, and that the way to achieve this was through the Japanese vernacular. He believed, however, that translation into the vernacular was merely an interim aid that should be discarded once the goal of reading Chinese directly had been achieved. The fact that the vernacular rendition was said to be merely a 'guide' was based on an awareness that reading while relating the written Chinese text to a vocal representation in Japanese is not the same as relying solely on the mind and eyes when reading (visual reading).

2. *Kiyô no gaku*—that is, studying Chinese as a modern language: In the preface of *Yakubun sentei* Sorai pointed out the limitations of the *yaku* method and presented what he regarded as a better alternative. This was his well-known advocacy of reading Chinese as Chinese, with the original pronunciation, intonation and word order. Sakai comments that "in Tokugawa society to propose such a new way of reading was to initiate a radical change in the regime according to which Chinese canonical writings had been interpreted." (1992:214). Sakai concludes that *kiyô no gaku* "occupies a highly significant locus in the new discursive space. . . . translation as postulated in *kiyo no gaku* was adopted by an increasing number of writers in the eighteenth century, and it expanded the possibility of disseminating ancient writings." (1992:229).

3. *Kobunji no gaku* 古文辞学 (School of Ancient Rhetoric): Another major influence on Sorai and a highlight of his period as a literati in his forties was
his encounter sometime after 1700 with the works of the 16th-century Chinese writers Li Panlong 李攀龍 (1514–1559) and Wang Shizhen 王士禎 (1526–
90), both of whom advocated returning to the expression of classical Chinese.
Their ideas led to the development of Sorai's new theory, known as *Kobunji
no gaku*, whose goal was to understand ancient Chinese texts in their original
form, without the aid of later commentaries. Earlier Sorai had argued against
paraphrasing Chinese in Japanese, but now he also argued against paraphrasing or "translating" classical Chinese into modern Chinese. Sorai stated that
his ultimate goal was to read the Confucian "Six Classics" in the original Chinese, rather than by the *kundoku* method, which hindered comprehension
of the true meaning, and without relying on interpretations by the great Chinese Neo-Confucianists, which he regarded as a sacrilegious variation.

Sakai writes that Sorai's *kobunji no gaku* and *kiyô no gaku* both "rejected the
multilinguistic coexistence of languages, and were formed on the premises that
hybrid languages such as the 'Japanese way of reading Chinese' (*wakun*), or the
Japanese methods of annotating literary Chinese, be completely excluded. Ogyû
had to separate the two contrasting figures of languages to translate from and
into in order to introduce the regime of translation and the schema of cofigu-
ration." (1997: 66)

Manifesting the attitude of inferiority that is often found in countries on the
periphery of a nation that is perceived as being more culturally advanced, Sorai believed that Chinese was superior to Japanese because it was the language
of the country where the sages were born. In his view, however, contemporary
Chinese was inferior to the classical language. Sorai admired classical Chinese
because of its beautiful literary style and monosyllabic nature, which he equated
with elegance and civilization, and he was critical of the polysyllabic Japanese
language and its need for particles. Yet Sorai's attitude toward the Chinese language did not consist of unqualified veneration. He admitted that it was the
content of Confucian texts that was important, not their language, writing that
"The Way is grand and profound, but the language (*go*) is only words (*gengo*)"
(Yakubun sentei I, 4a, Zenshu, II, 6a; tr. Minear 1976: 74). As Minear notes, "the
effect of his point is to strip the Chinese language of any claim to continuing superiority. As the language of the sages, Chinese is worthy of deep respect; but the
tie between message and medium is not indissoluble." (1976: 74)

It is rather ironic that Sorai's own writings were not always free from the conventions of his time. Sakai comments that ". . . Ogyû published many of his works in *yomikudashibun*, and most of his treatises in Chinese were annotated with the *wakun* he so vehemently denounced." (1992: 245n). This is somewhat similar to the difficulties faced by postcolonial writers when choosing what language to write in.

Sorai was not totally alone in his opposition to *kundoku*. Some other scholars also advocated reading Chinese texts without regard for the reading marks—i.e., from top to bottom directly. One such critic was Dazai Shundai 太宰春台 (1680–1747), a Confucian scholar who studied under Sorai and inherited his vernacular approach. In *Wadoku yôryô* 倭読要領 (1728) Shundai argued that Japanese who read Chinese texts using *kambun kundoku* do not realize that the Japanese reading actually hinders an understanding of the meaning. He emphasized that sound has primacy over writing—i.e., it is only with speech that writing becomes possible—and he advocated that scholars first study the Chinese pronunciations before learning *kundoku*. Sorai's view that Chinese should be regarded as a separate entity from Japanese was also shared by the historian and diplomat Amenomori Hôshû 雨森芳洲 (1668–1755), who was a proficient speaker of both Chinese and Korean. There was a group of like-minded critics of *kundoku* who formed the Sorai school, and their criticisms marked a turning point for *kambun kundoku* and translation in the Edo period. Saitô maintains that until then the pretense that *kundoku* was an interpretation of the meaning had been preserved to a certain extent, but after these criticisms *kundoku* was gradually simplified (1996b: 143).

Despite such supporters of Sorai's views, Dore is correct in pointing out that

> The full Sorai doctrine had few adherents, and even he admitted that it was an ideal difficult to attain. His arguments against the traditional method of 'upside-down reading' had more weight than his claim that Japanese students should start on a par with Chinese students by learning contemporary Chinese, and they could be met by a less radical solution—reading the Chinese text straight through in the original Chinese order, using only Chinese loan-words with their Japanese pronunciation. [...] A compromise which went part of the way towards meeting Sorai's objections to the mechanical equation of the Chinese words of the original texts with the Japanese words which the characters were conventionally used to write was to avoid such words as far as possible when construing the text and keep to the Japanicized pronunciation of the Chinese words—a device which helped to preserve a sense of the foreignness of the text and to ensure that words would be treated on their Chinese merits.   (1965: 135)

Thus *Yakubun sentei* met with a mixed reception. It attracted many students, but also much criticism. The argument that Chinese texts should be read in Chinese, not in *yomikudashi*, seems only natural, but met with resistance. Whether because of this opposition or not, in later years Sorai was somewhat reluctant to be associated with *Yakubun sentei* and he abandoned his earlier interest in translation.

Nevertheless, Sorai had paved the way for conventional translations from Chinese into the contemporary vernacular, something which had been virtually nonexistent until then. Morris also comments that "the emergence in the eighteenth century of a new regime of translation made it possible—in actual conditions of linguistic and social diversity—to conceive of a single 'Japanese' language and ethnos capable of claiming a continuous history, and to *represent* translation as occurring between two autonomous entities susceptible to nationalization." (1997: xvii–xviii). Thus 18th-century Japan witnessed the start of a paradigm shift in how Chinese texts and the Chinese language were accessed and perceived by Japanese readers, thereby representing a watershed in the history of translation in Japan. It took time for this reconceptualization of translation to filter through and become widespread in translation practice, and it was really only in the 20th century that the changes initiated by Sorai became the norm in translation from Chinese, superseding the long-established decoding norm nurtured by the practice of *kambun kundoku*. Of Sorai's three steps, it was the first—translation into vernacular Japanese rather than *kundoku*—that represented the most important reconceptualization from the viewpoint of translation. This step, which appears so trite from our viewpoint, was revolutionary in its time, introducing a new[12] method of translating Chinese after over a thousand years of *kundoku* as the mainstream approach, and it was to have an important effect on translations from European languages as well.

Notes

1. Miller (1986: 22–3) describes how Chinese words were borrowed into Japanese, even when there was an existing Japanese word:

... not only could a given Chinese character be used to write the borrowed Chinese word *shän* [mountain]—now appearing in Japanese in slightly altered phonetic guise as *san*—but it also became possible, if a writer wished to do so, for this same Chinese character to be used to write the Japanese word *yama* [mountain] as well. [...] This orthographic innovation, which in effect now brought into the Japanese writing system all the problems of approximation involved in any exercise in translation from one language to another, opened an enormous new area for the employment of Chinese characters in writing Japanese texts.

2. *Yomikudasu* means to vocalize – even if this is sub-vocalization in the mind.

3. Characters evolved in Japan on the basis of Chinese characters but used phonetically rather than for their meaning.

4. Kornicki notes that "What is significant about this multiplicity of print languages in pre-modern Japan is that they did not form a simple hierarchy that can be correlated with levels of educational or cultural attainment. The choice, for example, between *kanbun* and formal written Japanese was an ideological one as much as a linguistic one, representing a choice made between sinological and nationalistic orientations." (1998: 33–34)

5. Japanese names are written here in the usual Japanese order, with the family name first. In accordance with Japanese custom, famous figures such as Sorai are referred to by their given name.

6. Ken-en-juku , the Miscanthus Patch Academy, in Kayabachô.

7. Minear comments that this is "a mocking reference to the *okurigana* and *kaeriten* with which Japanese readers, from Kibi down to the present, decorate a Chinese text." (1976: 14)

8. *Yakubun sentei* was based on the notes of Sorai's lectures in 1690 or 1691. He made various changes before it was published 20 years later with a preface added. It contains a comprehensive Chinese-Japanese dictionary and a textbook on Chinese composition. In it Sorai grouped together verbs and adjectives with similar meanings and clarified by way of new "translations" in simple Japanese different Chinese words that under the traditional *kun* method would have been rendered by one and the same Japanese word. As an example in which the meaning was not fully conveyed because of the practice of *kundoku*, Sorai cited the homophones 視, 観, 覧 and 察, which are all pronounced *miru* in Japanese, thereby obscuring the semantic differences amongst these Chinese words (Sugimoto 1996: 145).

9. "What can be translated of Chinese words is only the meaning. And what can be spoken of the meaning is only the bare bones. The sonorous and brilliant character of Chinese words cannot be translated." (Letter to Hori Keizan, 1740; quoted in Minear 1976: 7).

10. Sorai evinced virtually no interest in other languages. In the preface to *Yakubun sentei* he wrote "In lands like Holland, in which human nature differs from the normal, there are indeed languages which are difficult to understand; they are like birds calling and animals roaring; they do not approximate human feelings. But when it comes to China and Japan, all things are similar." (tr. Minear 1976: 65). As Minear comments, "It would be difficult to find a better example of ethnocentrism".

11. *Kunyaku shimô* (Yoshikawa renders this as *Clarifying the Ambiguous Points in Japanese Kun Rendering* [1983: 111]) was one of Sorai's early works, and it focused on difficult grammatical terminology. Like *Yakubun sentei*, this was a Chinese-Japanese character dictionary for people carrying out the *yakubun no gaku* method that Sorai proposed for reading Chinese works. Using many examples, these dictionaries explain how different Chinese characters should be rendered into Japanese colloquial speech.

12. There had been occasional conventional translations before then, but it was not until now that they began to have any impact or become widespread.

Works cited

Adejunmobi, Moradeweun. 1998. "Translation and Postcolonial Identity: African Writing and European Languages". *The Translator*. 4, 2, 163–181.
Backus, Robert L. 1983. "Kambun", *Kodansha Encyclopedia of Japan*. Vol. 4, 123–124.
Baker, Mona. 1998. "Introduction". *Routledge Encyclopedia of Translation Studies*. London and New York: Routledge, xiii-xviii.

Bassnett, Susan and Harish Trivedi, eds. 1999. *Post-colonial Translation: Theory and Practice.* London and New York: Routledge.

Bedell, George. 1983. "History of Japanese Language Studies", *Kodansha Encyclopedia of Japan.* Vol. 4, 30–32.

Crawcour, Sydney. 1965. *An Introduction to Kambun.* Center for Japanese Studies, The University of Michigan, Ann Arbor.

Dore, R. P. 1965. *Education in Tokugawa Japan.* Berkely and Los Angeles: University of California Press.

Engels, Yukino. 1998. *A Study of Oranda Tsuji: in Preparation for an Extended Study of Translation History in Japan through Oranda Tsuji.* A dissertation submitted to the University of Manchester Institute of Science and Technology for the degree of MSc.

Genette, Gérard. 1997. *Palimpsests. Literature in the Second Degree.* Trans. C. Newnan and C. Doubinsky. Lincoln: University of Nebraska Press.

Hermans, Theo. 1999. *Translation in Systems: Descriptive and System-oriented Approaches Explained.* Manchester: St. Jerome Publishing.

Ishikawa, Kyûyô 石川九楊. 1998. "Shinsetsu Nihongo wa kô shite tsukurareta" 新説・日本語はこうして作られた」. *Chûô Kôron* 中央公論. 1365, 284–305.

Kamei, Hideo 亀井秀雄. 1991. "Honyaku to bôkun — "Shôsetsu shinzui" kenkyû (5) 翻訳と傍訓 ー『小説神髄』研究（五）. *Hokudai bungakubu kiyô* 北大文学部紀要. 40-1, 65–118.

Katô, Shûichi 加藤周一. 1982. Untitled article in "Bungaku no hiroba" column 文学のひろば『ホンヤク』. *Honyaku.* Tokyo: Iwanami Shoten, 274–5.

Katô, Shûichi 加藤周一. 1983. *A History of Japanese Literature Volume 2: The Years of Isolation.* Trans. by Don Sanderson. London: The Macmillan Press Ltd.

Katô, Shûichi 加藤周一 and Maruyama, Masao 丸山真男 et al. 1991. *Honyaku no shisô – Nihon kindai shisô taikei 15* 翻訳の思想 日本近代思想体系15. Tokyo: Iwanami Shoten.

Keene, Donald. 1987. *Dawn to the West: Japanese Literature in the Modern Era.* New York: Henry Holt and Company.

Kitamura, Ichirô. 1993. "Problems of the Translation of Law in Japan". *Victoria University of Wellington Law Review Monograph 7* (ed. and tr. from French into English by A. H. Angelo).

Kojima, Noriyuki 小島憲之. 1966. "Kundokushi no ichimen" 訓読史の一面. *Endô hakase kanreki kinen Kokugogaku ronshû Kyôto Daigaku Kokubun Gakkai* 遠藤博士還暦記念国語学論集 京都大学国文学会. Tokyo: Chûô Tosho Shuppan, 181–196.

Kondô, Masaomi and Judy Wakabayashi. 1998. "Japanese tradition". *Routledge Encyclopedia of Translation Studies.* London and New York: Routledge, 485–493.

Kornicki, P. 1998. *The Book in Japan – A Cultural History from the Beginnings to the Nineteenth Century.* Leiden, Boston, Koln: Brill.

McEwan, J. R. 1960/61. "Some Aspects of the Confucianism of Ogyû Sorai". *Asia Major.* Vol. VIII. B. Schindler, ed., 199–214.

Mehrez, Samia. 1992. "Translation and the Postcolonial Experience: The Francophone North African Text". In Lawrence Venuti, ed. *Rethinking Translation.* London and New York, Routledge, 120–138.

Mezei, Kathy. 1998. "Bilingualism and Translation in/of Michèle Lalonde's *Speak White*". *The Translator.* Vol. 4, No. 2, 229–247.

Miller, Roy Andrew. 1986. *Nihongo: In Defence of Japanese*. London: The Athlone Press.

Minear, R. H. 1976. "Ogyû Sorai's Instructions for Students: A Translation and Commentary". *Harvard Journal of Asiatic Studies*, 36, 5–81.

Miyoshi, Masao. 1974. *Accomplices of Silence – The Modern Japanese Novel*. Berkeley: University of California Press.

Morris, Meaghan. 1997. Foreword to Naoki Sakai. *Translation and Subjectivity: On "Japan" and Cultural Nationalism*". Minneapolis and London: University of Minnesota Press, ix–xxii.

Rabinovitch, Judith N. 1996. "An Introduction to *hentai kambun* [Variant Chinese], a Hybrid Sinico-Japanese Used by the Male Elite in Premodern Japan". *Journal of Chinese Linguistics*, vol. 24 (1), 98–127.

Robinson, Douglas. 1997. *Translation and Empire: Postcolonial Theories Explained*. Manchester: St. Jerome Publishing.

Saitô, Fumitoshi 斎藤文俊. 1996a. Personal communication, 12 June 1996.

Saitô, Fumitoshi 斎藤文俊. 1996b. "'Kaitai shinsho' Honyaku to kambun kundoku" 『解体新書』翻訳と漢文訓読 (Kanbun-Kundoku-Methods Used in the Translation *Kaitaishinsho*) *Jôhô bunka kenkyû*情報文化研究 3, March 1996, 137–146.

Sakai, Naoki. 1992. *Voices of the Past – The Status of Language in Eighteenth Century Japanese Discourse*. Ithaca and London: Cornell University Press.

Sakai, Naoki. 1997. *Translation and Subjectivity: On "Japan" and Cultural Nationalism*". Minneapolis and London: University of Minnesota Press.

Satô, Hiroaki. 1994. "Using a Foreign Language", *The JLD Times*, 3 (2), pp. 1, 10–12.

Satô, Tamotsu. 1983. "Poetry and Prose in Chinese", *Kodansha Encyclopedia of Japan*, vol. 6, 193–197.

Sugimoto, Tsutomu 杉本つとむ . 1996. *Seiyô bunka kotohajime jikkô* 西洋文化事始め十講. Tokyo: Surî nettowâku.

Toury, Gideon. 1995. *Descriptive Translation Studies and Beyond*. Amsterdam and Philadelphia: John Benjamins.

Tsukishima, Hiroshi 築島裕. 1965. *Heian jidai no kambun kundokugo ni tsukite no kenkyû* 平安時代の漢文訓読語につきての研究. Tokyo: Tôkyô Daigaku Shuppankai.

Twine, N. 1991. *Language and the Modern State: The Reform of Written Japanese*. London and New York: Routledge.

Wakabayashi, Judy. 1998. "Marginal Forms of Translation in Japan – Variations from the Norm". In L. Bowker et al. *Unity in Diversity? Current Trends in Translation Studies*. Manchester: St. Jerome Publishing, 57–63.

Woodsworth, J. 1994. "Translators and the Emergence of National Literatures" in M. Snell-Hornby, F. Pochhacker, K. Kaindl eds. *Translation Studies: An Interdiscipline*. Amsterdam: John Benjamins, 55–63.

Yamashita, Samuel Hideo. 1985. *Compasses and Carpenter's Squares: a Study of Ito Jinsai (1627–1705) and Ogyu Sorai (1666–1728)*. Ann Arbor, Mich.: University Microfilms International.

Yoshikawa, Kôjirô 吉川幸次郎. 1973. "Kaisetsu 'Sorai gakuan'" 解説 徂徠学案. *Nihon shisô taikei 36 Ogyû Sorai*. 日本思想体系36 荻生徂徠, 629–739.

Yoshikawa, Kôjirô 吉川幸次郎. 1983. *Jinsai, Sorai, Norinaga – Three Classical Philologists of Mid-Tokugawa Japan*. Tokyo: Tôhô Gakkai.

CHAPTER 8

Translationese in Japan

Yuri Furuno
The University of Queensland

Introduction

Historically, translation in Japan has been largely dominated by the desire to import new ideas and information from abroad, and throughout Japan's history foreign texts have been regarded as extremely valuable and important. In the area of English–Japanese translation, particularly in non-fiction texts, where the translator is introducing foreign ideas and information to Japanese audiences, 'adequacy' or the adoption of source text norms has traditionally played a more important role than 'acceptability' or adoption of target culture norms (Toury 1995). This was especially so after Japan was defeated in World War II. In order to revive its power as a nation Japan needed ideas and information from the West. Rather than conforming to the target culture norms, 'adequacy' or full-adoption of source text norms in translation continued to be popular, for Japan had a higher regard for Western culture than its own at that time. For Japanese readers, it seems that acquiring new ideas or information from the West was so important that the 'acceptability' of the product — that is, authenticity and naturalness of the language — was considered to be of secondary importance. In fact, the Japanese writing style for translated texts called *honyakuchō* (translationese), which replicates the original grammar and idioms, has long been accepted in Japan and does not have as many negative connotations as in English (Wakabayashi 1996: 899–904). As a notable Japanologist and Japanese–English literary translator, Donald Keene, puts it,

> The Japanese have rather different tastes in translation, often enjoying the foreignness of the idiom, which may persuade them that somehow, miraculously, they are reading a work in a language they do not know.   (Keene 1992: xiv)

This acceptance of foreignness on the part of Japanese readers, or the adoption of an adequacy norm in translated works, seems to have existed throughout Japan's history. Since the main goal of translation in Japan has been 'adequacy', the approach to translation studies in Japan has concentrated on searching for linguistic errors — i.e. the analysis of mistranslations.

Modern theories of translation, including Toury's concept of norms, have received virtually no attention in Japan, so the very idea of 'acceptability' in translation has not been properly investigated. Applying Toury's framework to the investigation of Japanese readers' tolerance of 'translationese' may shed new light on attitudes towards the 'acceptability' of translation in Japan today, and may show to what extent the traditional norm of 'adequate' translation is supported by the Japanese today as a proper translation approach.

Historical background

The history of Japanese translation started with Chinese-Japanese translation dating back to when Japan sent its first official envoy to China in AD 57. At that time Japanese people did not have a script to write their language, so the sound and meaning of Chinese characters were adopted to write Japanese words. Reading Chinese texts in order to import culture, new information and ideas was extremely valuable and important for Japan, and the reading method called *kambun kundoku* (interpretive reading of Chinese) was developed from the sixth to the eighth century. It uses grammatical indicators and markers to help Japanese readers decipher Chinese texts. Readers have to know the meaning of Chinese characters to be able to use this method. It was a direct means of construing a Chinese text into Japanese, and required close attention to the original text (Twine 1991: 39). This later contributed to the literal translation of Western languages into Japanese.

The first European language to arrive in Japan was Portuguese in the sixteenth century, followed by Dutch in the early seventeenth century, but the inflow of foreign texts was limited because of Japan's seclusion policy (1639–1853). It was not until 1853 that Japan formally opened its doors to the modern world. This led to a flood of imports of English, French, Russian and German works, and it was considered vital at that time to translate foreign texts so as to learn from the West. Translators at that time coined many neologisms by using combinations of Chinese characters to express the new concepts from the West. For instance, Nishi Amane[1] (1829–1894), a Japanese philosopher, is known to have coined neologisms for the words "philosophy", "logic", "psychology", "ethics", "phenomenon", "subject" and "object" during the early Meiji period (1868–1911) to help the Japanese understand the new foreign concepts needed after the Meiji Restoration (1867). Fukuzawa Yukichi (1834–1901), one of the leading translators/ educators at that time, also helped produce neologisms for social concepts such as "society" and "individual" (Yanabu 1982:18–33). During that period, new ways of writing were also accepted as necessary to express these new ideas, and translators were under no pressure to express the original ideas in a way that conformed to the target language (Wakabayashi 1998: 488–489).

However, according to Yanabu Akira (1998), these efforts in coining accept-able expressions for Western ideas were not entirely successful, as the meanings of the neologisms created during the Meiji period are still not properly grasped by Japanese readers to this day. Yanabu explains this as the 'cassette effect' (1976: 23–41), suggesting that the newly coined neologisms gave the impression that they were of absolute validity, and Japanese readers had a blind acceptance im-posed on them without fully understanding their meaning. In other words, Yanabu questions the acceptability of neologisms coined during this period. Most Japanese scholars (e.g. Shimizu 1959; Sigumoto 1961), however, admire the efforts of translators at the time for their achievement in cleverly utilizing Chinese characters to express modern Western concepts in Japanese.

Translators during the Meiji period not only coined neologisms but also often deliberately replicated the grammar and style of the source texts. For example, pronouns — which were unnecessary and rarely used in Japanese, where these forms had a somewhat different function – were inserted into translated texts to conform to the source text usage, and long English noun clauses were liter-ally and unnaturally translated into Japanese. Writers such as Natsume Soseki (1867–1916), who was himself also a translator, developed and promoted this new 'translationese' style. Despite their unnaturalness, neologisms and trans-lationese gained acceptance among Japanese writers and audiences, who were searching for an innovative style of written Japanese that would reflect the new times and could replace the heavily Chinese-influenced style of the past, which was far removed from the everyday spoken language.

The following are two contrasting views on translationese by leading Jap-anese novelists representing the Taishō (1912–1925) and the Shōwa periods (1926–1987). Tanizaki Junichirō (1886–1965) criticized translationese in the early Showa period as a "monstrous style", saying:

> I often see essays on economics by scholars in popular journals such as *Chūō Kōron* and *Kaizō*, but I wonder how many readers truly understand them. These essays are written with the expectation that readers have a good knowledge of the original language. Such essays look Japanese, but actually they are monsters of the foreign language. It is even harder to comprehend them than the original texts. I would

> call them the worst example of Japanese sentences. (*Bunshō Tokuhon* 1934: 74, my translation)

Writing twenty-five years later, however, Mishima Yukio (1925–1970) recognized the popularity of translationese:

> We now write Japanese compositions with translation-like expressions. Before the war, translationese was criticized, but not any more. Translationese is now the mainstream writing style, and authentic Japanese style is rare nowadays. Once translated concepts were limited to sophisticated philosophical thought, but they have been popularized and our everyday life is now influenced by imported concepts. (*Bunshō Tokuhon* 1959, 1973: 30–31, my translation)

After 1885 translations became more literal than in the early years of the Meiji period (Kondo and Wakabayashi 1998: 489), and Tanizaki was critical of the excessively source-oriented translations of his time. But after World War II Mishima acknowledged the prevalence of translationese, stating that it had become a part of the Japanese language.

Another way of importing foreign words into Japanese is transliteration, or the replacement of the foreign sounds with the nearest Japanese phonetic equivalent using the *katakana* syllabary. This practice started with borrowing from Portuguese in the 16th century and from Dutch during the 17th and 18th centuries. Beginning in the Meiji period, and especially after World War II, however, the proportion of loan words from English increased rapidly, and English is now estimated to represent 80–90% of all loan words in Japanese (*imidas* 1993). Of all 65,000 listings in a popular standard Japanese dictionary (*Sanseidō kokugo jiten* 1989), there are 7,100 (almost 11%) loan words. Transliteration does not require any effort to be made to convey the meaning of the original, but simply replaces the foreign sounds with Japanese sounds.

The current trend

In the last twenty years or so, however, Japanese translators and publishers have increasingly commented on the 'unacceptability' of much Japanese translations, arguing that translated texts should not just be faithful to the original, but should also be acceptable to Japanese audiences at large (Bekku 1985). As seen in a survey I conducted and in the articles and essays on translation by professional translators and publishers reviewed in this paper, greater naturalness in the writing of translated texts seems to be in demand and is being promoted in recent years in Japan.

In September 1978 a popular Japanese monthly translation journal, *Honyaku no Sekai* (The World of Translation),[2] started a regular column called "Critique of Defective Translations" by a professional non-fiction translator, Bekku Sadanori (1927–). In his articles Bekku not only picks on translation mistakes but also criticizes the unnaturalness of translated language, advocating acceptability in translation. This column remained popular among professional translators and students till June 2000. At the same time *Honyaku no Sekai* often featured round-table discussions amongst publishers and translators and conducts interviews with professional translators on translation problems. One of the round-table discussions, entitled "Finding Linguistic Errors in Translation is like a Witch-hunt" abhorred the nit-picking of mistakes in translation and concluded that, rather than just pursuing linguistic faithfulness to the original text, translation should also be discussed from the aspect of target-language expressions (*Honyaku no Sekai* 1983: 8–9).

A recent translation textbook called *Honyaku no Hōhō* (Methods of Translation, 1997) by a group of university lecturers takes issue with the literal translation method taught at high school English classes in Japan. It advises translation students to convey the meaning of texts in natural Japanese rather than just follow the original syntax and rely on the word-for-word equivalents listed in English–Japanese dictionaries (Sugawara 1997: 35–40). It advocates free rather than literal translation.

The above examples suggest that Japanese translation norms today are moving away from a source text orientation and taking the acceptability of translated texts more seriously than before. This shift toward a target text orientation, however, does not seem to have prevented the continued popularity of transliterating English and other foreign words into Japanese.

Transliteration runs counter to the recent shift in translational norms from 'adequacy' to 'acceptability'. Even though it is the closest phonetic representation of the source language and not at all natural or authentic Japanese, Japanese people seem to accept loan words as new expressions. There are several Japanese dictionaries specializing in loan words and they need to be constantly updated because current terms are increasing every year. This dependence on transliteration bears a resemblance to the traditional *kambun kundoku* method of transposition (Wakabayashi 1998: 58), which required readers to attend closely to the original language.

Thus it would seem that while Japanese readers' preference today may be for a more natural style and flow of the language, individual words may still remain foreign and opaque to the audience. Does this represent a basic contradiction?

To find out more about reader expectation and preferences, a survey was conducted in the reception of translationese.

A survey on translationese

In order to begin investigating why there has been a shift in translation norms in Japan, in 1998 I undertook a preliminary survey into the level of tolerance of 'translationese' and the general expectations towards translated texts. This survey suggested that while contemporary Japanese readers generally expect, though not necessarily desire, translations to read unnaturally as Japanese, the same readers cannot easily distinguish between translated and non-translated texts in their actual reading. This suggests a discrepancy between readers' expectations of translations and the contemporary reality.

The following section reports on the result of the survey undertaken in December 1998 at two translator training institutions in Tokyo — ISS (*Ai Esu Esu*) and Inter School. As a preliminary investigation into translationese, instead of choosing random respondents, I chose a group presumed to be more responsive to the questionnaire. While translation students can on the one hand represent general readers, they are also much more aware of translations than Japanese audiences at large.

1. Demographic Composition

Forty-five trainee translators from both institutions responded to the survey. Of the 45 respondents, 51% were aged under 34, and 49% were aged between 35 and 55, so that both the younger and middle-aged populations were represented. The group consisted primarily of females (42 of the 45 respondents). This gender bias was not a part of the survey design, but a reflection of the higher participation rate of women in translation training classes in Japan in general.

2. Methodology

Respondents were asked to assess sets of current Japanese non-fiction texts on the same topic by different authors and taken from popular journals of similar standards (*Bungei Shunjū*, *Chūō Kōron* and *Shūkan Shinchō*). The articles were grouped into two sets (T-1 & O-1 and T-2 & O-2), each consisting of one translation (T) and one original (O) text. No indication was given as to which were the translated texts. Firstly, respondents were asked to compare the naturalness and clarity of expression of the selected texts. Secondly, they were asked to identify the translated texts and explain their reasoning in terms of perceived differences between translated and non-translated texts. Thirdly, respondents were asked about their general preferences in translation, between "literally faithful" to the original (or 'adequate') and 'natural and readable' as a target text (or 'acceptable'). Finally, respondents' opinions were sought on the effect of translation on Japanese written expression — i.e. whether translations have enriched the Japanese language.

3. Results

Comparison of T-1 and O-1

T-1 was a translation, while O-1 was an original Japanese text. Fifty-nine-and-a-half percent of the respondents identified O-1 as more natural Japanese, but when asked to identify the translated text, only 42% correctly selected T-1 (see Table 1). Thirty-one percent picked both T-1 and O-1 as a translation, indicating that it was difficult to distinguish between the translated and non-translated texts. This could either mean that the translation is in authentic and natural Japanese, or that translationese has become such a part of Japanese writing style that readers can no longer tell the difference between the two writing styles.

Table 1. T-1 and O-1 comparison

	T-1 (%)	O-1 (%)	Not sure which (%)
More Natural	36	59.5	4.5
Clearer	34	50	16
ID translation	42	27	Both: 29
			Neither: 2

The most frequently cited reason for identifying a particular text as a translation was the poor flow of the language. This is a general expectation towards translations in Japan, because of its literal translation tradition. The second common reason given was the overall impression and stiffness of the language. The use of loan words was not cited by any respondent as a reason for identifying a text as a translation. The topic of the texts used for this comparison was the Japanese bureaucracy and the frequency of loan words was correspondingly low, which might explain the lack of reference to them.

Comparison of T-2 and O-2

T-2 (a translation) and O-2 (an original text) were on the social issue of juvenile delinquency in Japan. T-2 was chosen as a typical sample of 'translationese' style and was expected to be identified more readily as a translation, but as this comparison was on the second page of the survey, less than 87% of respondents answered it. Of these, only 23% found T-2 more natural than O-2, but when asked to identify the translation, just under half of the respondents (48%) identified T-2 correctly as a translation (6% more than the case of the T-1/O-1 comparison). Surprisingly, 26% picked both T-2 and O-2 as translations, indicating that translationese is not easily identified (see Table 2). The first three reasons for picking the translated text were the same as in the T-1/O-1 comparison, i.e. poor flow, overall impression and stiffness. However, 8% chose the high frequency of *katakana* loan words as their reason for identifying the translated text. T-2 (the translation) contained passages describing the social situation in the United States, and it is possible that the use of *katakana* is more influenced by the content of the text than by the writing style.

Clarity of language

The original Japanese texts collected more votes for clarity of expression than the translated texts in both comparisons. This was especially apparent when comparing T-2 and O-2, where the original Japanese text collected 56% of the votes while the translated text gained only 31% (see Table 2). This preliminary result suggests that original Japanese texts tend to be much clearer for Japanese readers than translated texts. This is contrary to one of the universals of translation in the West, the 'explicitation' factor (See Laviosa-Braithwaite in Baker 1998, 289), which suggests that the target text becomes more explicit than the source text because of the process of interpretation.

Table 2. T-2 and O-2 comparison

	T-2 (%)	O-2 (%)	Not sure which (%)
More natural	23	56	21
Clearer	31	56	13
ID translation	48	18	Both: 26
			Neither: 8

Reasons for identifying particular texts as translations

The most popular reason given for identifying a particular text as a transla-tion — that is, poor flow or unnaturalness of the language – remained un-changed in both T-1 vs. O-1 and T-2 vs. O-2 comparisons. However, I suspect that the second most popular reason given — overall impression — could hold the key in the final decision in identifying translated texts. Even though re-spondents overwhelmingly cited poor flow or unnatural language in particular texts, the variable of overall impression of a text reduces the percentage of cor-rect identification. The overall impression of a text could be influenced not only by the style of the language but also by the content of the text, the logic of the arguments and the use of loan words. As a result, the successful identification of a translated text does not match the percentage of votes given for such domin-ant characteristic as translationese, poor flow or unnaturalness.

The following is a selection of particular comments (free response) made by respondents as regards to the reason for identifying a text as a translation, thereby articulating respondents' particular *image of translationese*. Their com-ments will be discussed below in relation to the linguistic characteristics of the Japanese language.

- *A clear subject, unlike original Japanese sentences*
  Authentic Japanese sentences often do not state the subject of the sentence, and readers usually infer it from the context, so it would be unnatural in Jap-anese to indicate subjects clearly each time.
- *Too many commas*
  This indicates that there are many noun phrases in a sentence, often a charac-teristic of English–Japanese translations. This makes a Japanese sentence un-natural, long and unclear.
- *English-like structure or logic*
  This is the result of the traditional literal translation approach.
- *Too many pronouns*
  Pronouns are not usually used in authentic Japanese sentences unless for in-dicating concrete objects or directions. The use of pronouns for abstract con-cept was introduced through the translation of Western literature. Hence it is one of the distinctive indicators of translationese.
- *Repetition of key words*
  In order to avoid frequent use of unnatural pronouns in translation, proper

nouns may be used repeatedly. This may also be a reflection of the literal translation approach which follows the syntax of the source language.

'Adequacy' vs. 'acceptability'

Respondents were asked in the latter part of the questionnaire their opinion on 'adequacy' and 'acceptability' in translated texts in general, and whether they thought translated texts should pursue fidelity to the original norm or readability for the target audience. Three options were given: (1) translations should be faithful to the original even if the resulting text becomes somewhat unnatural, (2) it is better to have a readable text even if the translation does not follow the structure of the original, (3) not sure which is better. Respondents were then asked to give their reasons for choosing 1, 2, or 3.

A preference for the first option, which suggested the pursuits of adequacy in translation was supported by only 5% of the respondents, while a preference for the second option favouring 'acceptability' or readability in translation was supported by a majority of 57%. Thirty-eight percent chose the third option, "not sure" (see Table 3). This reflects some uncertainty in choosing between source-oriented and target-oriented (Toury 1995) translation, but the overall result shows that the initial norm of "acceptability" now prevails in Japan.

Table 3. Adequacy and acceptability (%)

Translation should be faithful to the original	5
Better to be readable	57
Not sure which is better	38

After stating their preferences, respondents were asked to comment on their choices. Their comments indicate that the adoption of the initial norms of "adequacy" or 'acceptability' depends on the type of text as well as on the kind of audience for whom the translation is produced. The texts used for this survey were non-specialized journal articles aimed at general readers. Therefore 'acceptability' was generally valued much more than 'adequacy'. Nevertheless, comments made by respondents who were not sure of their preference between the two initial norms reveal more sophisticated or complex considerations and should be pursued further. For example, one comment was that it is acceptable for legal or academic papers to be in unnatural language; another comment was that specialized translations should be literally faithful, but general translations should be acceptable/readable.

The influence of translation on the Japanese language

The final question posed to respondents was whether Japanese expression has been enriched by translation. Twenty-seven percent of respondents answered in the affirmative, 25% thought Japanese has lost its 'Japaneseness' or originality, and 48% responded that it is impossible to judge whether translation has enriched Japanese (see Table 4). These results indicate that translation is perceived as having both enriched the Japanese language and contributed to a certain loss of 'Japaneseness' in general. Even though almost half of the respondents were not sure of the influence of translation on Japanese language style, there were slightly more positive than negative comments on the overall influence of translations on the Japanese language. Some respondents commented that the question was too broad and it would be better if the field of translation had been specified. This is a valid comment, as the response could well be expected to be different for, say, literary and technical translations.

Table 4. The influence of translations (%)

Japanese has been enriched	27
Has lost its Japaneseness	25
Unsure	38

Conclusion

Although the acceptance of 'adequate' translation on the part of Japanese readers — or the adoption of the source text norms in translated texts — has existed throughout Japan's history, both the survey results and a preliminary review of Japanese publications on translation revealed that in recent years the pursuit of 'acceptability' in translation has gained ground over the traditional pursuit of 'adequacy'. The traditional English–Japanese literal translation method, which was considered to be faithful to the original, has been criticized in recent years by writers, professional translators and translation educators, who argue that literally faithful rendering of the source text does not convey its message, and that a translation should be expressed in natural Japanese.

Source-oriented translation was acceptable to the Japanese when it served the purpose of importing ideas and information from abroad. Overly 'adequate' translation was long tolerated, but with Japan's economic success and its renewed social/cultural confidence in the 1970s and 1980s, Japanese translators, publishers and readers have increasingly commented on the 'unacceptability' of much translated Japanese, arguing that the translated text should not only be literally faithful to the original, but should also be expressed in natural Japanese. The rate of tolerance towards translationese by Japanese readers seems to have become lower than before. As Mishima pointed out, translated ideas are no longer solely for the highly sophisticated class but also for the general population (1959, 1973: 38). Translation has been popularized, and readability is becoming a major concern for Japanese readers today.

The popularity of transliteration in Japan today, however, seems to run counter to the shift in translation norms from adequacy to acceptability. The root of this practice dates back to the Japanese writing tradition of direct adoption of Chinese characters and the *kambun kundoku* reading method. Although the preference of Japanese readers today may be for more naturalness in style and flow of language, retaining the 'foreignness' of individual words does seem permissible. The preliminary survey I conducted suggests that the use of *katakana* loan words does not contribute to the identification of translated texts.

The survey result also suggests that while contemporary Japanese readers generally expect translations to read unnaturally as Japanese, the same readers cannot easily distinguish between translated and non-translated texts. This may be understood as the result of the call for naturalness in translations in the last twenty years in Japan having been answered to some extent, and translations for the general reader today are more readable or their *translationese* style is not as obvious as in the past. An alternative explanation is that translationese has been prevalent in Japan for so long that it has become a part of the Japanese language, which accounts for the difficulty in distinguishing authentic Japanese from translated language in some cases. Both of the explanations provided above may explain why readers find it difficult to identify translated texts; they also account for the discrepancy between readers' expectation and the reality of translation today.

As shown in this preliminary survey result, while the initial norm of 'acceptability' in translation now prevails in Japan, in the eyes of readers, texts written originally in Japanese are still more readable and natural in style than the translated texts. In other words, stylistic differences between original texts and translations still exist in Japan today. Translationese or the source-oriented written style introduced through translation of Western languages, therefore, is yet to be fully accepted or naturalized as Japanese.

In response to the contemporary readers' increasingly target-oriented expectation towards translated texts, the traditional source-oriented translation approach and writing style may continue to change. Since the way the Japanese language itself evolves and the stylistic preferences of the reading public provide the overall linguistic environment for translations, further study is necessary to investigate the interplay between the change of the Japanese language and the perception of "translationese" in Japan in a broader framework.

Notes

1. Japanese names in this paper follow Japanese custom, with the family names coming before given names.
2. First published in 1976, the magazine changed its name and its orientation in 2000.

Works cited

Bekku, Sadanori.1985. *Honyaku to Hihyō*. Tokyo: Kōdansha.

Honyaku no Sekai. Ed. 1983. "Round-table discussion: Goyaku Hihyō wa Majogari ka (Finding Linguistic Errors in Translation is like a Witch-hunt)". *Honyaku no Sekai*, 8–9, 71–84.

Imidas. 1993. *Gairaigo Ryakugo Jiten (A Guide to Foreign Terms and Abbreviations)*. Tokyo: Shūeisha.

Keene, Donald. 1992. "Translation and Comparative Literature". Cornelia N. Moore and Lucy Lower, eds. *Translation East and West: A Cross-Cultural Approach* 5: *Literary Studies East and West*. Hawaii: University of Hawaii Press.

Kenbo, Hidetoshi et al. eds. 1989. *Sanseido Kokugo Jiten*. Tokyo: Sanseido.

Kondo, Masanori and Judy Wakabayashi. 1998. "Japanese Tradition", in M. Baker and K. Malmaakjaer, eds. *Encyclopedia of Translation Studies*. London & New York: Routledge, 485–494.

Laviosa-Braithwaite, Sara. 1998. "Universals of Translation", in M. Baker and K. Malmaakjaer, eds. *Encyclopedia of Translation Studies*. London & New York: Routledge, 288–291.

Mishima, Yukio.1973. *Bunshō Tokuhon*. Tokyo: Chūō Kōron Sha.

Shimizu, Ikutarō.1959. *Ronbun no Kakikata*. Tokyo: Iwanami Shoten.

Sugawara, Katsuya. 1997. "Eiwa Jiten Katusyōhō", in H. Kawamoto ed. *Honyaku no Hōhō*. Tokyo: Tokyo Daigaku Shuppankai, 31–43.

Sugimoto, Tsutomu. 1961. "Kidai nihongo no seiritsu". *Kokugogaku* 46, 52–68.

Tanizaki, Junichirō. 1934. *Bunshō Tokuhon*. Tokyo: Chūō Kōron Sha.

Toury, Gideon. 1995. *Descriptive Translation Studies and Beyond*. Amsterdam/Philadelphia: John Benjamins.

Twine, Nanette. 1991. *Language and the Modern State: The Reform of Written Japanese*. London/New York: Routledge.

Wakabayashi, Judy. 1996. "Translation Theory in Japan: Familiar Ideas or Fresh Insight?" *XIV World Congress of the Fédération Internationale des Traducteurs (FIT), February 1996, Melbourne Australia*: Vol. 2 .899–904.

Wakabayashi, Judy. 1998. "Marginal Forms of Translation in Japan: Variations from the Norm". Lynne Bowker, Michael Cronin, Dorothy Kenny and Jennifer Pearson, eds. *Unity in Diversity?: Current Trends in Translation Studies*. Manchester: St. Jerome.

Yanabu, Akira. 1976. *Hon'yaku towa nanika*. Tokyo: Hōsei University Press.

Yanabu, Akira. 1982. *Honyakugo Seiritsu Jijô*. Tokyo: Iwanami Shoten.

Yanabu, Akira. 1998. *Honyakugo wo Yomu*. Tokyo: Maruyama Bungei Tosho.

CHAPTER 9

The selection of texts for translation in postwar Japan

An examination of one aspect of polysystem theory

Noriko Matsunaga-Watson
The University of Queensland

Introduction

Japan has a long history of introducing both fiction and non-fiction works from other cultures through the medium of translation. In particular, there have been several 'translation booms' since World War II and translated works regularly occupy a high position on bestseller charts. Translation is a well-established genre in Japan and has achieved steady popularity. Drawing on polysystem theory, this paper investigates the patterns of Japanese cultural imports by examining the source languages, genres and authors selected. The scope of the paper covers works listed as bestsellers in Japan's *Publishers' Yearbook* 出版年鑑 published from 1953 to 1998, although obviously this excludes many translations that appeal to a limited audience or that are perceived to be of lesser value. *Publishers' Yearbook* is an annual publication containing information and statistics on publishing activities, and its data is reliable in terms of its consistency.

The paper focuses on the dynamics of the postwar bestseller market in the post-Occupation period (i.e. since 1952). The Occupation period immediately after World War II is excluded because during this period Japan's publishing activities were under strict censorship and sponsorship by the Occupation authorities. This paper focuses on internal factors influencing the publishing of translated works rather than on such externally imposed factors.

In order to obtain a good grasp of the dynamics of Japan's polysystem, the scope of this paper covers both fiction and nonfiction works. The objective is to examine the validity of polysystem theory's views on text selection in the case of one particular target culture, Japan. The paper also identifies the characteristics of certain genres within the Japanese book market that are currently filled largely by translated works.

Theoretical framework

According to polysystem theory as postulated by Even-Zohar (1990a: 47), translations will take place when one or more of the following conditions are met:

1. when the polysystem of the target culture is not yet established;
2. when the polysystem of the target culture is peripheral or weak;
3. when the polysystem of the target culture is at a crisis or turning point.

Even-Zohar also hypothesizes that texts are selected for translation for the following reasons: the prestige of the source language text, and/or the dominance of the source culture (1990b: 66–68).

This paper examines whether these hypotheses regarding the emergence of translation and text selection are applicable to postwar Japan. It also discusses other possible explanations for the emergence of translation and for text selection in a particular polysystem — that is, the polysystem consisting of bestsellers on Japan's book market.

The polysystem theory's hypothesis that selection is conditional upon the prestige of the source language text or the dominance of the source culture suggests that translation activities are controlled by the status and power of the source language and culture. Translation can be thus hypothesized as a push-driven activity where the target culture remains rather passive in receiving texts for translation. This paper will attempt to demonstrate, however, that translation activities are not always carried out simply to compensate for the weakness of the target culture or to complement the shortcomings of the fiction or non-fiction polysystem in the target culture. In the case of bestseller translations in Japan's post-Occupation period, it seems that the target culture is actively seeking palatable products that satisfy the audience.

In this paper the term 'bestseller' is defined as book products that are sold in large quantity for a relatively short time, for example, one year. When a certain book is sold for a longer period of time, this is defined as a 'longseller' regardless of the quantity sold.

Japan's book industry

Japan has a population of approximately 125 million, with an official literacy rate of 100%. Most students complete senior secondary education, and tertiary education is widespread. The number of potential consumers for book products in Japan is therefore large. According to *Publisher's Yearbook* (1982), Japan was rated the third leading nation in terms of publishing activities, after the United States and the former Soviet Union. While the number of publications does not necessarily indicate that a nation is culturally mature or advanced, it does at least present one aspect of the scenario in which book products in general are produced and consumed. According to the 1998 *Publishers' Yearbook*, the number of newly printed books in 1997 was 62,336 titles, approximately 40% of the total number of books in print. Book sales amounted to approximately US$ 9.78 billion.

Over the past forty-five years the total number of new books has been increasing by at least a few percent each year and sometimes by as much as 19% (e.g., 1955 and 1986). The industry as a whole has shown positive growth except for the following years: 1957, between 1959 and 1961, 1973, 1985 and 1987. Corresponding to the growth of the entire industry, the total number of fiction works, including new titles and reprints, has also been on the increase, usually standing at a healthy 20% of the total. Other genres competing with literature are general publications, philosophy, history, social science, natural science, technology, industry, art, linguistics, children's books and textbooks. In general, Japan's book industry and publishing performance have been vigorous. It is remarkable that the industry has managed continuous growth. However, the recent economic recession in Japan may lead to industry restructuring that will affect this positive performance.

Economic recessions were recorded in 1955 (deflation), 1959, 1964, 1976, 1982, 1994 and 1998. No correlation is evident between these recession years and the publishing industry's years of negative growth. The publishing industry has on the whole been active and maintaining its growth. Such a situation on the production and distribution side should provide a diverse market that is constantly filled with new book products. This is a positive and encouraging situation for book consumers, as greater variety could be expected to stimulate a potential growth in demand.

This $ 9.78 billion industry has been maintained and operated by 4,612 publishers throughout the nation. The information about size is given later. The majority (3,608) are located in the Tokyo area and most were established in the postwar era.

Table 1 shows the differing sizes of Japanese publishing houses, and Table 2 shows their size according to the number of employees. As these tables show, publishing houses vary greatly in size, and this diversity has the potential to cater for a range of tastes.

Table 1. The number of companies according to capital size

Capital	Number of companies
−4,400	11
4,500–8,849	26
8,900–17,700	17
17,800–26,500	233
26,600–35,400	29
35,500–44,200	65
44,300–88,500	1,412
88,600–177,000	433
177,100–265,500	204
265,600–354,000	93
354,100–442,500	109
442,600–885,000	136
885,100–	169
Unknown	1,675
TOTAL	4,612

Exchange rate: ¥113–US$ 1 (as of August 1999)
Source: *Publishers' Yearbook* (1998: 361)

Table 2. The number of companies according to the number of employees

Number of employees	Number of companies
−10	2,183
11–50	1,023
51–100	224
101–200	127
201–10000	121
1001–	37
Unknown	897
TOTAL	4,612

Source: *Publishers' Yearbook* (1998: 361)

Bestsellers in the post-occupation period

Figure 1 shows the top fifty bestseller translations on the domestic bestseller market from 1952 to 1997. Entries are divided into fiction and non-fiction categories. Translations have constantly appeared on the bestseller charts since 1952, the first year of this study, although the number was small until 1973 in both categories. The total number of translated bestsellers under survey was 139, con-

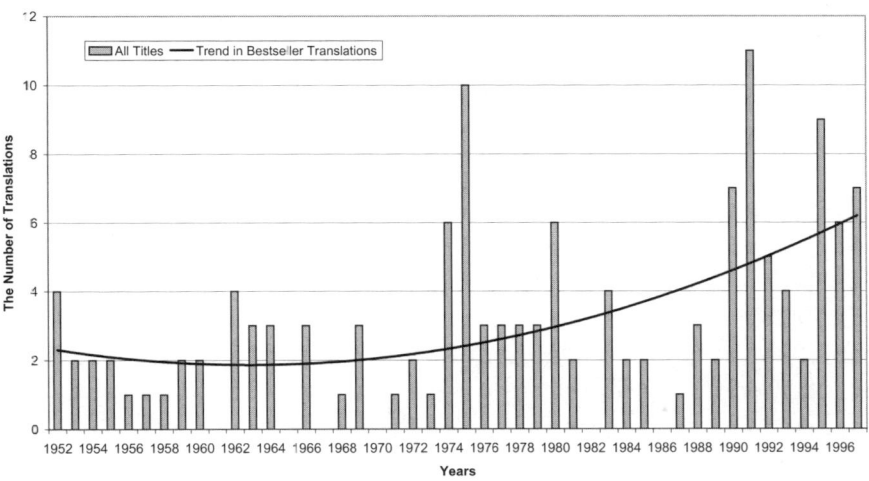

Figure 1. Number of translations per year

sisting of eighty-two fiction and fifty-seven non-fiction books. On average, 3.1 translations were constantly listed on the annual top-50 bestseller chart — more than 6% of the total number of bestsellers (although there were no translations on the bestseller chart in the years 1961, 1965, 1967, 1970 or 1982).

Figure 2 shows the fiction category, combining both literary masterpieces and popular novels for entertainment purposes. Literary masterpieces were predominantly sold as part of a series, which were popular in the early postwar years. After some time, however, the boom in such multi-volume works diminished — according to *Publishers' Yearbook*, the boom peaked in 1967 and ended in 1970. The fiction category in general appeared dormant between 1965 and 1973, and also between 1981 and 1987.

However, the number has risen dramatically since 1990, with 38 translated fiction bestsellers between 1990 and 1997. Nearly 46% of translated fiction bestsellers in the whole post-occupation period were concentrated within the space of these eight years. Globalization and the new age of information may have played an important role resulting in this significant figure. Figure 5 shows that tastes shifted to popular novels in the fiction category in this period. Many popular novels were promoted in conjunction with newly released movies of the same title. In this way, the interaction with external polysystems such as other media can act as an additional factor influencing Japan's publishing industry. This mixed-media interaction and the commercial force seem to have changed the definition of the term 'prestige' in the publishing arena. Translated works on

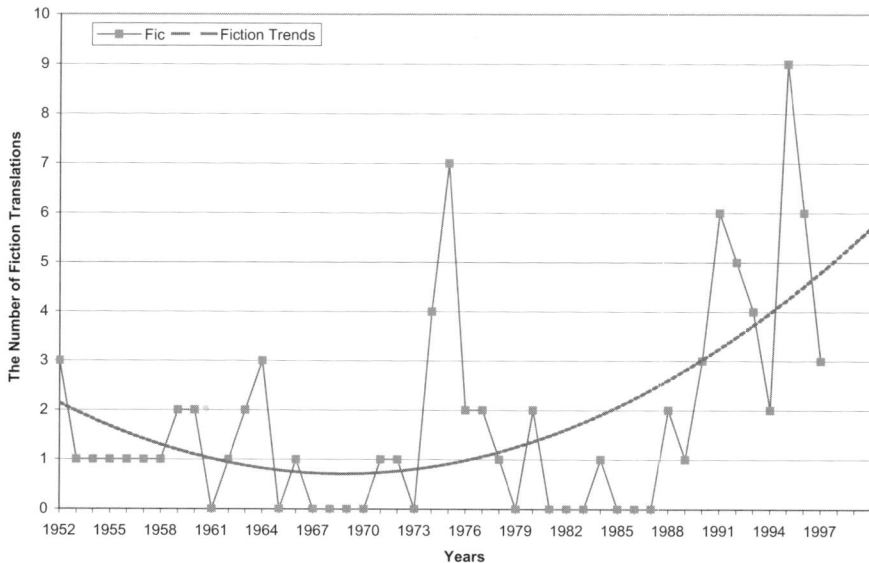

Figure 2. Trends in fiction translations

the bestseller chart are now regarded as consumable products for the purpose of entertainment. 'Prestige' no longer refers just to lofty canons such as the classics.

Figure 3 shows that the non-fiction category has appeared consistently on the bestseller chart since 1952, although the overall number of non-fiction translations was small. The number was particularly concentrated between 1978 and 1991, when there were a considerable number of business-related translations on Japan's bestseller chart. The sub-categories making up the non-fiction genre are mainly business-related works about management and administration, as well as futurology, *Nihonjin-ron* 日本人論, science in general and astronomy in particular, technology in artificial intelligence, and social and political issues. *Nihonjin-ron* deals with the issue of the identity of the Japanese in contrast with other races and cultures. The popularity of *Nihonjin-ron* works can be seen as a culture-specific boom driven by Japanese audiences. This may support the argument that the target culture also takes the initiative in text selection. The *Nihonjin-ron* boom lasted for six years, between 1972 and 1978, coinciding with the strong interest in management, administration and futurology. Astronomy became popular in 1981 and 1991, when Stephen Hawking played a major role in drawing general attention to this rather specialized topic. Figure 4 shows an

alternation between business and other non-fiction topics, which possibly reflects the fad nature of business management in modern times.

Both the fiction and non-fiction categories appeared constantly on the bestseller chart from 1952 onwards, but the overall number was small until the mid-
1970s, when translation showed signs of emergence on the bestseller chart. Although the fiction category had a relatively stronger presence, the non-fiction
category also featured consistently until the mid-1970s. Fiction was relatively
dominant between 1974 and 1978, then non-fiction took over the dominant
position till 1991. Fiction re-emerged in 1988. Since the appearance of many
translations on the bestseller chart in the mid-1970s, the tendency seems to be
that when translated fiction is selling well, non-fiction sales remain quiet, and
vice versa. This alternating trend is also characterized by a transition period
when interest is equally divided between two categories, such as between 1976
and 1977, and between 1988 and 1991.

English is also the single most dominant source language in the non-fiction
category, as Figure 7 shows. Fifty-four of the total 58 entries were written in English. The major contributor was again the United States, which has been exer-
cising its cultural, political and economic power in the international arena. Not
only its strong international presence, but also the proximity between Japan
and the United States might have reflected strongly in the book industry. This
outcome seems to be a partial reflection of the dynamics resulting from these

Figure 3. Trends in non-fiction translations

external yet closely related polysystems. The four other entries were originally written in Chinese, Russian, Italian and Spanish, and were also on political or sociological topics, indicating that interest focuses strongly on such issues.

In the fiction category, entertainment novels have been gaining in popularity since the beginning of 1990. In terms of individual authors, Sidney Sheldon has had 17 bestsellers in the sub-category of entertainment novels since his first work was listed on the bestseller chart in 1988. Sheldon is the only author appearing on the bestseller chart repeatedly, and the number of his titles has been increasing every year, a remarkable pattern never observed before. Sheldon's name seems to be equated with entertainment for general readers in Japan. These works do not fall into the category of conventional translation — *chôyaku* 超, or hyper-translation, is the term coined to describe the new approach adopted in the translation of Sheldon's works. In the name of translation, *chôyaku* alters the original freely to create an entertaining effect. Some might argue that this is not a new approach, but merely adaptation under a different name. However, Sheldon is still treated as the author, and his name is important for publishing purposes. It is simply that the translators of his works are given wide latitude by the publisher. The term *chôyaku* is printed on the cover of Sheldon's works in Japan, functioning as a caption to attract consumers.

Frederick Forsyth has been popular since his first work appeared on the bestseller chart in 1973, followed by other works in 1980, 1984, 1989 and 1991. His name has also become well established in the market. In the same sub-category

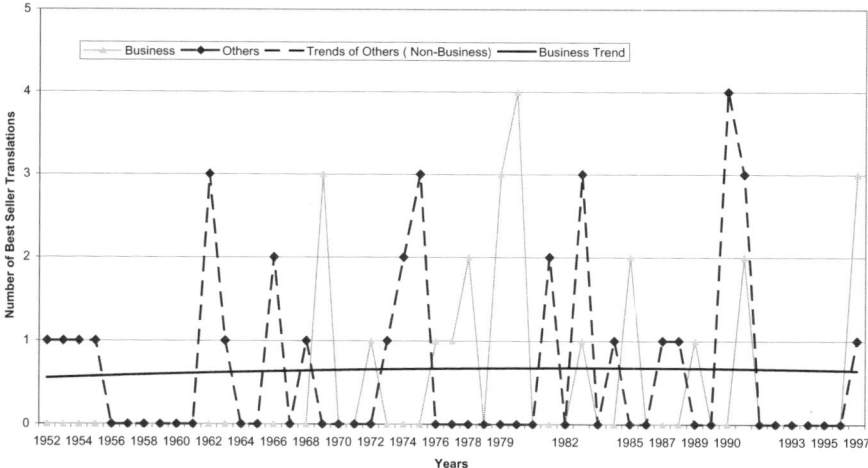

Figure 4. Non-fiction by sub-category

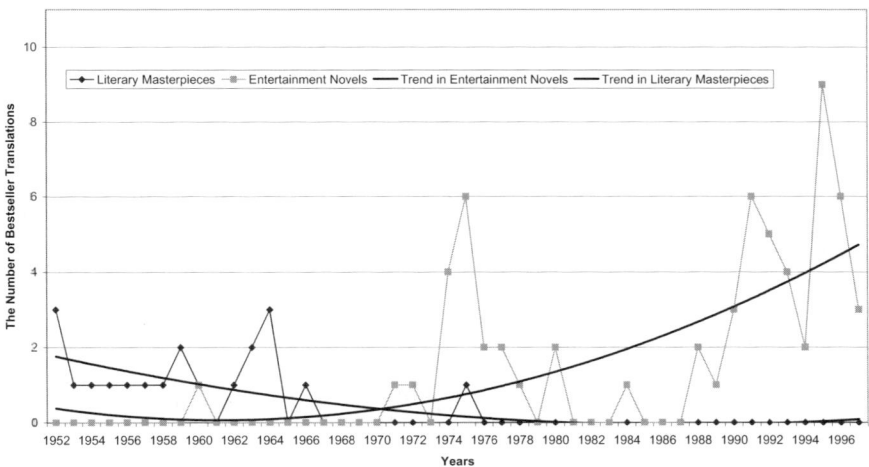

Figure 5. Fiction by sub-category

of entertainment novels, Graham Hancock is a new author who appears on the bestseller chart with two entries in 1996 and one entry in 1997. Although he is a relatively new name, he seems to have captured audience attention. Jostein Gaarder was listed in both 1995 and 1996 with the single entry *Sophie's World* ranking number one and nine respectively. The original was written in Norwegian, and represented the sole case in which a work in a language other than English became both a bestseller and a longseller. The author was quite unknown in Japan when the book was released, but it achieved great success, even though it is described as not easy to read. Philosophy or intellectual works in general are an attractive theme for Japanese readers. This particular work may have been consumed for its intellectual image, which may actually have been enhanced by the fact that it is a translation.

Jonathan Livingston Seagull by Richard Bach was a number-one bestseller in 1974. Part of the reason for its success is believed to be the choice of a famous Japanese author, Hiroyuki Itsuki, as translator. Most of the entertainment novels seem to be short-lived. Those works that are successful in the fiction market seem to be linked with more intensive publicity in the mixed media. For instance, Robert James Waller appeared on the bestseller chart for three consecutive years from 1993 with *The Bridges of Madison County*, the original work of the movie of the same title.

In the non-fiction category, the eminent futurologist Alvin Toffler appeared in 1981, 1990 and 1991, while Carl Sagan appeared in 1980 and 1981 in the field of astronomy and Stephen Hawking appeared in both 1990 and 1991. Although

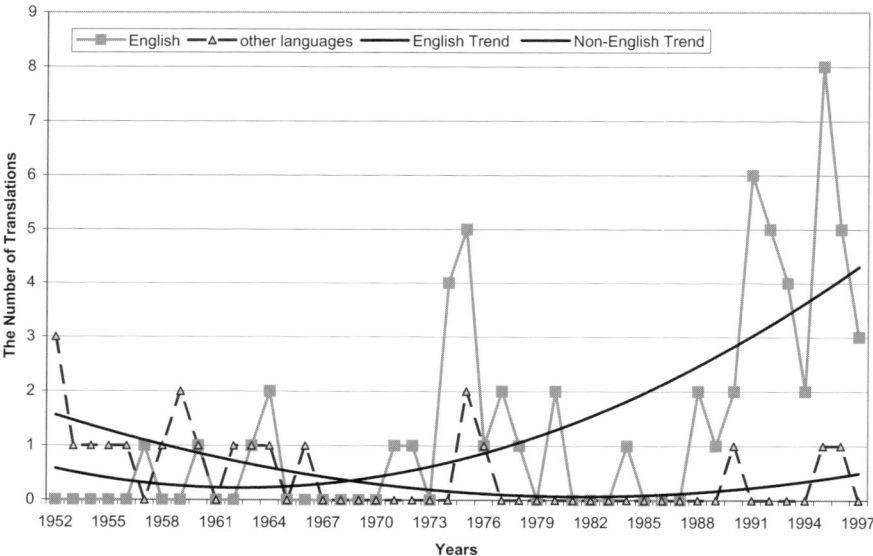

Figure 6. The number of fiction bestseller translations by source language

Joy Adamson is classified in the non-fiction category, the two entries listed on the bestseller chart in 1962 were probably read as stories. In the nonfiction category, a certain topic or issue seems to attract attention among general readers, such as business administration and management, forming a boom which lasts for at least a few years.

In terms of source language, the eighty-two entries in the fiction category are broken down to sixty-one from English, eight from French, six from Russian, one each from German, Italian and Chinese, and four from other European languages. The fifty-seven nonfiction works include fifty-two from English, and one each from Chinese, Russian and Italian. Figure 5 shows that literary masterpieces making a solo dominant category between 1952 and the mid-1960s were mostly from works written in French and Russian. As Figure 6 shows, English has been the major source language, with works from the United States outnumbering those from other English-speaking countries.

Trend analysis and grounds for text selection

In the 1950s Japan's literary polysystem was still largely influenced by the European macro polysystem. Literary masterpieces were selected for translation and accepted in the Japanese literary polysystem. The dominance of the European macro system, in particular French, seemed to be influencing Japan's polysystem in its text selection. This dominance of the source culture and prestige of the source text, such as works categorized as classics and prizewinning works, appeared to be a major ground for text selection in Japan's polysystem.

Subsequently, the American polysystem has become more influential in Japan. The United States occupies the central position in the international arena in terms of politics, economics, diplomacy and culture. As Japan became more influential in the international arena as its economic status improved, the proximity between the United States and Japan increased in this central arena. The longer interaction occurs between two polysystems, the more a common ground can be created. From a historical point of view, translation once was a national project in the Meiji period (1868–1912), aimed at absorbing new concepts from the 'better and more advanced' outside world — that is, the West. Translation has been an important means of introducing new information since then, and more and more common ground has been created over the years.

In both cases, the selection of texts for translation in Japan seems to have been influenced by the international market, with the exception of the *Nihonjin-ron* boom, which was a culture-specific interest in Japan. In the early stages, the dominance of the source culture and the prestige of the source text may have

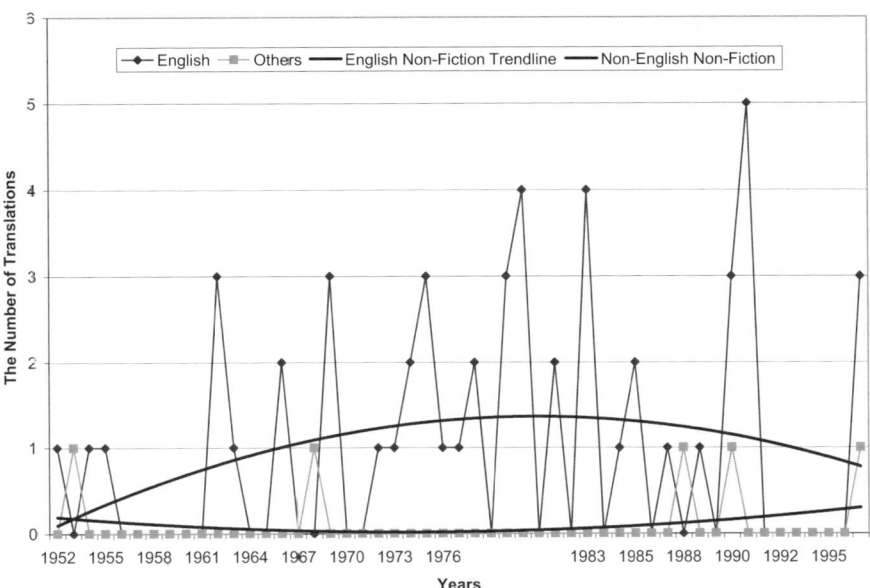

Figure 7. The number of non-fiction translations by source language

been a major factor determining text selection. Once a sufficient infrastructure, knowledge, information, tools (dictionaries), trained translators and market acceptance as well as positive expectations were acquired, translation became a more effective tool to increase variety in the market. Japan's polysystem has become closer to the American polysystem in the 1990s. The grounds for text selection for translation appear to be predominantly whether the text constitutes a consumable product for entertainment purposes.

Conclusion

Polysystem theory hypothesizes three conditions for the emergence of translation: when a literary polysystem in the target culture is (a) young, (b) weak or peripheral, or (c) at a crisis point. In both the fiction and the non-fiction categories, translation as one of the established genres seems to secure a solid position in Japanese polysystem. In this case study, one aspect of Japan's polysystem consisting of translated works suggests that translation may emerge and preserve its position once it is accepted by the audience within the polysystem. From the production point of view, the more translations are produced, the better infrastructure can be built for more effective production. More variety coupled with publicity in the mixed media, expectations and attention from consumers may increase. This feedback may reflect the decision making on the production side. The popularity of entertainment translations in the 1990s may be partly explained by this upward spiral.

The major factors determining text selection for translation as hypothesized in polysystem theory are the prestige of the source language text and the dominance of the source language culture. These factors appear applicable to the situation in the fiction category in the early 1950s. However, this pattern changed as time elapsed. This may be because the tastes of general audiences shifted away from such 'prestigious' works as the classics. This trend seems to have appeared in the early 1970s when the tastes and expectations of Japanese audiences became more diversified. In response to this change in public expectations, book production started to be carried out based on the concept of providing a greater variety of products. However, the polysystem hypothesis seems still applicable to Japan's situation. As the industry and the taste of the audience changed according to the time, what 'prestige' involves may have also changed.

In conclusion, commercial factors and other external polysystems such as politics, economics, and international relations may play an important role in explaining the emerging pattern of translation and the grounds for text selection for translation in the case of Japan's modern polysystem consisting of bestseller translations. Further study will be carried out to investigate the factors driving reader interest — the book or the media, the cultural mood or the country's psychological environment.

Works Cited

Even-Zohar, Itamar. 1990a. "The Position of Translated Literature within the Literary Polysystem." *Poetics Today* 11, No.1 (1990): 45–52.

Even-Zohar, Itamar. 1990b. "Laws of Literary Interference." *Poetics Today* 11, No. 1 (1990): 53–72.

Shuppan Nenkan (Publishers' Yearbook). 1953–1998. Tokyo: Shuppan News-sha. 1953–1998.

Case studies from China

CHAPTER 10

Translation in transition

Variables and invariables

Lin Wusun
Chinese Translators' Association

Within my life span, I've used a pen, a typewriter and then a computer to write and translate. Though the switch from one to the other had caused me some pain and effort, each time it upgraded the quality of my work and increased my efficiency. Now I am having to switch again, this time continuing to use my computer but relying more heavily on translation hardware and software which are appearing on the market like mushrooms after a spring shower.

New translation tools

A whole range of translation tools have come about. There are, among others:

- Computerized dictionaries. The Web-based, multi-language dictionary Logos (www.logos.it), for example, is truly amazing. This magnum opus is freely accessible online with 7,590,000 entries in 150 languages, including Chinese. It gives complete definitions to the queried word, including the grammar with plurals, etymology, synonyms, and antonyms when possible. One can also find the context of the word within the Logos "wordtheque" library (*Language International* 1999: 8).
- Terminology data banks.
- Translation memory programs, which provide you with all translated texts you have done before on the computer so that you can make use of them when necessary.
- Bitext programs, which display the source text and the target text simultaneously in two columns side by side.
- Concordancers, software that retrieves instances where a word or expression is used in translation.

- Machine translation programs.
- Sound-sensitive hardware and software so that all you have to do is to talk to the microphone and your translation is put into your computer.

As a result of these latest developments, concepts and terms such as machine-assisted human translation (MAHT) and human-assisted machine translation (HAMT) have been devised (Delisle, Lee-Jahnke & Cormier 1999: 193).

Seven major trends

In a previous paper (Lin 2002), I listed seven major trends on the Chinese translation scene as the country was about to cross the threshold into the new millennium. These are:

1. Thanks to China's rapid economic development, the market looks promising for translators/interpreters. Demand now far exceeds supply.
2. The scope of translation/interpretation (hereafter T/I) continues to expand. Science-tech, business/trade, media, legal and other related T/I now make up the market's lion's share. Literary translation, on the other hand, dwindles in proportion.
3. Chinese translators/interpreters have to handle T/I both from and into their own mother tongue. This puts a higher demand on them.
4. Except perhaps in literary translation, there is shrinkage in the number of languages used compared with the three preceding decades from the 1950s to the 1980s. For example, among Asian languages, only Japanese and Korean now feature actively in translation work.
5. China's adhesion to the international copyright convention is having an impact on Chinese publications and hence also on the translators. The purchase of copyright from abroad often has a bearing on the type of books which are being translated.
6. The use of computers, translation and terminology software, Internet and email is spreading. This has opened new vistas for translators/interpreters in China. For example, the T/I market has expanded beyond national boundaries. Also, translation is now closely linked with information retrieving, and summaries are often called for instead of straightforward translation.
7. While there exists a top layer of first-class translators/interpreters, the general quality level of Chinese T/I is not up to the desired standard. In other

words, although the quantity of T/I increases by leaps and bounds, the quality seems to have gone down visibly.

This unhappy situation calls for co-ordinated efforts to upgrade translation teaching and to introduce an accreditation system for Chinese translators/interpreters on the basis of some kind of examination and other performance tests. In the following sections I should like to expand on trends number 2, 3, 6 and 7, emphasizing their impact on translation practice and teaching.

Variables in translation practice and teaching

Since many of China's university foreign language students will eventually enter the T/I market, we have to prepare them for the new challenges they are going to face. As the world is going through the process of globalization, the volume of T/I work is growing at a tremendous pace. With the development of new fields in inter-disciplinary studies and frontier science, there are many topics and terms which the translators/interpreters cannot be expected to be familiar with. Yet they do require T/I, and the job has to be done within a tight schedule. This situation calls for help from terminologists and consultation with specialists. Hence the development and use of terminology dictionaries and software is essential. Students would be in a disadvantageous position if they were not taught the use of these translation tools. The ability to make use of some of the tools listed above is absolutely necessary in an Information Age when competition is fiercer than ever before and the tempo of life has increased dramatically. This new requirement is what I call variables in translation practice and studies because some of the subject matters which professors are familiar with are no longer as significant as before while subjects with which they are unfamiliar are coming to the fore. And this process of change will undoubtedly speed up in the 21st century.

I must add that this situation is not unique to China. Throughout Europe and the United States, academics and translators/interpreters are calling for reforms in language and translation teaching. In Europe, for example, a program called POSI, stressing the importance of a more practice-oriented curriculum, is under serious study. Here in China too I would like to see some changes take place, such as the setting up of T/I colleges and departments, revamping the curriculum and introducing new textbooks and teaching methods.

Invariables in translation practice and teaching

Does it mean that all our previous knowledge about T/I is outdated? No, not at all. In this Information Age, I believe while students need to be familiar with new fields of knowledge and be capable of handling new tools, mastery of the basics in T/I has become more, rather than less, important. This is what I call the invariables in translation practice and teaching. To take full advantage of all the available new Information Technology (IT), students need to have a solid grounding in T/I skills. And for that, they need a thorough understanding of the source language (SL) and the ability to express themselves fluently in the target language (TL). In China, few people are bilingual, but acquiring both these capabilities is a prerequisite to quality T/I. Command of a foreign language cannot be achieved without a comprehensive understanding of the culture associated with the language. To achieve this, it is necessary both to study the history, philosophy and literature of that country or countries, and to live and study and possibly to work there in order to get a sense of the values, thinking process and way of life of the local people. With China opening to the world and the development of modern means of transportation, this latter requirement is now within reach to a good portion of Chinese language and translation students and perhaps to most translation scholars. The significance of this goal cannot be over-emphasized.

Here I would like also to stress the importance of mastering our mother tongue, the Chinese language. This is harder than it seems. In a world where television, computer and/or pop culture are occupying so much of our young people's time, when visuals are all pervasive, there is a malignant tendency to neglect the writing skill. People read and write less, not more. I am not a purist and I agree that languages need to change with the times. Yet one has only to peruse the Chinese press to realize how 'polluted' our language has become.

In the United States, we find an ongoing controversy over the same question and the appearance of advocates of so-called 'cultural literacy'. In China, too, we need to safeguard standard Chinese from the onslaught of sloppy use of our native language. While I am all for the teaching of translation studies in universities so that students can be initiated into both the hows and whys of T/I, they would not be able to really appreciate what the different theories are driving at without previous translation experience. For example, to understand the significance of target-oriented theories, you must have first-hand experience in handling pragmatic texts and receiving feedback from customers. In this respect, internship in translation companies is also indispensable. Just as the best way to learn swimming is to swim, so the best way to learn all the ramifications of the translation process is to work on a translation project. There is nothing that can compare with the good old master-student relationship, which our forefathers devised centuries ago. Don't get me wrong. I am not against translation studies, nor against the introduction of Western translation theories into China. All I am saying is the study of translation theories should come after translation practice and not before. A swimmer must be trained scientifically, but that can only be done in a pool and not on the ground.

Conclusion

To conclude, translation is experiencing a process of unprecedented transition. It has become closely linked with information retrieving and an important part of the knowledge industry. As the translation market places new demands on translation practitioners, and as information technology is providing brand new tools for our profession, so must translation practice and teaching make adjustments, revamp and break new ground. Break down the Great Wall between the practitioners and the academics. Let the former constantly summarize their new experiences and learn from the academics. Let the latter come out of their ivory tower and march with the times.

There are two English sayings which seem to be contradictory to each other and yet are very pertinent to our topic: "One is never too old to learn," and "Old dogs can't learn new tricks." Let us old-timers strive to learn "new tricks" while we help the novices to learn both old and new. Herein lies the future of our profession.

Works cited

Lin, Wusun. 2002. "Translation in China and the Call of the 21st century". In Eva Hung ed. *Teaching Translation and Interpreting 4.* Amsterdam/Philadelphia: John Benjamins.

Delisle, Jean, Lee-Jahnke, Hannelore and Cormier, Monique eds. 1999. *Translation Terminology*. Amsterdam and Philadelphia: John Benjamins.

Language International "World News Brief" 1999. *Language International* Vol. 11, No. 3.

CHAPTER 11

On annotation in translation

Han Jiaming
Peking University

Editor's note

Though most translators and translation critics would agree that assumptions about the reader's need often feature prominently in the process of translation, there is no necessary consensus as to what the reader's need is. Before one can address such need, one has first to address the question of who is the prospective reader. This article shows us that translators, editors and publishers may have different answers to this question, and that a published translation is often the result of negotiation between these different parties.

In terms of the translation of literary material, late 20th-century China presents an interesting situation in that until the late 1980s, there was practically no differentiation between popular literature and serious literature. As a result, translators and editors would often assume that the text should work for different strata of a wide readership whose knowledge of the text's background could vary greatly. Moreover, China's literary translation tradition, which became established in the early 20th century, has a strong utilitarian flavour: translated texts were considered instruction tools for social improvement, and the translator was seen as a transmitter of new knowledge (frequently equated with knowledge of the West). Nor did the translator feel that he had to be an invisible intermediary—one only has to recall how Lin Shu's generation of translators inserted personal comments into their translations to understand how they perceived their own role. All these had an impact on translation practices. When, after decades of isolation, China opened her doors again to the outside world in the early 1980s, many of these factors were just as relevant as they had been eight decades ago. It is therefore not surprising that a tendency towards the instructional and the didactic should reveal itself in the use of annotation—a method which by its very nature inclines towards the educational. The translator Zhang Guruo's use of annotation discussed in this paper should be placed in this context.

However, new elements have also come into play which changes the readership and its needs. As Chinese society moved from socialism to *de facto* capitalism, serious literature gradually lost its popular appeal. There is much greater differentiation among literary publications, with each type appealing to a different readership. Thus, constant adjustments have to be made in defining 'the reader' and his/her need.

The result is a much more diversified approach in assumptions about the projected readership: the norms of the 1980s were no longer sacrosanct at the end of the century. At the same time, translators or editors now have to address concerns other than the reader's need. Unlike their early 20th-century predecessors, PRC publishers today are bound by copyright regulations. This article shows us, through what is apparently a minor incident, how certain decisions are no longer in the hands of the translator and the editor.

Annotation is an important method in translation, especially in translating classic or scholarly works. In "Translation and Interpretation", I discussed the problem of translation redundancy and considered annotation as one way of avoiding translation redundancy, using as examples the late Zhang Guruo's translation of Henry Fielding's *Tom Jones* and David Hawkes' translation of *The Story of the Stone* (Han 1996). Recently, I co-translated *The Short Oxford History of English Literature* with two colleagues, and while reading the proof, my attention was drawn to the problem of unnecessary or unauthorized annotation. This surprising discovery led me to reconsider the issue of annotation. Consequently I re-read Zhang's translation of *Tom Jones* with careful attention to his annotations, and this re-reading made me aware that annotations are often, but not always, necessary. A distinction between the two, taking into consideration the nature of the text to be translated and the background of the target readership, will make the translation more informative and readable.

The basic uses of annotation

Almost all Chinese textbooks on translation mention annotation as an important method used to clarify difficult points, to provide background information, or to discuss specific allusions. In my class on English-Chinese translation, I have used two textbooks: *A Textbook of English-Chinese and Chinese-English Translation* compiled by Ke Ping, and *A Collegiate Course in English-Chinese Translation* compiled by Wang Zhikui et al. Each textbook has a section or subsection on annotation. Ke Ping notes that annotation can be used in three situations: (1) when translating classic or scholarly works, the translator may use annotation to preserve the multiple meaning of the original work; (2) when the original expression has allusive meanings, the translator may help the reader with annotation; (3) most often, annotation is used to provide background cultural information for the reader of translated literature. At the end, Ke Ping remarks, "Annotation is a method which makes it convenient for the translator to illustrate the implied meaning of the text, but in literary translation, annotation should not be too liberally used; otherwise the reader's interest may be disrupted." (1993:112; my translation). Wang Zhikui et al. also point out that annotation may be used to provide information on cultural background and to solve special rhetorical problems such as puns (1995:133). If we reassess the use of annotation in many well known Chinese translations according to the above-mentioned criteria, we will find cases where the use of annotation is questionable.

A case study: translated fiction

Here, for the purpose of illustration, we will examine the use of annotation in Zhang Guruo's Chinese version of Henry Fielding's *Tom Jones*. The first chapter of the novel is two to three pages in length; in Martin C. Battestin's annotated edition three-and-a-half pages, with five footnotes. Zhang's version runs to more than six pages with eight notes. Of the eight, one is about Bayonne and Bologna, two cities having a good or bad reputation respectively for making sausages (1993:6); one is on the Roman Emperor Heliogabalus (1993:8); and one is a reference to strong Italian seasoning (1993:9). I would classify these three as necessary notes which provide information on the cultural background of the source text, without which the Chinese reader's understanding of the passage might be hindered.

There are, however, footnotes which aim at providing information which exceeds the criterion of necessity. One such case is the footnote stating that the famous couplet "True Wit is Nature to Advantage drest, /What oft' was thought, but ne'er so well exprest" is taken from Pope's *Essay on Criticism* (1993:6). The translator goes on to illustrate what "wit" meant in the eighteenth century. This note, which is well over one thousand words long, is unquestionably learned, but for the ordinary Chinese reader, it is not very useful, whereas for scholars of English literature it is somewhat redundant. It therefore seems that much of the more detailed information could have been excluded without affecting the reader's understanding of the story.

Another example of a similar nature is related to the words "calipash and calipee", referring to "the edible substances found, respectively, under the upper shell and inside the lower shell of a turtle" according to Battestin's annotation (1975:32). In addition to this information, Zhang's footnote also provides details about the Alderman of Bristol whose gluttony was proverbial, as well as the evolution of the institution of the alderman in English history; the note is over eight hundred words long. Here again the note is certainly informative, but for the average reader of this novel, the benefit seems to be minimal.

There is a third category of annotation that goes beyond what we assume to be the normal boundaries of explication. Our first example is a long informative note on "humanity" provided by Zhang, listing the contrasting views of Hobbes and Shaftesbury and Fielding's different responses to them (1993:5). Since the general argument is not dissimilar to the traditional Chinese dispute over whether human nature is good or evil, the average Chinese reader would not have gained substantially in his understanding of the author's message. What this footnote supplies is information on the author's philosophical standpoint and its contexts in this argument. The question is: is a footnote the best vehicle for conveying such information?

The same question applies to the two remaining footnotes in Chapter 1 of *Tom Jones*. In one of them Zhang discusses his reasons for rendering the words "wit or wisdom" as "明達之識或明哲之智", citing alliterative effect as a reason for his choice (1993:4). In another he explains his rendering of the word "gibbeted" is a paraphrase (1993:7). While the discussion of translation approaches and choices might be of interest to some readers, it is best that such information or argument be presented in the preface or colophon rather than in isolated footnotes. For readers who are interested in what concerns the translator in the process of translation, a systematic discussion illustrated with examples taken from the translation would have been far more illuminating than a random mention in an occasional footnote, while for the average reader who, we assume, is more concerned with the story itself, footnotes elaborating on matters of approach may be too disruptive.

To sum up, of the eight footnotes provided in the first chapter of Zhang's version of *Tom Jones*, we may say that three are necessary, two serve a purpose but are overdone, and three are more suitably placed elsewhere. Here the major consideration is obviously how we define the extent of "necessary background information". To answer that question we need to define, however vaguely, the translation's target readership. Our assumption here is that most readers of fiction read for pleasure, not for instruction. In that case, if the annotations are too heavy, the potential reader may be scared away.

The translator has to gather a lot of the background information about the text both prior to and during the process of translation While all this information has a bearing on how the translation is done, he has to be selective about what to include in the footnotes, what to leave out, and what other forms of communication there may be for more detailed cultural information which may only be indirectly relevant to the story.

I propose that our main criterion in making such a judgment should be the reader's need: annotation should be provided to such a degree that the reader will not encounter substantial obstacles, while not to be the extent of appearing overly intrusive. As David Hawkes remarks, "though footnotes are all very well in their place, reading a heavily annotated novel would seem to me rather like trying to play tennis in chains" (1977: 12). While I do not agree with Hawkes' categorical rejection of annotation, I nevertheless think the point he makes is important. Thus, admirable though Zhang's translation and his wide learning may be, I have to say that sometimes his annotations seem to go a bit too far.

A different context

In translating classical literature the translator is primarily responsible to the reader because the authors are long dead and the copyright long expired. But with translating modern or contemporary work, the situation is somewhat different, for here the translator often has to take the demand of the copyright holder (be it the author, his literary estate or the original publisher) into consideration. Here I will use my personal experience as the co-translator of a scholarly book to illustrate how, paradoxically, considerations for the reader's need may not always be a decisive factor in the use of annotation.

When I was first asked to translate the chapters on seventeenth- and eighteenth-century literature in *The Short Oxford History of English Literature*, I was instructed to produce a close or literal translation of the text, but that I could add some necessary notes both to clarify difficult points and to present the views of Chinese scholars. There is of course a marked difference between a work of literature and a work of scholarship, though the latter may discourse on literature. The nature of the work is also significant in our consideration of how and whether to annotate. Accordingly, I added several footnotes. My annotation can be classified into three categories: first, clarifying obscure points; second, offering elaboration on specific problems; and third, presenting variant views in relation to the writer's.

Notes in the first category include those on the "Habsburg, Bourbon, Gonzaga, and Medici rivals", "the Pillars of Hercules", "Pilate" and other similar phrases.

The purpose is to give the Chinese reader information which is essential for the understanding of the relevant passages.

An example from the second category is a note on "wit". I translated this term as "巧智", and in the note I wrote:

> Wit is one of the most widely used concepts in poetry writing and criticism in the seventeenth and eighteenth centuries. It could mean genius and intellect, poetic talent, special choice of expressions, creation of images, and especially the skill of expressing striking ideas in paradoxes. It is tentatively rendered as "巧智", but "机智", "睿智", "才智" could be used, too.

Another example is about *Robinson Crusoe*. In discussing this book, Sanders writes: "Robinson Crusoe 'of York, Mariner' gives over only some two-thirds of his narrative to his life on his desert island, but the account of those twenty-eight years forms the most compelling section of his experiences." (2000: 445). I added a note to the effect that "only" and "but" probably should be omitted to provide a clearer logic. Since Crusoe gives two-thirds of his account to describe his experience on the desert island, it is not surprising that it should be the most compelling section. Instead of glossing over this in translation by omitting the word "only" and "but", I added a footnote.

The third category of annotation is more complicated. Since the editor at first expressed a kind of encouragement for personal or critical views on the book, I added some footnotes to that effect in my manuscript. For example, in the note on Crusoe mentioned above, I continued:

> In Sanders' commentary on *Robinson Crusoe* in this paragraph, his emphasis on the theme of religion is correct, but it is not fair for him to attack critics who have seen Crusoe as a primitive colonialist. In fact, most Anglo-American critics have always emphasized Crusoe's character as a bourgeois individualist and the theme of religion, and only in the last decade or so have more critics begun to examine his image as a primitive colonialist from the perspective of post-colonial studies.

I offered this note as an assessment of Sanders' view and also to provide information on more recent development in the field.

Another annotation provided for a similar purpose is on Aphra Behn, the first English woman who made a living by her pen:

> Earlier literary histories did not pay much attention to Aphra Behn. But since the 1980s critical works on Behn have flourished in England and America, and now she is generally held to be one of the most important English writers in the late seventeenth century.

These two notes both provide supplementary information, with the first being more critical; they both are quite valid. But in the final proof-reading stage

I decided to delete them. That decision was made because according to the contract signed by the People's Literature Press (Renmin wenxue chubanshe) and Oxford University Press, no alteration of the meaning of the text is allowed, and annotation must be kept to the minimum. Indeed, the clause against alteration meant that I had to let an apparent error remain in the book. The publication date for John Dryden's *All for Love* is known to be 1678, but Sanders gives the date first as 1678 and later as 1677. Clearly this is a slip on the writer's part, but I was advised to keep the error and add a note instead of simply correcting the error.

There were, however, other instances when a decision about annotation was indeed made based on the projected readership of the book. For example, a copy editor added a footnote to Bacchus, the god of wine in Greek and Roman mythology, to my translation of this book. After I pointed out to him that the book's intended readers — teachers and students of English literature — would have prior knowledge of Bacchus, the footnote was dropped. This demonstrates that in deciding whether to use annotation, we have to consider the potential readers for the book and take what they know and what they need to know into account.

Concluding remarks

To conclude, annotation is an important tool in translation. Since the current trend is for many translations to be quickly and poorly done, we should encourage translators to engage in more research and to provide annotation where necessary in translation. But this does not mean that the more footnotes there are, the better the translation. Annotation should only be used judiciously; only those that are essential for the reader's understanding of the text should be added. There is little point in repeating common knowledge or demonstrating the translator's own erudition for its own sake.

Works cited

Fielding, Henry. 1975. *The History of Tom Jones, a Foundling*. Ed. Martin C. Battestin and Fredson Bowers. Middletown: Wesleyan University Press.
Fielding, Henry. 1993. *Qier Tangmu Qiongshi shi (The History of Tom Jones, a Foundling)*. Tr. Zhang Guruo. Shanghai: Shanghai yiwen chubanshe.
Han, Jiaming. 1996. "Translation and Interpretation: Translation Redundancy Reconsidered." *Perspectives: Studies in Translatology* 1: 113–126.

Hawkes, David. 1977. "Preface". In Cao Xueqin. *The Story of the Stone*, Vol. 2. Tr. David Hawkes. London: Penguin Book.

Ke, Ping. 1993. *A Textbook of English–Chinese and Chinese–English Translation*. Beijing: Peking University Press.

Sanders, Andrew. 2000. *Niujin jianming Yingguo wenxueshi* (*The Short Oxford History of English Literature*). Tr. Gu Qinan, Han Jiaming, Gao Wanlong. Beijing: Renmin wenxue chubanshe.

Wang, Zhikui et al. 1995. *A Collegiate Course in English–Chinese Translation*. Jinan: Shandong University Press.

Index

'assumed translation' 5
acceptability xi, 4, 62, 107, 147–151, 153, 156–159
Adamson, Joy 170
adequacy 91, 102, 107, 147, 148, 151, 153, 156–158
affective memory 114
Afrikaans x, 19, 22–39
Amenomori, Hôshû 141
American Dream, the 93
An, Shigao 47, 58, 60, 61
annotation xii, 137, 183–189
Antoine, André 113, 114
apartheid x, 22, 26–29
Asia (see also China, Japan, Korea) xii, 45, 61
    East 46
    Central 46–50, 60–62
Asian languages (see also Chinese, Japanese, Korean) 47, 48, 178
autonomy/autonomous 92, 93, 96, 97, 100, 104, 107, 142

Bach, Richard 169
Baoyun 49
Battestin, Martin C. 185
Beckett, Samuel 115
Behn, Aphra 188
Bekku, Sadanori 151
Belgium 117
bestseller 161–170, 173
Bible x, 12–14, 23–26, 68
    New Testament 13, 25, 26, 29, 82
    Old Testament 13, 25, 27, 35
Bible Society 24–26
Bible translation x, 12, 19, 23–28, 35
Bonavia, David 85
Book of Mormon 11–13
borderland x, 43–49, 52–58
    cultural x, 43–45, 48, 52, 53, 56
    geo-political 45, 46, 49, 50
    institution-based 45, 50–52, 54, 57
    socio-political 45, 52, 53, 55, 57
Britain/British/Anglo xi, 12, 19–24, 62, 67, 68, 85, 112–115, 188
Brodie, Fawn 13, 16
Buddhism/Buddhist 45–50, 56, 60–62, 135

Calvinism 26, 69
Carey, William 68
Chang'an 49, 59, 60
China vii–xiii, 43–62, 67, 69–87, 91, 94, 102, 105, 109, 127, 134, 135, 137, 138, 143, 148,

178–181, 183
Chinese x–xiii, 43–62, 69–72, 75, 76, 79–87, 91–93, 95, 100, 106–109, 121–143, 148, 149, 158, 168, 170, 177–180, 183–188
Chopin, Kate 91, 96, 97, 106, 108
Chôyaku 168
Christianity 67, 82, 85, 86
comparative analysis 19
Confucius/Confucian 48, 62, 75, 82–85, 101, 136, 140, 141
connotations 73, 91, 95, 101, 103–108, 147
Copeau, Jacques 112, 114
copyright 116, 178, 184, 187
Crawford, T. P. 82
Crommelynck, Fernand xi, 111–118
cultural change x, 3, 19, 43, 45, 57, 58, 86
cultural differentiation 30
cultural repertoire 3, 4, 9
cultural-political transformation 19
culture planning ix, 4, 9, 16

Daigen jûsoku 137
Dao'an 49
Dazai, Shundai 141
De Tocqueville, Alexis 93, 108
deletion/delete 29, 30, 35, 38, 189
Descriptive Translation Studies viii, ix, 19, 28
Dharmaraksa of Dunhuang 47, 59
Dryden, John 189
Du Toit, S. J. 24
Dutch 19–28, 116, 148, 150
Dzhabayev, Dzhambul 14

education ix, xi, 48, 68, 73, 75, 78–81, 162
English vii, xii, 8, 11, 12, 15, 22, 23, 67, 68, 70, 71, 92, 102, 103, 105, 109, 111–114, 116, 117, 147–151, 155, 157, 167, 169, 170, 181, 184–189
epistemology 26
Europe 15, 20, 21, 44, 46, 50, 52, 111, 112, 114, 148, 170, 171, 179
evangelism 67–69
explication/explicate 29–39, 130, 186

fiction 12, 57, 62, 161–165, 167–170, 172, 185, 186
fictitious translations (see also pseudo-translations) ix, x, 4–15
Fielding, Henry 184–186
French x, 8, 10, 11, 20, 62, 67, 93, 111–113, 117, 148, 170, 171
Fukuzawa, Yukichi 149
fundamental nature 96, 99, 105

Gaarder, Jostein 169
Gakusoku (Instructions for Students) 136
generalization/generalize 29, 35, 75
German 9–11, 20, 67, 69, 75, 116, 148, 170
government ix, xii, 22, 23, 26, 49, 51, 52, 54, 55, 57, 58, 75–81, 83, 86, 87
Graves, Roswell H. 69, 72, 84–86
Greek 12, 24, 25, 29, 32, 34–39, 79, 92, 93, 189
Grossvogel, David 112, 113

hakaseketen system 122
Hancock, Graham 169
Hawkes, David 184, 187
Hawking, Stephen 166, 169
health care 75, 79–81
Hebrew 8, 12, 13, 24, 25, 29–39
hentai kambun (variant Chinese) 125
Herring, D. H. 82, 83
Hipps, John Burder 72
hiragana script 122, 126
Hiroyuki, Itsuki 169
Holmsen, Bjarne Peter 9, 10
Holz, Arno 10, 11
honyaku (translation) 127, 129
host culture viii, ix, 5–7, 43–45, 48–51, 56–58
hybrid language 130, 131, 140

identity x, 5, 10, 27, 35, 47, 57, 91–108, 134, 166
imperial decree style (*semmyôtai*) 125
individualism/individual 8, 9, 70, 79, 84, 91–98, 101, 103, 104, 107, 108, 149
information technology 180, 181
integrity 94, 95, 97–99
intensification 29, 35
Israel 27, 32, 35
Italian 67, 93, 114, 116, 168, 170, 185

Japan xi, 45, 77, 82, 121, 122, 124, 126, 127, 129, 130, 135–137, 142, 143, 147, 148, 152, 158, 159, 161–163, 167, 169, 171
Japanese xi, 62, 121–143, 147–159, 161, 163, 166, 169, 171, 172, 178
japanized reading 128, 139
Jesuit/Society of Jesus 24, 50–57, 61, 62

kaeriten 121, 143
kambun (the Chinese way of writing) 122, 124–135, 138
kambun kundoku (Japanese reading of Chinese) xi, 121–135, 141, 142, 148, 151, 158
kambun yomikudashi (Chinese written out as Japanese) 121
katakana 122, 125, 150, 154, 158
Ke, Ping 184
Keene, Donald 130, 147
Keet, B. B. 24
Ken-en tôwa (The Chinese conversation group

of the Ken'en school) 135, 139
kiyô no gaku (the 'learning of Nagasaki translators') 138–140
Kobunji no gaku (School of Ancient Rhetoric) 140
konsequenter Naturalismus 11
Korea 45
Korean 141, 178
Kumarajiva 47, 59, 61
kunten reading marks 121
Kunyaku shimô 139, 143
kutôten punctuation 122

Leone, Sergio 114
Lewis, D. B. Wyndham 112, 113
Li, Panlong 140
Liangzhou/Hexi 45, 48–50, 58
loan words 141, 150, 151, 153–155, 158
Logos 177
Luther, Martin 67

Macpherson's Ossianic poetry 15
Marcel, Gabriel 115
Masanov, Iurij 8
Mauriac, François 116
Medhurst, Walter Henry 54
Meiji Restoration 148
Mignon, Paul-Louis 116
Mishima, Yukio 150, 158
missionary/missionaries x, 13, 50–52, 54, 56, 67–87
monk-translators 48, 61
Mormon/Church of Jesus Christ of Latter-day Saints 11–13
Mortier, Gérard 117

Natsume, Soseki 149
naturalism 10, 11, 114
Nida, Eugene 25
Nihonjin-ron 166, 171
Nishi, Amane 148
non-fiction 147, 151, 152, 161, 162, 164–167, 169, 170, 172
Norwegian 9, 11, 169

Ogyû, Sorai 135–143
Okajima, Kanzan 135, 136
okototen diacritics 122
Owen, Jesse Coleman 78

Papa Hamlet 9–11
paraphrase 29, 32, 35, 186
Parenin, Dominicus 51
philosophy 20, 75, 78–81, 84, 85, 92, 100, 148, 163, 169, 180
Pope, Alexander 185
Poteat, Gordon 82, 83
Potok, Chaim 91, 98, 99, 107

Poupeye, Camille 113
Pruitt, Anna 72, 79, 83, 86
pseudo-translations/pseudo-translate ix, 4–15
Pym, Anthony 43, 44, 53

Radcliffe, Ann 8
readership xii, 57, 134, 183, 184, 186, 189
realism 26, 27, 114, 115
reconciliation vocabulary 28, 35
redundancy 50, 184, 185
religion vii, 70, 71, 74–76, 84–86, 99, 100, 188
Robinson Crusoe 188
Russian 8, 10, 14, 15, 111, 116, 148, 168, 170

Sagan, Carl 169
Sanders, Andrew 188, 189
Sanskrit 47, 48
Saunders, J. Roscoe 72
Schaller, Michael 85
Schlaf, Johannes 10, 11
self x, 91–109
self-discovery 98
selfishness 100, 101, 108, 109, 116
self-reliance 95, 98, 104
Shanghai 53–55, 57, 58, 62, 69
Sheldon, Sidney 168
Shostakovitch, Dmitri 14, 15
Shōwa 149
Silk Road 46, 48, 56
Smith, Joseph 11–14, 16
social consciousness x, 27–29, 34, 35
social relationships 75, 81
Souday, Paul 115
soul 67, 85, 91, 95–98
Southern Baptist 69, 70, 72, 75, 82–84, 86, 87, 116
Soviet Union 14, 15, 22, 163
Stanislavski's Method 114, 115
Staughton, William 68
substitution/substitute 29–31, 33, 35–38
Sutra (Buddhist scriptures) 45–50, 56–61

Taishō 149
Tanizaki, Junichirō 149, 150
terminology 33–39, 108, 143, 177, 179
   software 178, 179
tertium comparationis 29
text selection xi, 52, 161, 162, 166, 170–173
The Castle of Otranto 15
Toffler, Alvin 169
Tom Jones 184–186
Toury, Gideon ix, 127, 148
translation vii–xiii, 3–15, 19, 24–30, 35, 40, 43–
   45, 47, 49–62, 70–72, 75, 79, 81, 83, 84, 86,
   87, 91, 92, 95, 100–108, 111–117, 123–143,
   147–159, 161–173, 177–181, 183–189
   computer/machine vii, 178
   conceptualization of, from Chinese 135, 142

culturally-oriented 43, 55–57
   mental 127, 131
   prototypical 126, 131–134
   accreditation 179
   communities 44
   history x, 15, 43–45, 55, 57, 129, 142, 147,
      148, 157, 161
   memory programs 177
   norms viii, xi, 15, 28, 57, 127, 142, 151,
      152, 158
   software 177, 178
   teaching 179–181
translation theory (see also Descriptive
   Translation Studies) viii, xii, 129, 132, 138,
   140, 148, 180, 181
   polysystem viii, xi, 161, 162, 172
   source-oriented viii, xi, 25, 28, 30, 35, 150,
      151, 158, 159
   target-oriented 25, 30, 151, 159, 180
translational relationships 5
translationese xi, 132, 147–155, 158, 159
translators/interpreters (T/I) vii–xii, 7–14, 25,
   26, 43–50, 53–62, 68, 102–107, 112–114,
   127, 129, 132–136, 138, 147–152, 157, 158,
   168, 169, 172, 177–179, 183–189
Tynjanov, Jurij 10

United States 68, 70, 96, 98, 101, 109, 112, 154,
   163, 167, 170, 171, 179, 180
unnaturalness 149, 151, 152, 155, 156, 158

vernacular 23, 24, 134, 138, 139, 141, 142
Volkov, Solomon 14

wabun (classical Japanese) 124, 126, 130
Wadoku yōryô 141
Walker, Roy 113
Waller, Robert James 169
Walpole, Horace 15
Wang, Shizhen 140
Wang, Zhikui 184, 185
wayaku (translation into Japanese) 127
Weissbrod, Rachel 8
Western Region 45, 48–50, 56, 58–61
Whitman, Walt 91, 93, 95–99, 101, 104–106, 108
World War II xi, 75, 147, 150, 161

Xiongnu 46, 60

Yahalom, Shelly 8
Yakubun sentei (A Guide to Translation) 137–
   143
Yanabu, Akira 149

Zhang, Guruo 183–187
Zhi Qian 47, 48, 58
Zhu Fonian 49

In the series *Benjamins Translation Library* the following titles have been published thus far or are scheduled for publication:

13 DELISLE, Jean and Judith WOODSWORTH (eds.): Translators through History. 1995. xvi, 346 pp.

14 MELBY, Alan K. and Terry WARNER: The Possibility of Language. A discussion of the nature of language, with implications for human and machine translation. 1995. xxvi, 276 pp.

15 WILSS, Wolfram: Knowledge and Skills in Translator Behavior. 1996. xiii, 259 pp.

16 DOLLERUP, Cay and Vibeke APPEL (eds.): Teaching Translation and Interpreting 3. New Horizons. Papers from the Third Language International Conference, Elsinore, Denmark, 1995. 1996. viii, 338 pp.

17 POYATOS, Fernando (ed.): Nonverbal Communication and Translation. New perspectives and challenges in literature, interpretation and the media. 1997. xii, 361 pp.

18 SOMERS, Harold (ed.): Terminology, LSP and Translation. Studies in language engineering in honour of Juan C. Sager. 1996. xii, 250 pp.

19 CARR, Silvana E., Roda P. ROBERTS, Aideen DUFOUR and Dini STEYN (eds.): The Critical Link: Interpreters in the Community. Papers from the 1st international conference on interpreting in legal, health and social service settings, Geneva Park, Canada, 1–4 June 1995. 1997. viii, 322 pp.

20 SNELL-HORNBY, Mary, Zuzana JETTMAROVÁ and Klaus KAINDL (eds.): Translation as Intercultural Communication. Selected papers from the EST Congress, Prague 1995. 1997. x, 354 pp.

21 BUSH, Peter and Kirsten MALMKJÆR (eds.): Rimbaud's Rainbow. Literary translation in higher education. 1998. x, 200 pp.

22 CHESTERMAN, Andrew: Memes of Translation. The spread of ideas in translation theory. 1997. vii, 219 pp.

23 GAMBIER, Yves, Daniel GILE and Christopher TAYLOR (eds.): Conference Interpreting: Current Trends in Research. Proceedings of the International Conference on Interpreting: What do we know and how? 1997. iv, 246 pp.

24 ORERO, Pilar and Juan C. SAGER (eds.): The Translator's Dialogue. Giovanni Pontiero. 1997. xiv, 252 pp.

25 POLLARD, David E. (ed.): Translation and Creation. Readings of Western Literature in Early Modern China, 1840–1918. 1998. vi, 336 pp.

26 TROSBORG, Anna (ed.): Text Typology and Translation. 1997. xvi, 342 pp.

27 BEYLARD-OZEROFF, Ann, Jana KRÁLOVÁ and Barbara MOSER-MERCER (eds.): Translators' Strategies and Creativity. Selected Papers from the 9th International Conference on Translation and Interpreting, Prague, September 1995. In honor of Jiří Levý and Anton Popovič. 1998. xiv, 230 pp.

28 SETTON, Robin: Simultaneous Interpretation. A cognitive-pragmatic analysis. 1999. xvi, 397 pp.

29 WILSS, Wolfram: Translation and Interpreting in the 20th Century. Focus on German. 1999. xiii, 256 pp.

30 DOLLERUP, Cay: Tales and Translation. The Grimm Tales from Pan-Germanic narratives to shared international fairytales. 1999. xiv, 384 pp.

31 ROBERTS, Roda P., Silvana E. CARR, Diana ABRAHAM and Aideen DUFOUR (eds.): The Critical Link 2: Interpreters in the Community. Selected papers from the Second International Conference on Interpreting in legal, health and social service settings, Vancouver, BC, Canada, 19–23 May 1998. 2000. vii, 316 pp.

32 BEEBY, Allison, Doris ENSINGER and Marisa PRESAS (eds.): Investigating Translation. Selected papers from the 4th International Congress on Translation, Barcelona, 1998. 2000. xiv, 296 pp.

33 GILE, Daniel, Helle V. DAM, Friedel DUBSLAFF, Bodil Ringe MARTINSEN and Anne SCHJOLDAGER (eds.): Getting Started in Interpreting Research. Methodological reflections, personal accounts and advice for beginners. 2001. xiv, 255 pp.

34 GAMBIER, Yves and Henrik GOTTLIEB (eds.): (Multi) Media Translation. Concepts, practices, and research. 2001. xx, 300 pp.

35 SOMERS, Harold (ed.): Computers and Translation. A translator's guide. 2003. xvi, 351 pp.

36 SCHMID, Monika S.: Translating the Elusive. Marked word order and subjectivity in English-German translation. 1999. xii, 174 pp.

37 TIRKKONEN-CONDIT, Sonja and Riitta JÄÄSKELÄINEN (eds.): Tapping and Mapping the Processes of Translation and Interpreting. Outlooks on empirical research. 2000. x, 176 pp.

38 SCHÄFFNER, Christina and Beverly ADAB (eds.): Developing Translation Competence. 2000.
xvi, 244 pp.

39 CHESTERMAN, Andrew, Natividad GALLARDO SAN SALVADOR and Yves GAMBIER (eds.):
Translation in Context. Selected papers from the EST Congress, Granada 1998. 2000. x, 393 pp.

40 ENGLUND DIMITROVA, Birgitta and Kenneth HYLTENSTAM (eds.): Language Processing and
Simultaneous Interpreting. Interdisciplinary perspectives. 2000. xvi, 164 pp.

41 NIDA, Eugene A.: Contexts in Translating. 2002. x, 127 pp.

42 HUNG, Eva (ed.): Teaching Translation and Interpreting 4. Building bridges. 2002. xii, 243 pp.

43 GARZONE, Giuliana and Maurizio VIEZZI (eds.): Interpreting in the 21st Century. Challenges and
opportunities. 2002. x, 337 pp.

44 SINGERMAN, Robert: Jewish Translation History. A bibliography of bibliographies and studies. With
an introductory essay by Gideon Toury. 2002. xxxvi, 420 pp.

45 ALVES, Fabio (ed.): Triangulating Translation. Perspectives in process oriented research. 2003.
x, 165 pp.

46 BRUNETTE, Louise, Georges BASTIN, Isabelle HEMLIN and Heather CLARKE (eds.): The Critical
Link 3. Interpreters in the Community. Selected papers from the Third International Conference on
Interpreting in Legal, Health and Social Service Settings, Montréal, Quebec, Canada 22–26 May 2001.
2003. xii, 359 pp.

47 SAWYER, David B.: Fundamental Aspects of Interpreter Education. Curriculum and Assessment.
2004. xviii, 312 pp.

48 MAURANEN, Anna and Pekka KUJAMÄKI (eds.): Translation Universals. Do they exist? 2004.
vi, 224 pp.

49 PYM, Anthony: The Moving Text. Localization, translation, and distribution. 2004. xviii, 223 pp.

50 HANSEN, Gyde, Kirsten MALMKJÆR and Daniel GILE (eds.): Claims, Changes and Challenges
in Translation Studies. Selected contributions from the EST Congress, Copenhagen 2001. 2004.
xiv, 320 pp. [EST Subseries 1]

51 CHAN, Leo Tak-hung: Twentieth-Century Chinese Translation Theory. Modes, issues and debates.
2004. xvi, 277 pp.

52 HALE, Sandra Beatriz: The Discourse of Court Interpreting. Discourse practices of the law, the
witness and the interpreter. 2004. xviii, 267 pp.

53 DIRIKER, Ebru: De-/Re-Contextualizing Conference Interpreting. Interpreters in the Ivory Tower?
2004. x, 223 pp.

54 GONZÁLEZ DAVIES, Maria: Multiple Voices in the Translation Classroom. Activities, tasks and
projects. 2004. x, 262 pp.

55 ANGELELLI, Claudia V.: Revisiting the Interpreter's Role. A study of conference, court, and medical
interpreters in Canada, Mexico, and the United States. 2004. xvi, 127 pp.

56 ORERO, Pilar (ed.): Topics in Audiovisual Translation. 2004. xiv, 227 pp.

57 CHERNOV, Ghelly V.: Inference and Anticipation in Simultaneous Interpreting. A probability-
prediction model. Edited with a critical foreword by Robin Setton and Adelina Hild. 2004. xxx, 268 pp.
[EST Subseries 2]

58 BRANCHADELL, Albert and Lovell Margaret WEST (eds.): Less Translated Languages. 2005.
viii, 416 pp.

59 MALMKJÆR, Kirsten (ed.): Translation in Undergraduate Degree Programmes. 2004. vi, 202 pp.

60 TENNENT, Martha (ed.): Training for the New Millennium. Pedagogies for translation and
interpreting. 2005. xxvi, 276 pp.

61 HUNG, Eva (ed.): Translation and Cultural Change. Studies in history, norms and image-projection.
2005. xvi, 193 pp.

62 POKORN, Nike K.: Challenging the Traditional Axioms. Translation into a non-mother tongue. 2005.
xii, 166 pp. [EST Subseries 3]

63 JANZEN, Terry (ed.): Topics in Signed Language Interpreting. Theory and practice.
xii, 355 pp. + index. *Expected October 2005*

64 ENGLUND DIMITROVA, Birgitta: Expertise and Explicitation in the Translation Process. ca. 275 pp.
Expected October 2005

A complete list of titles in this series can be found on **www.benjamins.com/jbp**